Turkey and the European Union

Turkey and the European Union

The Politics of Belonging

Lucia Najšlová

BLOOMSBURY ACADEMIC

LONDON • NEW YORK • OXFORD • NEW DELHI • SYDNEY

BLOOMSBURY ACADEMIC
Bloomsbury Publishing Plc
50 Bedford Square, London, WC1B 3DP, UK
1385 Broadway, New York, NY 10018, USA
29 Earlsfort Terrace, Dublin 2, Ireland

BLOOMSBURY, BLOOMSBURY ACADEMIC and the Diana logo
are trademarks of Bloomsbury Publishing Plc

First published in Great Britain 2021
This paperback edition published in 2022

Copyright © Lucia Najšlová, 2021

Cover design by Jade Barnett

A catalogue record for this book is available from the British Library.

A catalog record for this book is available from the Library of Congress.

ISBN: HB: 978-1-8386-0266-6
PB: 978-0-7556-3998-4
ePDF: 978-1-8386-0267-3
eBook: 978-1-8386-0268-0

Typeset by Deanta Global Publishing Services, Chennai, India

To find out more about our authors and books visit www.bloomsbury.com
and sign up for our newsletters

To my mother, who taught me to love the Mediterranean.
To Tarik and Zuzana. To the many people working and living
somewhere in EU-Turkey relations, who have felt misunderstood,
but have not given up looking for common language.

Contents

Acknowledgments

I wrote this book because I believe that exclusion is wrong. I wrote it also because I believe that humans and the institutions they (we) built often exclude *others* without knowing how it feels to be locked out. This book has been drafted, redrafted, put on hold, forgotten, and rediscovered. It has had, like any book, many versions and eventually came to life mainly thanks to colleagues, friends, and strangers, who kept reminding me that the story is worth telling. Responsibility for the final shape including the flaws is mine, of course, but the sections, chapters, paragraphs, sentences—none of this could have appeared without a long list of others. I am grateful for precious mentorship, encouragement, and also acceptance that things would still be alright if this does not get written. The early ideas feeding this manuscript came around the middle of the first decade of the twenty-first century, when some in the EU were celebrating its big bang enlargement and others were mourning it. This was the time when "post-socialist" states were let in, and things started to look optimistic for Turkey, too. Since that time, I have had the opportunity to spend over a decade traveling across various places on the European map, and to assemble fragments of (partially) enlarged EU-rope, all of which have eventually pointed toward the theme of *belonging*, a word I consider defining for Europe at the time of writing.

The list of individuals and institutions that supported this work is long. The Faculty of Social Sciences at the Charles University in Prague, the Faculty of Social and Economic Sciences at the Comenius University in Bratislava, the Research Center of the Slovak Foreign Policy Association in Bratislava, the Institute for European Politics EUROPEUM and Institute of International Relations in Prague have been generous with travel and research grants and collegial support. I have greatly benefited from visiting fellowships at the University of Oslo and the Koç University in Istanbul and I am grateful to Yunus Emre Vakfı for covering part of my early Turkish language education. Earlier versions of parts of this manuscript have been presented to audiences at the University of North Carolina at Chapel Hill in January 2017, the Stockholm University Institute of Turkish Studies in Spring 2017, the EWIS workshop "Resilience and Hope in a World in Relation" in summer 2019 and at several seminars and summer schools convened by the Charles University in Prague. I am grateful to conveners and participants of these workshops and seminars.

Numerous individuals shared their time and observations and provided great advice throughout the process. They should not be held responsible if I have misunderstood their stories and recommendations, but they do deserve credit. First, it is the many diplomats, NGO workers, writers, citizens, and strangers, working or living somewhere in Turkey-EU relations, for sharing their experience, in confidence, that it has been put to good use. As is the convention of the genre, their names have been changed in text. Specific name attribution appears only when the speaker was making a public statement. Second, it is the academic colleagues who provided advice when inchoate versions started appearing on page. The late IR scholar Lucia Antalova Seybert once noted that the most important thing in doing research is coming to terms with understanding, that one might (and probably will) be proven wrong. The writer Maria Golia reminded me, many times, that books have their own clock, they can take a lot of time, and we better choose ideas we are ready to spend that time with. Professor David Chandler of the University of Westminster has been very generous with his time, knowledge, and encouragement; I thank him for stimulating conversations, reading lists, and respectful (dis)agreements. Emre Hatipoğlu of Sabanci University provided a crucial guidance, perhaps just with one sentence. As I was not sure, on one Budapest afternoon, whether I'm looking at the EU from Turkey, or at Turkey from the EU, he asked: "Why don't you inhabit that in-between place? That is also a place." Pages then started making more sense. Writing of Professor Rebecca Bryant has provided an important compass in thinking about temporalities of belonging. The present book has benefited from research of many scholars, most of whom I never met. If I were to name three books that have been foundational for learning to think about Europe ethnographically, it would be Rebecca Bryant's *Imagining the Modern*, Cris Shore's *Building Europe,* and Mehmet Döşemeci's *Debating Turkey's Modernity.* Professor Milada A. Vachudova of the University of North Carolina at Chapel Hill and Professor Petr Kratochvíl of the Institute of International relations in Prague have been very generous with encouragement and several reminders, that "the perfect is the enemy of the good." Anthropologist Martin Fotta repeatedly asked me to keep in mind that a researcher's task is not to look for what *is not there* and criticize the lack, but instead to try to understand what *is there* and why. I am pretty sure I am not following the recommendation thoroughly, but I try. My mentors have provided all kinds of valuable advice, and while they come from a range of intellectual backgrounds, there was one reminder most of them tried to convey, in various ways—that there is not really a blueprint for how a book should look like. At various stages of making of the argument, I have benefitted from conversations with Eleni Diker, Alexander Duleba, Beril Eski, Associate

Professor Başak Yavçan of the TOBB University in Ankara, Professor Ahmet Evin of Sabanci University, Andrej Findor, Tarik Günersel, Martin Kanovský, Petr Kratochvíl, Hans Ingvar Roth and Paul Levin of the Stockholm University Institute of Turkish Studies, Selcen Öner of the Bahcesehir University, and Ayşen Üstübiçi of the Koc University. Friends and colleagues at the V4Revue and at UPCES have been a great source of support.

Professor David Chandler of the University of Westminster, Dr. Pelin Ayan Musil and Professor Petr Kratochvíl of the Institute of International Relations in Prague, Eda Dağoğlu of History Department at the Koç University in Istanbul, Dr. Andrea Purdeková of Bath University, Dr. Egemen Bezci and Dr. Jan Adamec have been very generous with their time and attention when last-minute panicked chapters here and there arrived at their desk. Thank you! I am very grateful to Dr. Jan Pospisil for inspiring conversations, reading the whole text, and encouraging me not to rewrite it into a more classically structured and styled book. I am quite certain that this work would not have appeared in its present form had it not been for the confidence expressed in it by Tomasz Hoskins, Nayiri Kendir, and the editorial team and reviewers at the I.B. Tauris/ Bloomsbury. The encouragement of a house whose production I have admired for many years has been crucial for turning drafts into a manuscript.

Note on Spelling

One of the primary obligations of authors and editors is to make manuscripts not too confusing for the readers. This includes adherence to a particular style. It is sometimes suggested that bookwork can be divided into two components—the content and the form (style). In an increasingly complex world, the content/form binary is contestable. For example, according to the Chicago Manual of Style (CMS), "terms that denote regions of the world or of a particular country are often capitalized, as are a few of the adjectives and nouns derived from such terms." The guideline is followed by examples: the West, western, a westerner (of a country); the West Coast; the West, Western (referring to the culture of the Occident, or Europe and the Western Hemisphere); west, western, westward, to the west (directions). Yet, when speaking about E(e)asts and W(w)ests, it is not so easy to separate culture and geography. In an interconnected world, geographies are rarely free of politics and culture, and culture and politics are rarely a product of just one geography. Moreover, it is difficult to know whether people and places described in the present manuscript would like to see themselves as western (geographically) or Western (culturally) or whether they would use such marker at all. This difficulty, even impossibility, to separate things eastern from things western is one of the subjects of this book. Thus, the usage in this book tries to follow the style manual, but in some places, it leaves it up to the reader to consider whether the capitalization makes sense. We tried to keep them to a minimum, following another CMS guideline, which suggests it is better to avoid excessive capitalization.

Abbreviations

AKP	Justice and Development Party
CoE	Council of Europe (not an EU institution)
JAP	Joint Action Plan
EEC	European Economic Community
EP	European Parliament
EU	European Union
MFA	Ministry of Foreign Affairs
OSCE	Organization for Security and Cooperation in Europe
RoC	Republic of Cyprus
TES	Turkey-EU statement
UN	United Nations
V4	The Visegrad Four (Visegrad Group)

Introduction

Toward the end of the second decade of the twenty-first century, headlines about Turkey and EU were dominated by news of severe diplomatic tensions and disappointments voiced by many people in their respective societies. In one conversation held at that time with a representative of an EU-based foundation, who had for many years worked with partners in Turkey, my interlocutor suddenly noted matter-of-factly: "And some people there are still talking about membership, can you imagine?"[1] I was about to say something like "Yes, you are right, that is strange," the way we show that we are listening and encourage our partner to continue talking. But as he finished the sentence, I could not. It made perfect sense to me why they would, especially now, discuss membership. In Turkey-EU relationships,[2] moments when people suddenly waver, whether to ask for a clarification or give an explanation are in fact not rare. Here, my interlocutor clearly expected me to know that accession was, at the moment, out of the question. I expected him to know that it could not have disappeared from discussions, especially not in Turkey.

Turkey has been, together with Greece, the first country with which the emerging EU (EEC) signed agreements on association in the 1960s, which mostly focused on common trade but already offered a window of opportunity for membership. After a few decades of associate status, the EU member states gave a green light for the beginning of talks on accession in 2004. The run-up to this moment had generated a lot of hope and controversy. While the value of cooperation has rarely been questioned, debate about membership, a relationship based on much firmer rights and obligations than the present framework invites strong opinions for and against. The vote to open formal negotiations on membership has not resolved the dispute over whether membership should become a reality. It did, however, provide a new script that navigates what interlocutors from both sides can do. There is now a new set of rules, guiding how the relationship is supposed

---

[1] We met, geographically, at the EU "side," that is why he says "there."
[2] I use the terms "relations" and "relationships" interchangeably. It used to be the convention of the genre to speak of "relations" when states were involved and of "relationships" when these concerned individuals. The lived experience has made this convention outdated.

to *happen*. But while there is a fixed beginning, and a rather finite set of questions that the diplomatic representations need to discuss, there is no deadline for their closure. Thus, every single event in the relationship is an opportunity to validate or reject the other. In the fifteen years since their opening, the accession talks have been pronounced dead on multiple occasions.

At the time of writing, the notion that Turkey's membership is not "realistic" dominates the conversations on the relationship. And yet, the negotiations continue. This book approaches Turkey-EU relations as a theatrical stage, on which their protagonists offer, accept, and reject their many differences. Much of that conversation revolves around difference as something negative and impossible to bridge. But Turkey is already firmly on the map: it will either be a member or a partner. The possibility of Turkey *not being anything* is not part of the script. And so we see a lot of commentary and analysis on policy developments in the diplomatic relationship.[3] We read texts about past injustices and texts stipulating that we have to pragmatically consider our future options. At the time of writing, "transactionalism" is one of the trending words, with some analysts and policy makers suggesting that Turkey and EU have to have a concise balance sheet of what they could do together and for each other. Others object that such tradesman attitude spoils the essence and misses the bigger picture.

The present book does not compete with the newsreel. It will not shout. It offers an ethnography of the many misunderstandings in EU-Turkey relations, and an insight into what happens, if belongings are denied. Ethnographic perspectives, those that prioritize the nuances of what people tell (and do not tell) each other when they meet, are not a new genre in Europeanist research. Scholars in various disciplines have worked hard to show us the background of what the anthropologist Cris Shore calls "building Europe"[4] or political geographer Merje Kuus called "geopolitics of expertise."[5] The space is already open for thinking about Europe beyond slogans and official narratives. The bookshelves holding Turkey/EU tags can also pride themselves with an emerging library of manuscripts that inspect the relationship from places where it happens, such as Elif Babül's meticulously researched account of unexpected transformations

---

[3] The list could potentially be very long, let me name a few policy institutes that have a long-standing interest and regular publications covering the current developments in EU-Turkey relations: Instituto Affari Internazionali in Rome, Istanbul Policy Center (affiliated with the Sabanci University), International Crisis Group, EDAM in Istanbul, SWP in Berlin, GMF, European Stability Initiative, Carnegie Europe.

[4] Cris Shore, *Building Europe: The Cultural Politics of European Integration* (London and New York: Routledge, 2006).

[5] Merje Kuus, *Geopolitics and Expertise* (Chichester: John Wiley and Sons, 2014).

brought with EU-funded aid programs.[6] The present manuscript does not go deep into one specific site of interaction between representatives and citizens of Turkey and the EU member states; it is not a story of a group of people tied by one place and time. It prioritizes the width, or the multiplicity, and tries to grasp how fragments of interactions at various sites inform our knowledge of the international framework of the relationship. Stories are in the spotlight here, but they would not make sense unless placed in the dominant international narratives. This book takes the risk that walking between the disciplines and conventions could in fact help the participants of the relationship see not just the oft-noted differences, but also similarities in their pursuits.

The lines of differentiation discussed here are not always as visible as border checkpoints. As one influential scholar of politics observed, we often *imagine* the communities we live in and have a sense of "us" even with people we have not met in our lifetime.[7] One such community is often called *European* and an easy way to begin a conversation on Turkey *and* the EU is to suggest that the former is not European. Europeanness is puzzling and so is the process of its recognition. It also has a violent history. While its meanings have evolved over time and space, in everyday conversation, the word "European" often appears as a verdict of clear and unchanging set of traits of a person or a country. Such understanding is often promoted in official narratives of the Union and its twenty-seven member states. *Being European* can also be thought as a way of seeing the world and shaping that world, similar to how many scholars suggest to think of other belongings.[8] Being European can well be, as the anthropologist Marilyn Strathern proposed to think about gender, "a substitute for other things,"[9] in this case, the political and cultural notions of democracy or modernity.

Being European can mean different things, depending on who is speaking and when. Yet we know with certainty that if a state is to become a member of the EU, the standing members have to *see* it as European. But the perspective can change in a moment—no dictionary or law stands above political consensus in member states and between them. From the vantage point of the Brussels institutions, the states in EU's geographic proximity are all neighbors and partners and some could become members. A "yes" answer to the question whether a state is European qualifies it to be considered as a potential member.

6   Elif Babül, *Bureaucratic Intimacies* (Stanford: Stanford University Press, 2017).
7   Benedict Anderson, *Imagined Communities* (London, New York: Verso, 2006).
8   Michael Billig, *Banal Nationalism* (London: Sage, 1995); Marilyn Strathern, *Before and After Gender* (Chicago: HAU Books, 2016); Fiona Robinson, *The Ethics of Care: A Feminist Approach to Human Security* (Philadelphia: Temple University Press, 2011).
9   Strathern, *Before and After Gender*.

In official documentation of the relationship, Turkey did get this yes, it has been recognized as European, otherwise accession talks could not have been opened. And yet, it is precisely this question that remains unsettled and unsettling.

Belonging (to Europe) is difficult in the absence of a federal system that would clearly establish and enforce rights and obligations. To be sure, the EU member states do have their own federal structure, but there is no system of institutions including a constitution, government, and court, holding all *European* states accountable.[10] Europeanness is negotiated in a cacophony of everyday interactions of many interlocutors. This is not a new thing to say. What hopefully *is* new is the way I show the consequences of this disorder. The central lens, one that brings all the conceptual detours together, is belonging. Questions of belonging go hand in hand with questions of understanding/comprehension. Because one cannot belong if they are not understood and if they do not understand. And if there is no grand narrative and no one institution that can be held accountable for Turkey-EU process, then we need to turn to the many individual protagonists. They are not familiar with all the developments that have an impact on the "big picture" of the relationship. They often find themselves in a limbo, hesitating whether to provide an explanation (lecture their counterpart) or ask for a clarification. In other words, individual protagonists of the many EU-Turkey relationships often suffer from empathy fatigue. That fatigue certainly is also a product of the fact that they often find themselves defending categories they did not choose. Because, if the European Union can, arguably, guarantee its citizens a higher degree of protection of their rights than is the case in neighboring states, why would one choose *not to be* a European?

In Turkey, ideas about Europe and later discussion about institutional membership therein have been an important part of state-building. Europe, or "the West," was on horizon well before the establishment of the present Turkish republic. The Ottoman policy makers adopted several legal and cultural codes from Western Europeans. Throughout the twentieth century, the conversation became more intense and complex. Many more voices could now be heard. As Mehmet Döşemeci showed in his seminal study of the first two decades of the association agreement, already this process made Turkey fully European.[11]

[10] Council of Europe (CoE), a human rights organization almost twice the size of the EU (47 members), is more of an international organization than a federation. Moreover, while CoE's rules are binding, the states that blatantly disrespect them can still be members. That of course can in principle be said about EU members as well, but as far as respect for rights goes on the EU territory, the EU members are doing better than CoE members.
[11] Mehmet Döşemeci, *Debating Turkey's Modernity: Civilization, Nationalism and the EEC* (Cambridge: Cambridge University Press, 2013).

Europe or the West—being there, being like it—is a powerful mobilizing theme, it has many nuances, it is neither unequivocally embraced nor shunned.

We could say many similar things about how Turkey has mattered to making Europe—both as an idea and an institution.[12] As Paul Levin observed, Turks and Muslims have often been discussed as "fictional characters"—fulfilling other roles in storytellers' narratives.[13] European integration has been, from its onset, a future-oriented process. Successive waves of inclusion of new member states and federalization of more and more sectors of the economic and social life have been justified by a future benefit for all. The future of the Union is often imagined with the French word *finalité* and Turkey is a common case on which the desirable ends are demonstrated. Every year federal institutions and the member states announce "new commitments" and "new tools and principles." The march toward novelty does not erase the older layers—several authors pointed out similarities and continuities with earlier modes of governance.[14] In fact, the past is often needed to justify the projects in the making. How would a debate about the future of the EU look if Turkey was not referenced in it?

In this book, we will spend some time with the archives. Regardless of whether one is a candidate or a neighbor, the thick body of EU policy documents addressing relations with these states embarks from an axiom: that they are on a linear track, the closer they come to the Union, the more modern, democratic, prosperous they become. It has, however, become increasingly evident that the development clock does not stop ticking once a state becomes a member. Perhaps more importantly, the clock can start ticking backwards: a wave of nationalist antidemocratic movements is on the rise around Europe, and they seem to be more vocal and successful in pushing their demands through than movements campaigning for rights-based cooperation.

These developments can be observed both in the EU and its neighborhood and, thus, a number of European integration scholars have called for revisions of notions of linear progress and the EU's leading role in the process. The notion of "enlargement as the strongest foreign policy tool" has until recently been very popular in the debates on EU relations with neighbors. The optimistic thesis has been largely based on the 2004 eastern enlargement. There is, however, a

---

[12] Iver Neumann, *Uses of the Other: The "East" in European Identity Formation* (Minneapolis: University of Minnesota Press, 1999). Paul T. Levin, *Turkey and the European Union: Christian and Secular Images of Islam* (New York: Palgrave Macmillan, 2011).

[13] Levin, *Turkey and the European Union*, 1.

[14] Hartmut Behr, "The European Union in the Legacies of Imperial Rule? EU Accession Politics Viewed from a Historical Comparative Perspective," *European Journal of International Relations* 13, no. 2 (2007): 239–62. Ian Klinke, "European Integration Studies and the European Union's Eastern Gaze," *Millennium: Journal of International Studies* 43, no. 2 (2015): 567–83.

growing evidence questioning EU's possibility to deliver all the good things, including security, prosperity, and democracy. Recent texts on the current lives of eastern enlargement show that, while membership *did* have a transformative effect, it did not provide the type of rights-based order many expected. We are then entering a discordant conversation. On the one hand, the EU citizens and potential citizens expect it to provide rights. On the other, they are not sure, whether it can deliver. It has been suggested from several places that instead of "leading by example," the Union started "leading by recommendation." Instead of *showing* how things should be done, it *tells*. Suggestion that the Union is leading by example to advance human rights elsewhere has been challenged especially on the grounds that such strategy obscures role of national (self) interest in its foreign policy.[15]

But if the ground is unstable in narratives that used to make sense of European politics, is it even possible to provide a coherent account of Turkey-EU relations? Perhaps we could structure our effort by policy clusters and talk about what the two are doing together (or against each other) in trade, energy, migration, or security. If we go down this road, sooner or later we will meet two words: interests and identities. A reference to "common interests" is a part and parcel of any policy-oriented work, whether it comes from a pen of a diplomat or a scholar. Why otherwise should one care about anything with "Turkey and the EU" in a title, if common interests would not be assumed or expected? With identities, things are a bit more complicated. The question of identity, how similar or different these two are, is rarely absent from the conversation on interests and what one wants from the other. In fact, assumptions of similarity and difference drive strategic calculations. In the second decade of the twenty-first century, Turkey and EU developed a migration partnership. This was in a period in which most of the involved diplomacies have been reluctant to move forward the accession process; in other words, they were reluctant to work toward a structure that would provide the same rights and obligations to all of its members. There is a long trajectory documenting preferences for partnership rather than membership.[16] And it is precisely in the more recent migration-related developments (discussed in the final chapters of the present book) that we see how partnership and membership do not add to each other—they

[15] Kalypso Nicolaïdis and Robert Howse, "'This is My Eutopia ...': Narrative as Power," *Journal of Common Market Studies* 40, no. 4 (2002): 767–92; David Chandler, *Empire in Denial: The Politics of State-Building* (London: Pluto, 2006). Kalypso Nicolaïdis, Berny Sèbe and Gabrielle Maas (eds.), *Echoes of Empire: Memory, Identity and Colonial Legacies* (London and New York: I.B.Tauris, 2015).
[16] Mehmet Uğur, *The European Union and Turkey: Anchor-Credibility Dilemma* (Aldershot: Ashgate, 1999).

can be mutually exclusive. If Turkey was considered as potentially "the same" or at least similar, the EU governments could have hardly hoped that it would accommodate, within a very short time-span, more refugees than any single EU country, as it happened in the wake of the Syrian exodus in recent years.

So by now we know that both the EU and Turkey have a special place in mutual imaginaries. Before we go further, let us put on the record the notion of uniqueness, which often comes up in conversations on the relationship, and this pertains to their individual protagonists and also to what is between them. Many observers of Turkey have highlighted its uniqueness, a country between East and West, and until recently "Muslim but democratic." Several scholars have observed the many problems such an approach presents. Uniqueness can after all be determined only in comparison and narrowing down our vision to one actor perhaps also makes us underestimate the dynamics between various interlocutors in the conversation. It may not let us see similarities in their conduct.[17] Yet uniqueness is not imposed by writers—the makers of Turkey have engaged in this narrative as well, references to it appear in the official communication of Turkish institutions and everyday remarks *"biz bize benzeriz"* (we resemble ourselves).[18] Likewise, political manifestos and academic texts about the European Union, often note its sui generis nature.[19] And then there is the question of the relationship, when it is often suggested that Turkey is the most "controversial" candidate for membership. Uniqueness is used both as an argument for why the EU rejects Turkey and why it should include it. Dwelling on difference and certain notions of the exclusive "we" in fact makes Turkey and EU, and people who study them, very similar.

It is this cacophony of differences that gradually merge into what I call architectures of similarity. Makers of both Turkey and the EU have invested a lot into sculpting political projects that emphasize some differences and obscure other. And while there might be many layers of "we" within the respective national communities, some types of "we" cross boundaries, no matter how rigid the border checkpoints are. Belongings are not locked within the confines of one's respective nation-state. What hopefully makes this book a contribution is that it is written based on an observation of the relationship from several vantage

---

[17] Paul T. Levin and Sinan Ciddi, "Interdisciplinarity and Comparison in Turkish Studies," *Turkish Studies* 15, no. 4 (2014): 557–70; Murat Somer, "Theory-Consuming or Theory-producing? Studying Turkey as a Theory-developing Critical Case," *Turkish Studies* 15, no. 4 (2014): 571–88; Daniela Kuzmanovic, *Refractions of Civil Society in Turkey* (New York: Palgrave Macmillan, 2012).

[18] Suraiya Faroqhi, *Approaching Ottoman History: An Introduction to Sources* (Cambridge: Cambridge University Press, 1999).

[19] William Phelan, "What is Sui Generis about the European Union? Costly International Cooperation in a Self-Contained Regime," *International Studies Review* 14, no. 3 (2012): 367–85.

points. It presents fragments from conversations with European diplomats and NGO workers. It walks us through archive documentation of the accession process and migration partnership. It enters places that reveal similarities rather than just differences between the protagonists. Exploring spaces between the declarations, perceptions, and practices of "being European," it hopes to contribute to a wider debate on reading differences.

On the "Two Sides": Whose Relationships?

The easiness with which we use the phrase "Turkey-EU relations" can sometimes obscure the fact that there are many different relationships within this framework. Most commonly such phrase is used to refer to diplomatic relations of the states involved. Yet authors covering the main contours of inter*national* relations often note that this is a difficult endeavor. The EU is after all a partnership of twenty-seven societies. These are represented by their respective governments and parliaments and discuss wider European developments through nuances of their earlier (national) experience. Their (recent) histories have been written as national, and current events are read through the national lenses. The member states are not planets of their own—they are linked by federal institutions and other networks of debate and action. But the nuances of the debate and resulting hierarchies of priorities are products of national political processes.[20] Understanding the EU relations with any other state, including Turkey, then requires navigation in a strange terrain in which Turkey is auditioning to become a member of the Union, not of its parts (member states), but in order to get there, it has to win the case in all of these separate parts. The final yes or no is a result of the complex national debates. And while the federal institutions have been set up to speak and act on behalf of all states and citizens, many other voices make claims to such a representation. It is precisely this cacophony, one similar to the politics of nation-states, that matters. Turkey and the EU are similar, in that their many public spheres produce competing visions on national or European unity, and voice different expectations of how "the other" should unite.

---

[20] My point here is not to dismiss literature on "supranationalism" and the role of transnational settings in creation of European policies. After all, the question of where the decisions take place is one of the central preoccupations in EU studies and I am not sure it has been conclusively answered. I emphasize however that major issues are discussed in member states, through the optics of their lived pasts and planned futures.

But what do relations really mean? Sharing a space? Having a good conversation? Helping each other? And how much is a relation(ship) a result of choice as opposed to being stranded together and looking for a way of handling the situation? One could go deep into the fragments of everyday encounters between various participants of Turkey-EU relations. But regardless of whether we hear a representative of an NGO, a diplomat, or a citizen without a public role, we are always bound to come back to the *international* framework. The relations we will see in this book happen at the border, when one does not need just a passport, but also visa and an invitation that precedes them. They happen in parliaments when a legislator proposes a motion to suspend accession talks. They happen in squares, at political rallies, when a Turkish politician pledges that Turkey will follow "EU standards" or announces that Turkish standards are much better, and it is the EU who should be following. Turkey-EU relations also happen in living rooms, when people watch ministers, professors, and actors speaking on TV and nod, laugh, or despair at their remarks.

Regardless of the many settings in which the EU-Turkey conversations happen and how fragmented they are, some type of commonality is always at the backdrop. The polities discussing this relationship are often called "divided" or "fractured." But while Europeanness is internally contested, we already know that a new state can *only* become a member of the bigger whole. European integration often happens in the language of wishes, *how things should be.* There is a specific nuance if those wishes come from the outside. The latter *need* the EU to speak with one voice because only *one voice* can bring membership. The Union is mysterious to its own citizens including the long-term students of European integration because its rule-making is so complex. But it is one thing to be lost in the many rules and procedures, and quite another to demand accountability and articulate wishes on how things *should work.* Demands for unity and quick decisions are placed even when the speaker is well aware of what prevents the fulfilling those demands. The assumption of homogeneity or the call for other's swift action might not necessarily be placed with an expectation that the other will oblige. It can serve another purpose; it can simply be a message to one's own constituency. This then is the politics of belonging.

Some lines of separation in Turkey-EU relationships can often be misleading. They can freeze the protagonists of the relationship in categories in which they are not comfortable. They can also freeze them in categories that cannot explain the actual dynamics. The task then is not to compare, but to follow the relatedness. Only then can we learn more about the similarities at various sides of the many borders. As Kalioppe Amygdalou concluded in her study of post-

Ottoman Thessaloniki, a city in present Greece, and Izmir, a city in present Turkey:

> [I]t was not necessarily the French architects who advocated the imposition of a clear "Western," or "colonial" model, and it was not necessarily the local politicians who were protective of their local heritage. [. . .] Rather, we can witness a variety of interpretations of the "West," "us" and the "other," dictated by the needs of power, identity and legitimacy.[21]

The present book explores the notion emerging upon the realization that things and people can often belong to other places than we originally thought. Every text contains words that have contested pedigrees and thus can rarely do justice to all of their etymologies. That is why it needs one central word. In this book, the word is *belonging*. Belonging brings together a number of aspects related to (not) being a part of something. It has been studied by disciplines in social sciences and humanities, which explores the psychological and the social,[22] the cognitive and the emotional,[23] and the imagined and the material.[24] Importantly, belongings are a process, a movement between "being" that is already there and "longing" to arrive to that place.[25] The anthropologist Thomas H. Eriksen recently observed, that "no other part of social anthropology receives more interest from wider public sphere than those specializations that are concerned with social identity or identification."[26]

The present work is not meant to be representative of what citizens of Turkey and the EU as collectives think. Rather it is a journey through their misunderstandings. It presents a diverse set of objects—policy documents, photographs, movie clippings, and excerpts from the conversation. I found

---

[21] Kalliopi Amygdalou, "Building the Nation at the Crossroads of 'East' and 'West': Ernest Hébrard and Henri Prost in the Near East," *Opticon1826* 16, no. 15 (2014): 1–19, 14.

[22] Henri Tajfel and J. C. Turner, "The Social Identity Theory of Inter-group Behavior," in S. Worchel and L. W. Austin (eds), *Psychology of Intergroup Relations* (Chicago: Nelson-Hall, 1986); Serge Moscovici, "Questions for the Twenty-First Century," *Theory, Culture & Society* 7, no. 1 (1990): 1–19; Serge Moscovici, "Social Representations and Pragmatic Communication," *Social Science Information* 33, no. 2 (1994): 163–77. Stuart Hall (ed.), *Representation: Cultural Representations and Signifying Practices* (London, Thousand Oaks and New Delhi: Sage Publications and Open University, 1997).

[23] Daniel Kahnemann and Amos Tversky, "Prospect Theory: An Analysis of Decision Under Risk," *Econometrica* 47, no. 2 (1979): 263–91; Daniel Kahnemann and Amos Tversky, "The Framing of Decisions and the Psychology of Choice," *Science* 211, no. 4481 (1981): 453–8.

[24] Craig Calhoun, "Imagining Solidarity: Cosmopolitanism, Constitutional Patriotism and the Public Sphere," *Public Culture* 14, no. 1 (2002): 141–71; Craig Calhoun, "The Class Consciousness of Frequent Travelers: Towards a Critique of Actually Existing Cosmopolitanism," *South Atlantic Quarterly* 101, no. 4 (2002): 869–97.
    Christopher Lawrence, *Blood and Oranges: Immigrant Labor and European Markets in Rural Greece* (New York, Oxford: Berghahn Books, 2007).

[25] Elspeth Probyn, *Outside Belongings* (London: Routledge, 1996).

[26] Thomas Hylland Eriksen, *What is Anthropology?* (London: Pluto, 2017), 152.

"denied belonging," a sense of unjust and unjustified rejection to be one of the dominant frames of reading the EU among my Turkish interlocutors. This sense of rejection is often exploited in political campaigns. While campaigning on a future within the EU might be difficult in Turkey, mobilization on the fact of rejection is not. But reference to rejection is not always negative. One Turkish interlocutor, an engineer in his mid-fifties, told me, referring to the former French president who actively spoke out against Turkey's EU membership: "I actually like Sarkozy. At least he is honest." Those in the EU who object to the possible membership of Turkey often paint dark scenarios of how the EU would look like should a country *like that* become a member tomorrow. The German chancellor Angela Merkel was quoted suggesting that Turkey's membership would be "a catastrophe" and that certainly would be one of the more diplomatic statements from the rows of those who are skeptical about Turkey's possibility to belong. On the other hand, defenders of Turkey's EU bid remind that questioning its EU vocation alienates the Turkish public and slows down reforms that could make Turkey more compatible with the EU. Aspiration is crucial in this debate, and so are the rejections and recognitions. But what exactly is being recognized or rejected?

Belonging, Understanding, and Recognition

How does one write a book about the inability to understand without occasionally committing the same misdeed? Understanding complexity is difficult—we cannot always know all the details that shaped peoples' decisions. Writers are expected to explain why the protagonists are acting in a particular way and not in any other. Writers should explain why their protagonists do not always hear each other. Writers should also be honest if they do not have all the answers— that after all is one of the key differences between more conventional writing on politics and the ethnographic genre. As Anna Tsing has convincingly argued in her recent multi-sited ethnography, fragmented stories may well be the best thing to share, once the grand narratives have started falling apart.[27]

"I do not understand" is probably one of the least forgivable statements one can make when discussing politics professionally. "I do not know" often faces similar fate. Globalization has created the appearance that everyone can

---

[27] Anna Lowenhaupt Tsing, *The Mushroom at the End of the World: On the Possibility of Life in Capitalist Ruins* (Princeton and Oxford: Princeton University Press, 2015).

and does read or consume the same things. Yet the problem of understanding, comprehension of "the other," seeing them in contexts in which they act and speak, has yet to see its scientific breakthrough. The late writer Susan Sontag, building on Virginia Woolf's *Three Guineas*, a reflection on problems of saying "no to war," suggested: "No 'we' should be taken for granted when the subject is looking at other peoples' pain."[28] The novelist Zadie Smith, whose prose is set in relationships of people of diverse backgrounds, said in a recent interview: "It's something that's important to me, in fiction: imperfect knowledge. That's the reality of most people's lives—mine too."[29] The various settings of Turkey-EU relations abound with moments when people (including the present author) take universal knowledge for granted ("everyone has to know this") yet resist when they are categorized wrongly.

Belonging is what is at stake. There are many factors shaping who belongs and who is excluded. The one I prioritize in this book is the difficulty of understanding others in an increasingly complex world, or, in a world in which we are increasingly aware of the complexity. Because neither Turkey nor EU are single personas, the interactions between the two entities take place via a multitude of channels, including diplomatic meetings, NGO workshops, or spontaneous encounters. Thus, no participant of the relationship can possibly have all the knowledge about its other venues. Moreover, no participant of the relationship can have control of all the spaces in which Turkey-EU relations happen.

This brings us to an important point and that is the question of intentionality. Observers of EU-Turkey relations often make claims that take collective intentionality as a default. This could, for example, be, "EU rejects Turkey" or "Turkey refuses to reform." This is a common shortcut in journalism, but also in policy and academic writing. It is common, hence, there is a significant audience who is not disturbed by such shortcuts. And while brevity is often a must, it also solidifies the fiction of collective intentionality. The research presented in this book invites the reader to consider the complexity of conversations that happen in the EU-Turkey framework. Individual protagonists in the many spaces of EU-Turkey relationships do not regularly come together and come up with one position. The expectations of intentionality are then not born out of direct

---

[28] Susan Sonntag, *Regarding the Pain of Others* (New York: Picador, 2003).
[29] Cressida Leyshon, "This Week in Fiction: Zadie Smith," *The New Yorker*, February 3, 2013. See also Smith's short story "The Embassy of Cambodia" in February 11 (2013) issue of *The New Yorker*. In my view, this story demonstrates wonderfully how we often make assumptions without questioning them.

experience with the specific interlocutor involved. People commuting between the many sides in Turkey-EU relations are sometimes considered ambassadors of their national cultures. Thus, they are often categorized into boxes created without evidence that that particular interlocutor believes in what they are accused of believing.

The knowledge and understanding of what it means to *be European* mobilizes a variety of emotions, and has direct consequences for everyday life. Europeanness is contested and exclusive. If belonging is a question of choice, we also need to ask what happens if certain choices do not receive a green light. Turkey has already made cracks in the EU's self-narrative, by highlighting its reluctance to include Muslims.[30] Studies in international politics, for most part conducted from Euro/ West-centric positionality have only recently (re)discovered the ambiguity of Eastern agency.[31] It is one of the concerns of this book to think beyond the framework of the West as agenda-setting and the East as merely responding. It has often been suggested that Turkey is split between the "moderns," who are looking toward the West and support the country's integration into the European Union, and the conservatives, who look to (or stay in) the East. But in Turkey, one might well support, in principle, the integration process but be disappointed by how the governments are handling it. One might want to be a part of the EU, in principle, but disagree with a number of its specific policies. As far as aspiration is concerned, this does not make the Turkish (or any other candidate state) society different, in principle, from societies in the member states.

Belongings do not happen only here and there, but also now, before, and after. The question "Can/should Turkey become an EU member state" elicits a yes or no response. It also invites one to consider it as an event rather than a process. In negotiating the present, images of past and future are frequently deployed as evidence in support of impending decisions. For decades, narratives of Turkish intellectual life have revolved around the the theme of movement toward the West, catching up with it, and setting up defenses against it. *Time* is also at the core of western European debates on belonging and relating to others. For the modernization discourse to hold, someone has to be forward and someone backward. It is often suggested that the relationship should move faster. But what exactly does that mean? And does "not now" mean "never"?

---

[30] Bahar Rumelili and Viyacheslav Morozov, "The External Constitution of European Identity: Russia and Turkey as Europe-makers," *Cooperation and Conflict* 47, no. 1 (2012): 28–48; Levin, *Turkey and the European Union*.

[31] John Hobson, "The Postcolonial Paradox of Eastern Agency," *Perceptions* 29, no. 1 (2014): 121–34.

Ways of Seeing[32] and Ways of Telling

Ethnographic moments from Turkey-EU relations have played a key role in structuring this book and the search for interpretation had to cross many borders. The present manuscript owes a lot to reading across disciplines. Historians of ideas helped me comprehend how meanings of Europe, East, and West, and related knowledge apparatuses emerged; how they were co-opted to build polities in specific eras or time-spaces. Anthropological scholarship has been crucial in giving this manuscript wings—liberating it from conventions of writing about Europe in EU studies and reconciling the many puzzling moments in research and writing. In some academic traditions it is common to think of "data" and "theory" as separable parts of research and writing. Anthropologist Ruth Behar voiced concerns of many others who felt that such approach is limiting:

> The writings of Durkheim, Weber, Marx, and Foucault, among other works classified as "theory" are essentially ethnographic texts that have been anointed as theoretical. My sense is that we tend to automatically reach for the work of such European theorists, which our canon has legitimized as translocal and applicable to myriad situations beyond their original settings, without always thinking about the way this reproduces Eurocentric prestige hierarchies of knowledge in the academy.[33]

Research and writing are guided by numerous "aha" moments that occur unexpectedly, switches and twists, and it is often the personal encounters and sudden realization that one's believed truths are not accepted by the interlocutor that influence the structure of the text. Research frameworks need a "space for surprise," as the sociologist Nilüfer Göle advised.[34] One should travel between established frames and engage with moments of what the anthropologist Erwing Goffman called "astounding complex,"[35] faced by interlocutors who find out that events are not unfolding according to their expectations. In some academic

---

[32] "Ways of seeing" (or variations thereof) is a phrase often used to explain positionality in research, the fact that knowledge emerges from specific perspectives, or what Donna Haraway called "situated knowledges." A good introduction for a reader not familiar with this scholarship might be a book on visual art by John Berger et al., *Ways of Seeing* (London: British Broadcasting Corporation and Penguin Books, 2008).

[33] Ruth Behar, "Ethnography and the Book that Was Lost," *Ethnography* 4, no. 1 (2003): 15–39, 25.

[34] Nilüfer Göle, *The Forbidden Modern: Civilization and Veiling* (Ann Arbor: University of Michigan Press, 1996).

[35] Erwing Goffman, *Frame Analysis: An Essay on the Organization of Human Experience* (Boston: Northeastern University Press, 1974).

journals on international politics, vibrant debates on the role of writing and writers in the process of knowledge production are becoming unavoidable.[36]

Authors covering contested narratives often note that it is difficult not to "choose sides." Historian Onur Yıldırım, who authored a nuanced study on Greek-Turkish relations, put it well when he highlighted that writer's position is unlikely to be shaped only by a distinct set of documents or conversations undertaken for a specific research project. It is the whole context of his/her coming of age that matters.[37] Growing up and working in C(c)entral Europe has shaped much of the thinking behind the present book and so have the years of travelling between EU and Turkey. I have never had any serious doubt that Turkey and EU should work toward a genuinely *common* way of shaping their public space. And while this present manuscript hopefully presents views from "both sides," it certainly goes deeper into the dynamics in the EU.

(Hi)story-telling can well emerge in realizations of similarities in seemingly different contexts. "Thank you, European!" says a friend as I'm handing him an *ıslak mendil* (wet towel). We burst into laughter immediately and cannot stop. It is early spring, we have just finished breakfast at a lakeside restaurant in Ankara, and before making the gesture I watched him for a while struggle with pieces of food in his hands. It is not just what he says but how he says it—the expression on his face is pretentiously humble. Ours is a jolly laughter, one that connects. We are happy to see each other after a while, the air is a bit chilly, but not too cold. It is three of us at the table and after generous breakfast we are about to take a walk. Our only duty today is to enjoy each other's company and catch up on old conversations. But laughter does not always connect—it can also express distance.[38] In this case, just as it confirms our camaraderie, it inevitably voices a common jest for a certain idea of a relationship between "Europeans" and their southern or eastern neighbors, one in which the former is morally and intellectually superior, and the latter responds with a mix of submission and resistance. We can laugh also because we know that, as this friend put it in another conversation, "this is not about good/bad Europe and good/bad Turkey."

---

[36] Particularly productive have been the discussions on the pages of the journal *Millennium*, including these contributions: Vanda Vrasti, "Dr. Strangelove, or How I Learned to Stop Worrying about Methodology and Love Writing," *Millennium – Journal of International Studies* 39, no. 1 (2010): 79–88. Can Mutlu, "How (Not) to Disappear Completely: Pedagogical Potential of Research Methods in International Relations," *Millennium: Journal of International Studies* 43, no. 3 (2015): 931–41. Jason A. Rancatore, "It Is Strange: A Reply to Vrasti," *Millennium: Journal of International Studies* 39, no. 1 (2010): 65–77.

[37] Onur Yıldırım, *Diplomacy and Displacement: Reconsidering the Turco-Greek Exchange of Populations, 1922-1934* (New York and London: Routledge, 2006).

[38] Michael Billig, *Laughter and Ridicule: Towards a Social Critique of Humour* (London: Sage and Theory, Culture and Society, 2005).

And, it is even more complicated than that. The "European" author, while now an EU passport holder, was raised in a country that is not really "Western" in Turkish (or any other) narratives of Europe. It is postsocialist, post-Soviet, or "new" Europe—always with hyphens.[39] Being a liminal European, a one who got "certified" around the time of graduation from college, it thus felt familiar hearing "thank you, European," or variations thereof, expressed in different contexts, often in a less joking manner, to communicate a sense of injustice and of being misunderstood. It also felt familiar when sarcasm and denunciations of EU-rope were expressed almost in the same sentence, in which my interlocutors would lament the state of affairs in Turkey and express hopes that "the West" could help resolve some things—or at least not make them worse.

When the EU member states gave a green light to accession talks with Turkey in 2004, I was working as an analyst in a think-tank in Slovakia. This was a period of enthusiasm from eastern enlargement of the Union, a new beginning. Yet just as Eastern Europeans enjoyed the joys of inclusion, a shadow was flourishing, called an "enlargement fatigue," a suggestion that perhaps this was a too big and too early expansion for the old Union. Even in "postsocialist" states there was not a uniform consensus on further enlargement and Turkey had been viewed as a "no" case especially for politicians and commentators for whom Christianity as a religion and Christian democracy as a political movement were important points of departure. Yet I could not say that this sentiment *dominated* the policy rooms. On the contrary, support for deeper collaboration with candidates for membership and other neighbors was a key point in discussions of policy makers and think-tankers in Eastern and Central Europe.[40] Foreign policy institutes in "newly European states" were engaged in vibrant collaboration and offered free tribune for exchange of diverse opinions.[41] Even if priority attention was placed on the western Balkans and post-Soviet Eastern European states, which were for many reasons deemed "closer," it was perfectly acceptable, even welcome, if non-partisan policy institutes brought Turkey on agenda. It has not been the easiest thing to do, as Turkey-EU conversation had previously involved mainly the more Western countries, but not an impossible one.

[39] For recent debates about the "post" in post-socialism, see John Bailyn, Dijana Jelača and Danijela Lugarić (eds), *The Future of (Post)Socialism: Eastern European Perspectives* (Albany: SUNY Press, 2018).

[40] I use this term geographically. The next chapter discusses ideas behind map-making.

[41] This is not to say that mobilizations based on denying of belonging to "the other" (the Turk, in this case) were not a part of political life. They were. But smaller, face-to-face encounters of policymakers, journalists and academics did provide a room for constructive discussions in which diversity of voices could he heard and listened to.

The present author and number of other colleagues in the region strongly disagreed with the different standards applied to Turkey, and speaking in favor of accession talks was the only option that made sense. I felt that most of the counterarguments presented on the grounds of religious differences or economic development missed the crucial part about the accession process. Namely that it is something that evolves, an opportunity to negotiate differences. Visitors from Western European policy rooms who sometimes joined these discussions were often surprised to find such a support for Turkey in "new Europe." They were even more surprised to hear a confident explanation that Bratislava is also different from Berlin or Barcelona and yet all are in the EU. Colleagues from Turkey presenting their work to "newly European" audiences were free to air various views, including complaints of "having to explain themselves" to countries that popped up on EU map somehow unexpectedly. Local "Central Europeans" skeptical of Turkey's accession could point out their worries and hear responses, from other fellow "local" central Europeans, that their rejection of Turkey mirrors many a "Western European" thought about Czechs, Hungarians, and other Easterners.

And while a sense of "denied belonging" has shaped much of Turkish conversations on the EU with a renewed vigor after the talks on accession were suspended immediately after their opening, it seemed that even if the talks were restarted immediately, a range of contested issues would remain. The EU has been perceived neither as a default provider of progress nor as a model unambiguously worthy of emulation. When I set out to understand what shapes meanings of the EU/Europe in Turkey, I was quickly initiated into difficulties such process may involve. In the past decade I have spent several shorter and longer periods in Istanbul and have had the opportunity to discuss questions shaping this book in hundreds of conversations. The journey started in conversations with people who were used to translating Turkey for foreigners. For them, the joys of "discovering Westerners" and being tired of them went hand in hand. A young woman, to whom I was introduced by a common acquaintance welcomed me with "Hi, my name is Meliha and I do not like foreigners." At the time of our meeting she was working as a fixer for Western journalists and grew more and more frustrated with what she perceived as their lack of willingness to listen. And while I gradually met many other people, it was probably the experience of the writers, NGO workers, and others who have commuted between the various "sides" that has been guiding for the argument. But then the argument would not have emerged had it not been for the conversations with people who never did any such commuting. The conversations informing this work took place mainly in Istanbul, Prague, Bratislava, and Brussels over the decade 2007–17.

And while denied belonging and references to European rejection would come up in many of EU-related conversations in Turkey, this has not been the only reason for critique of the West. Western-ness mattered in a different way than experienced during westernization of Czechoslovakia. While in say the latter case it has been an anchor, a second pole to which policy making levitated after being on Moscow's orbit during the Cold War, in case of Turkey, the European/Western aspirations have been more of a stepping stone, a tool rather than a final destination.[42] A number of my interlocutors would sometimes remark a variation of: "*I accept that the EU is not taking Turkey in, but it could at least help it to become better governed.*" That said, I rarely heard Europe discussed as a model to be fully emulated.

This text is written from the middle of a whirlwind. The accession partnership is constantly disputed, and Turkey's very eventful domestic and foreign policy is making international headlines regularly. With more developments in western Europe, academics are joking that European integration courses might as well be renamed European (dis)integration. In the process of writing, I found myself envying historians digging into periods that have already seen some closure. I thought they might be more confident when making decisions about what belongs in the story and what does not, as they have the benefit of standing at the top of the mountain, with a view of all the streets and dead-ends below. But then, even for an experienced historian, choices do not come easy. As Norman Naimark noted: "The past is huge, it's endless."[43]

When anthropologists do "field research" they seek *immersion*. This means opening up to perspective of their interlocutors. The rise in international mobility of people, capital, and information, and the emergence of diaspora communities has opened debate about multi-sited ethnography. "The field" is not standing just for a geographic location anymore, as vibrant debates in anthropology suggest. The idea of travel between away and home has shaped much anthropological writing, with many studies emerging exactly from the benefit of the crack that happens in the process of leaving and coming.[44] In the case of this book, I cannot say I ever left "the field," because immersion is happening *in* the relationship. I do get different perspectives for thinking about EU-Turkey relations when I watch them from Prague or Istanbul. But while each of these addresses brings

---

[42] Of course, also in the "class of 1989/2004" there has been a diversity of perspectives on expectations from the EU membership.

[43] Norman M. Naimark, "How Historians Repeat Themselves," *Hoover Digest* no. 3 (2009), https://www.hoover.org/research/how-historians-repeat-themselves.

[44] Raelene Wilding, "Transnational Ethnographies and Anthropological Imaginings of Migrancy," *Journal of Ethnic and Migration Studies* 33, no. 2 (2007): 331–48.

up different ways of seeing, the primary "field" of immersion here has been the problem of understanding.

At the time of writing of this book, Turkey is nowhere near the formal accession into the EU. While the latter continues to be point of reference in Turkey's domestic debates, it is not necessarily a positive one anymore. Mainstreaming of nationalism and xenophobia around Europe has shaken some of the strongest pillars of the enlargement process—capacity of the EU to lead by example. At the same time, the Union is perhaps more introverted, considering a number of domestic challenges to its legitimacy. Turkey's harmonization with the EU law has been lukewarm. This book provides a screenshot of one era. While it highlights misunderstandings, it was written with aspiration that some form of better understanding is indeed possible.

Summary of Chapters

This book hopes to provide impulses for discussion about the future of European integration but refrains from scenario-building or giving tasks to participants of the process. Instead, it invites the reader toward exploring architectures of similarity, exactly because all that emphasis on difference in the(se) relationship(s) must become tiring at some point. Especially so, if some narratives of difference seem to be reproduced out of inertia, and in a way which conceals other differences more pertinent to lives of humans—and not addressed by policies.

In Part One, we will take a walk through orders and borders. It may seem so, that crossing intellectual spaces is somehow easier than overcoming physical barriers, but perhaps this is not the case. The part engages with the creation of knowledge, as a product of human curiosity, but also a result and tool of controlling narratives. Making sense of where things and people, including ourselves, belong is a common part of everyday life. It is also an objective of scientific inquiry. We categorize and are categorized. No matter if one focuses on books or maps, the act of searching for orders and our place in them seems inescapable. States including their federations need legitimation narratives. These do not always reflect the wishes of all of their citizens or residents. Moreover, such narratives sometimes establish differences that have not existed prior to their announcement. The chapters in this part take us through recent discussions of how the Ottomans/Turks and West Europeans imagined each other and how the discussions about the other helped glue their respective polities. A key question guiding this section is the one of choices: Will things and people fit comfortably in their assigned places just because we ask them to? And will we be allowed to belong just by the virtue of expressing such a wish?

Part Two enters straight into the accession process, a stage both novel in Turkey-EU conversations and one following the many past routines. The chapters in this part look at its scripts, formal and informal rules, some given, some contested. Thousands of pages have been covered, in diplomatic documents and think-tank briefs, with notes on progress in the relationship. The central axis of this conversation is the one of *a right*—a right to ask, a right to speak from inside. While there is no law that would validate this demand, such right is still claimed. The lack of conclusive laws in this situation provides a fruitful ground not just for expressing grievances, but also for their use for short-term political gains. Turkish and other European citizens now meet in a variety of constellations— from diplomatic summits through NGO projects. It is a part of the new script that one more binary comes to the forefront—it is not just Turkey and the EU, but also their many respective "civil societies." On the one hand, the support for more forms of interactions between the Turks and other Europeans can be lauded: many new understandings emerged in such dialogues, a lot of good faith was brought to the world. At the same time, it seems that the support of these "civil society" interactions postpones the eventual process of inter*national* inclusion ad infinitum. Expectations that nonstate actors would "democratize the state" have so far largely failed. This is mostly due to the absence of more solid prospects for the shared belonging between Turkey and the European Union. The civil society workers after all, however innovative ideas they may possess, are constrained by legal frameworks and policy structure. Rather than being empowered, they often find themselves unsafe in any discussion they enter—too "European" for Turks, too "Turkish" for Europeans. To advance this argument we turn to a story of Turkish Cypriots. The EU has suspended accession talks with Turkey shortly after their opening, stating different opinions on the Cyprus conflict as the main reason. While Cyprus is often presented as an obstacle in Turkey's EU path, it also offers analogies to the situation of Turkey. The EU approach to the Cyprus conflict and to negotiations with Turkey is conflated by the ambiguity with which "democracy" is seen as both a precondition and a consequence of EU relations with potential members. Parallels between a situation of Turkish Cypriots in an unrecognized state and lives of Turks, whose right to request insider status in the Union is also not recognized, provide a new perspective on the relationship.

Part Three focuses on "revival" of Turkey-EU diplomatic relations, announced with the adoption of "refugee deal" in Spring 2016. While the

EU-Turkey Statement, as the deal is officially titled, has been mostly promoted as an instrument of strategic cooperation separate from accession partnership, such separation is possible only in official documentation, not in everyday life of the relationship. Arrival of refugees was presented as something that gives boost to the relationship and yet it again pointed to the foundational problem. That problem is both between EU-Turkey and within their respective polities. To that end we focus on debates in one EU state often referenced as a "new member." Chapters in this section show the complexity of migration debate in post-2015 "crisis" Europe and offer ethnography from watching the "refugee deal" in Prague, Brussels, and Istanbul. Much writing on Syrian refugee crisis has centered on the rights of the refugees and perspectives of peace process in the Middle East. We have perhaps seen less accents on how the states' wrangling over numbers and agitated focus on border protection has gone against the spirit of the accession partnership—in which the EU (and members) are expected to help the candidate, not the other way round. Yet in the aftermath of the 2016 refugee deal, it is becoming less and less clear who is helping who. Moreover, strange hierarchies of rights have been proposed, such as when some activist campaigns suggested to "rescue" refugees from Turkey. Engaging with official records, ethnography, and journalistic coverage, I show how the policy has been shaped by elites informed by the wariness of the Middle East and indifference to societies who have been left to do the work of hospitality almost on their own. Such exclusion from the "common we" does not require active loathing—indifference is a sufficient ingredient.

In Coda, we turn to reflections on times and time-zones. We are used to counting time in categories we consider neutral. Yet, there is nothing apolitical about time—not just because of how the clocks and calendars have been invented, but also the purpose they serve today. It has been sometimes suggested that Turkey-EU relations should be speeded up. Diplomatic interlocutors often emphasize "Turkey must decide" or "Europe must choose." Such statements often come with suggestions that the other party should not procrastinate on its decisions; the earlier it makes the choice, the better. But what exactly does "things should start moving faster" mean? Who should act, how, and what will change, if the relationship would move "faster"? And what do such calls mean in a world that is already moving so fast that many of its participants, Eastern, Western, Southern, Northern, have trouble imagining they could *ever* catch up?

Part One

The Clock, the Compass, and the Typewriter

In the early spring 2010 a group of Istanbul residents, including a playwright and an engineer, organized a press conference to tell the world that from now on we should date our present epoch from the moment of the invention of the wheel some 4,000 years ago. "Such a switch would help mankind build on what connects it rather than divides," a writer behind the initiative said. "The current calendar is limiting," he continued, "in that it departs from one religion, one tradition." Shortly before the conference initiators found out that a group of creationists elsewhere in the world recently also added this same number to their calendar, something that made the present group emphasize that theirs is a strictly secular project. The conference was convened in a place called °360, a high-end club at night-time, restaurant at daytime, a few steps from Galatasaray Lisesi, a well-known elite high school in Beyoğlu neighborhood. The choice of the venue, °360 was symbolic—it literally offered a view into all four corners of the world and angles between them. On a second reading, perhaps it matters that the possibility to see all the angles of the world can be rather exclusive. Only few residents of the city could enjoy a meal at this venue, or would even consider finding out whether they could. But what was served at this occasion was the story, fairly revolutionary to my ears. It has never occurred to me before that one could just propose changing the calendar. I was surprised that very few journalists attended, and the initiative, read amidst the sounds of church bells and ezan, barely made headlines.

The signatories wanted to follow up with letters to the UN, Council of Europe and European Commission, but, by the time of writing of this book it did not happen. A few years later, one of its founders, Tarik Günersel, launched an *Earth*

Civilization Project, a call to "reconsider our collective existence on this planet."[1] In our many conversations, in which I sometimes skeptically compared calls to synchronize calendars to Esperanto, Tarik never seemed to have wavered or been discouraged that the idea is not (yet?) getting massive appeal, always claiming that even if one person listens to your thought, you've done your job. For him, the making of that appeal—how about we look at common beginnings—has been a way of exercising freedom, autonomy, and an act of exploring the possibilities of connection. As another signatory told me, "Turkey is now living a historic time," so it is a propitious moment for sharing the idea. Going all the way through with technicalities has not been the priority. The most important part was the creative process, the act of suggesting that there are more ways how humans can relate beyond what divides them. Tarik after all is a writer and at the time of announcing this initiative, he was also the chair of Turkish PEN.

The city of Istanbul is very rewarding if one wants to think about how we organize times and places. In fact, it provides many invitations to this journey. Synchronization of clocks and the difficulty thereof is a theme weaving through Turkish history. In the nineteenth century, Ottoman reformers pledged to bring the empire closer to Europe, a project of travel in time, rather than space, hence the frequent references to "catching up." Successive generations of politicians and writers have stocked whole libraries with dreams generated by this process and frustrations when Europe seemed a too difficult, even unreachable, destination. But it is not just texts—it is also visual monuments, spaces and their accessibility—that provide a perspective on being and becoming. It takes less than an hour to get from Sinan's sixteenth-century mosques in Sultanahmet to skyscrapers in Levent or the twenty-first-century gated communities, such as Mashattan in the Maslak area, the latter being a world fully self-sustaining, with its own restaurants, shops, and even a little lake. But such a journey does not neatly mark centuries and decades, from earlier to later; Istanbul's old and new are not laid out like in a museum catalogue. Perhaps the closest way of describing how they *are* laid out would be in the words of physicist Carlo Rovelli contending linear understandings of time: "The events of the world do not form an orderly queue like the English, they crowd around chaotically like the Italians."[2]

First-time visitors to the city are often surprised that what they find to be some of its most European neighborhoods are on the Asian continent, or that bar streets

---

[1] Tarik Günersel, "Earth Day and Earth Civilization Project," *Sampsonia Way*, April 17, 2014, http://www.sampsoniaway.org/fearless-ink/tarik-gunersel/2014/04/17/earth-day-and-earth-civilization-project/.
[2] Carlo Rovelli, quoted in *The Guardian*, "There is No Such Thing as Past or Future," April 14, 2018.

are just a few steps away from very pious quarters. The air-conditioned shopping malls selling a mix of brands from around the world including Turkey have not yet fully replaced street markets. While various "re-vitalization" projects have destroyed parts of earlier fabrics, nothing has so far erased the many reminders that the city has lived through different eras and political projects, new time-zones not only replacing each other but also co-existing. As the anthropologist Partha Chatterjee reminds us, "People can only imagine themselves in empty homogeneous time; they do not live in it."[3]

The three chapters in this part explore maps, time zones, and writers' decision-making; in short, how we organize what and who belongs where and why. The aim is to outline contours of the worlds into which *accession talks* entered at the beginning of the twenty-first century, to show the locations from which Europe(s), West(s), and East(s), have been imagined and lived, how they served in political contestations and the organization of knowledge. While the year 2004 opened a *new* stage, the life of the relationship has not been cut off from its pre-accession pasts, it builds upon them. I open this discussion with a review of the many nuances of belonging, and its other side (denial, withdrawal, rejection, absence). The second chapter follows with ideas that have shaped Europe's self-narrative as it started becoming an institution—the European Union. The third chapter reviews recurring themes in Turkey's debate about (not) being part of EU-rope.

---

[3]　Partha Chatterjee, "Anderson's Utopia," *Diacritics* 29, no. 4 (1999): 128–34, 131.

1

Belongings We Choose, and
Those That We Do Not

"Where should I put this?" one may ask at home when unpacking the shopping bags. "Where does he come from?" could be a common question inquiring about someone who just joined a group. "How did *this* get here?" is sometimes uttered in surprise when things are not where they are supposed to be. What and who belongs where are also basic questions we ask when we do research, organize libraries, or draft new articles. They guide our learning and ways in which we convey knowledge. Humans dream of becoming part of something, think and feel they are a part of something, yet writers sometimes get them wrong. Belongings are fought for, rewritten, contradictory, and, probably, inescapable. They also often come in binaries such as eastern/western, democratic/undemocratic, or developed/developing. The problem with binaries is that they force us to define one entity in terms of what it is not. But then, who invented binaries, and can we escape some of them?

The calls for adjustment of clocks, setting them to a common starting point, such as the one described in the opening of this part, connect profoundly to debate about possibilities of connectivity, togetherness, and solidarity. Writers living in various eras and geographies have asked for unity, so did founders of political projects, be they national or imperial. Claims to universalism, however, are often translated into institutional histories built on disagreements with and about various types of "others." The volume of commentary, political pamphlets, and scholarship produced in Istanbul, Berlin, Paris, Prague, and other places on a European map, in which authors watch "Turkey" from "Europe" or the other way around is enormous. It is now well-established that for Western Europeans and Turks alike, ideas about the imagined other helped to shape their "home" polities.[1] Imitating the others, frustrations at not being able to be like

---

[1] Levin, *Turkey and the European Union*; Neumann, *Uses of the Other*; Döşemeci, *Debating Turkish Modernity*.

them as well as denying membership, and coming to terms with this rejection, have shaped a sense of "we" for many human polities. Turkey and EU-rope are then no exception—although, arguably, they have featured in their respective imaginaries more frequently, than, say, Samoa has. Where specifically is this difference, why do we need to say Turkey *and* Europe?

Finding the Border, Writing the Border

There are several types of maps. The first atlases I recall from elementary school usually came with two versions of the world: physical/natural and political. The former would show mountains in brown color, lowlands in green, and rivers and seas in blue. The latter would get more colorful—every state got one color—and also more determined on beginnings and endings, as borders were emphasized with a line. What is not immediately obvious when we look at such a map is that it captures a state of affairs at the time of its publication. Digital era has made it much easier to produce maps and thus to see series of images that show how authority over territory[2] has been changing over time. While such sequences already give a hint that political units are impermanent, they reveal the results, not the process that led to reordering. When thinking about lines of separation, in the European context, it is helpful to engage with Maria Todorova's succinct description of the Balkans' becoming "European" exactly by un-becoming Ottoman, that is, as they started imitating the European nation-state.[3] Spaces shift in time, but the shifts do not just happen, they are made. Place-names reveal a bit more about histories of world-making.[4] The terms Near (Middle, Far) East, stayed with us from a recent era in which distances have been measured from Europe, and so has the taxonomy that refers to the cultural heritage of map makers.[5]

But neither the lines nor the names on the map provide the full story behind that seemingly clear order, such as which parliaments had to meet, whose armies moved, and who attended international conferences. Providing that story is the role of writers, but these also have to choose an angle, and countries sometimes

---

[2] Saskia Sassen, *Territory, Authority, Rights: From Medieval to Global Assemblages* (Princeton and Oxford: Princeton University Press, 2008).
[3] Maria Todorova, *Imagining the Balkans*. Updated edn (Oxford: Oxford University Press, 2009).
[4] So does positioning of a particular state or continent in the center of a map.
[5] A common example mentioned in debates on geographies of naming is the Pacific island of Rapa Nui, named Easter Island, when an eighteenth-century Dutch explorer visited it on this Christian holiday. For many European explorers this Euro/Christian-centric worldview was perhaps a natural standpoint as they were approaching worlds unknown to them from a point they came from and were familiar with.

end up categorized by their past. Some Eastern European states are often called postsocialist (or postcommunist) long after 1989, and two decades after that year the British weekly *The Economist* ran a blog "Eastern Approaches: Ex-communist Europe."[6] In many EU documents and policy-oriented commentary, countries are referred to according to the policy-making boxes they fall in such as "The EU has adopted Action Plans with each Eastern Partnership country."[7] Nomenclature comes with the one making the order.

Search for order, relationship between things, and clarity in conveying knowledge is at the heart of academic work. Scientists have explored how humans shape their belonging, but their work and assumptions underlying their inquiry have constituted and reified certain orderings of the world and the vocabulary in which it is common to think about it. Published texts, often results of multiple redrafts, strive to provide definitive or full answers, yet can rarely meet that ambition.

Several recent publications have critically examined the earlier portrayal of the Ottomans in Western historiography.[8] The historian Caroline Finkel observed that Ottoman elites were often reduced to a "theatre of the absurd"[9] and their actions judged by standards different than those of West Europeans. As the historian Daniel Goffman pointed out, Ottoman "militarism" was highlighted in such terms as if other states at that time did not have conquests and wars in their regular repertoire. What was deemed normal and acceptable for Western European nations was a sign of barbarism when Ottomans were scrutinized.[10] Certain reductions of Ottoman society migrated to Western social science literature to become *types* or categories for comparing social organization. It is undeniable that scientific production has been constrained by demands of political power of the day.[11] Narrating the Ottoman story via conflict, war, "decay,"[12] and

[6] When I interviewed the magazine's editor Ed Lucas in 2011, and asked him whether it would not seem strange if a column about Western Europe in Slovak magazine would be headlined "A window into post-colonial world," he said: "I agree and I have been fighting against such cheap labels for a long time. In 1939 the Economist did not have a correspondent for 'former Habsburg Empire'—although this was precisely 21 years after its break up, just like we are speaking today 21 years after collapse of communism. [. . .] Post-communist is not a very nice label but let us keep in mind that journalism needs brevity and one cannot start every article with an essay on terminology." (Zahranicna Politika 1/2011, translated from Slovak).

[7] "Eastern Partnership" is an initiative announced by the EU in 2009 to strengthen relations with Armenia, Azerbaijan, Belarus, Georgia, Moldova, and Ukraine.

[8] Revising the Eurocentric bias in earlier scholarship has recently become an urgent and long overdue part of agenda in several social science and humanities disciplines.

[9] Caroline Finkel, *Osman's Dream* (London: John Murray, 2006).

[10] Daniel Goffman, *The Ottoman Empire and Early Modern Europe* (Cambridge: Cambridge University Press, 2002).

[11] John Hobson, *The Eastern Origins of Western Civilization* (Cambridge: Cambridge University Press, 2004); Hobson, "The Paradox of Eastern Agency"; Behar, "The Book that was Lost."

[12] Faroqhi, *Approaching Ottoman History*.

disrespect for learning cannot really be separated from gradual creation of what Gerard Delanty called "Platonic-like vision of an immutable European ideal, the notion that the idea of Europe has always been linked to the values of freedom, democracy and autonomy."[13] That ideal was born in arguing with what it is not— and Turks/Ottomans have featured prominently in this narrative.[14]

While writing does not just *tell*, it also *makes* the world, the library of human curiosity has not yet been centrally organized. Texts can contribute to reification of separating lines unintentionally. In a preface to his *Age of Empire*, covering some forty years at the break of European nineteenth and twentieth centuries, the historian Eric Hobsbawm writes about his effort to

> [S]ee the past as a coherent whole, rather than (as historical specialization so often forces us to see it) as an assembly of separate topics: the history of different states, of politics, of the economy, of culture or whatever. Ever since I began to be interested in history, I have always wanted to know how all these aspects of the past (or present) life hang together and why.[15]

It is perhaps ironic, considering the book's title, that the Ottomans receive only a few passing references. Hobsbawm knew very well that those deemed non-European were perceived as "inferior, undesirable, feeble and backward, even infantile,"[16] thus his marginal attention to the Ottomans can hardly be seen as a product of intention to belittle. Yet writers make choices and even the most genuine effort to show "how life hang together" is bound to leave some parts missing, and unintentionally reproduce existing orders of things and places. Telling parts of the story, then, does not always mean siding with one of its protagonists. Reducing the universe of references does not have to be a mechanism of exclusion—it can be an act of pursuit of depth.

Where Do We Stand on the Meanings?

If we accept that texts emerge from times and places in which their authors lived, how do we think about appeals to humanity's common origins or purpose, such as the one for harmonizing our calendars described in opening of this part? How do we reconcile the positionality of the one behind the typewriter and an

[13] Gerard Delanty, *Inventing Europe: Idea, Identity and Reality* (Basingstoke: Macmillan Press Ltd, 1995), 2.
[14] Neumann, *Uses of the Other*, 40.
[15] Eric Hobsbawm, *The Age of Empire 1875–1914* (New York: Vintage, 1989).
[16] Hobsbawm, *The Age of Empire*, 79.

ontology that there is something common to all humans? Thinking about the world as if it were one place has been at the backdrop of calls to end (hostilities, war, racism, ecocide), and thus, also to begin anew. Just recently, cosmopolitan imaginaries have surged in writing about international politics in the 1990s.[17] This has been in response to growing interconnectedness of the world, where money and cultures could travel faster than before. It was also a celebration of the fall of the Berlin wall and first steps toward the EU's eastern expansion, or a process sometimes referred to as the unification of Europe. A famous moment from this time is Francis Fukuyama's declaration of the "end of history":

> The triumph of the West, of the Western *idea*, is evident first of all in the total exhaustion of viable systematic alternatives to Western liberalism. . . . What we may be witnessing is not just the end of the Cold War, or the passing of a particular period of postwar history, but the end of history as such: that is, the end point of mankind's ideological evolution and the universalization of Western liberal democracy as the final form of human government.[18]

As his book was widely debated, genocides in Rwanda and Bosnia rallied urgent calls for more resolute international action. "Citizen of the world" T-shirts have been proudly worn at many a European summer school or development education camp, yet they often attracted backlash for ignoring the privilege that comes with some passports.[19] Scholar of international relations David Chandler warned that calls for bringing responsibility for rights protection to international institutions at a time when rights were still tied to nation states might result in less rights exactly for those who ask for more. Moreover, "global civil society" was an unlikely candidate for enforcement of such rights.[20] In a similar argument, sociologist Craig Calhoun notes that in the plethora of texts that came into being with these discussions, a question that seemed to be marginalized has been the one of how to actually reconcile the cosmopolitanism of "frequent travelers" with the wishes of wider societies in which they live.[21] While the dichotomy of mobile elites and sedentary commons, often made in debates about globalization, might be a bit simplified, it probably is true that the world reveals different parts of itself to its observers, depending on their vantage points. It is probably also true that humans speak from very unique points, or

---

[17] At the time of writing, cosmopolitan imaginaries gained new strength in relation to climate change debates.

[18] Francis Fukuyama, "The End of History?" *The National Interest*, no. 16 (1989): 3–18, 3.

[19] See Calhoun, "The Class Consciousness of Frequent Travelers," 869–97.

[20] David Chandler, "New Rights for Old? Cosmopolitan Citizenship and the Critique of State Sovereignty," *Political Studies* 51 (2003); David Chandler, *Constructing the Global Civil Society: Power and Morality in International Relations* (London: Palgrave Macmillan, 2004).

[21] Calhoun, "The Class Consciousness of Frequent Travelers," 869–97.

what Nira Yuval-Davis calls "social locations" shaped by gender, class, ethnicity, and other layers of belonging. These social locations are constantly evolving and "not adding up but mutually constitutive."[22]

It then seems that in these diverse constellations of belongings, all in constant state of flux (oxymoron intended), appeals to something unifying come with accents on different particulars. Take Diogenes of Sinop,[23] who is often referenced for "the first" recorded declaration of "I am a citizen of the universe."[24] Yet, as we learn from scholars of Diogenes's life, that statement was born out of rejection of the emperor's or anyone's right to *offer* citizenship to others: he already belonged. His story, regardless whether it was really "the first" helps illustrate how belongings, including the cosmopolitan, emerge as a response, a critique of the state of affairs in one's own particular life-world. Diogenes is remembered as a Greek philosopher, Sinop is a province and a town on a Black Sea coast of present Turkey. In terms of the present calendar, the philosopher lived in the fourth century BC. Translated to present concerns, the *cosmos* to which he belonged was not a place inhabited solely by humans and I imagine he would really enjoy current debates in which duality of the human and the natural is becoming increasingly challenged, including in the debates around the concept of Anthropocene, which appears to be our new epoch, although we do not know when it started.[25]

We can well say that cosmopolitanism is a standpoint[26] through which writers convey their critique of the world. It can also be a language that allows political communities to justify their place in the world and viability of their goals. Writers working on the field of belonging, including those who opt for another vocabulary, such as identities or solidarities, often distinguish between "thick" and "thin," the more or less immediate, urgent, tangible as opposed to the more abstract or distant. But if we accept that belongings are mutually constitutive, locking someone into a specific bracket defined by one category does not make any sense. The mutuality of constitution also means that belongings are political and social—as Michael Billig emphasizes, they are not "inner psychological

---

[22] Nira Yuval-Davis, "Belonging and the Politics of Belonging," *Patterns of Prejudice* 40, no. 3 (2006): 197–214.

[23] Diogenes of Sinop, we learn, is sometimes confused with Diogenes Laertius, his chronicler.

[24] Darrin McMahon, "Fear and Trembling, Strangers and Strange Lands," *Daedalus* 137, no. 1 (2008): 5–17; A. A. Long, "The Concept of the Cosmopolitan in Greek and Roman Thought," *Daedalus* 137, no. 1 (2008): 50–8.

[25] Cameron Harrington, "The Ends of the World: International Relations and the Anthropocene," *Millennium: Journal of International Studies* 44, no. 3 (2016): 478–98.

[26] Calhoun, "The Class Consciousness."

states."[27] Where the "cosmopolitan" comes as very different from the book of genders, ethnicities, classes is in the aspiration to something all-embracing, something the other particular boxes can never provide.

Mapping of belongings can well continue through a dyad of reason and emotion.[28] The scholars who walked this way noted that saying something is "emotional" often means it is not "rational." One is often "Eastern," the other "Western." Jack Goody traced the "Western idea" through formative periods such as Renaissance, Enlightenment, and Reformation and observed that "the rise of the West" has often been explained by "the possession of a rationality not available to others."[29] In a related discipline, cognitive scientists Daniel Kahnemann and Amos Tversky proposed the theory of bounded rationality. Their series of experiments explored how framing of social situations matters for choices humans make; their results showed that under pressure, we seem to be more likely to build on what the authors call "reflexive knowledge," rather than deep reflection. Emotions and reason then work together, it is not one or the other.[30]

While every day might be a new dawn, the scientists from various disciplines are telling us that we do not simply *decide* on the meanings of social situations on the spot. If we sit at a table, accidentally drop our cutlery and ask for a new "Europe" instead of a "fork," it might start an interesting conversation but we will probably not be understood immediately. "Europe" will not be a "fork" just because we chose that it could be. The sociologist Erwing Goffman used the example of a hospital setting to demonstrate what he calls the "astounding complex." Doctors are expected to prescribe pills, perform operations, and the patients are the ones being treated. A role reversal would come as a surprise as things are supposed to be explained within an established system of frames:

> Individuals exhibit considerable resistance to changing their frameworks . . . in our society the very significant assumption is generally made that all events—

[27] Billig, *Banal Nationalism*. Billig works with the term "identity" rather than "belonging," but his conclusions are still relevant for the present text.
[28] Yuval-Davis, "Belonging and the Politics of Belonging" sees belongings as emotional attachments individuals have to their social locations.
[29] Jack Goody, *The East in the West* (Cambridge: Cambridge University Press, 1996), 11.
[30] Daniel Kahnemann and Amos Tversky, "The Framing of Decisions and the Psychology of Choice," *Science* 211, no. 4481 (1981): 453–8; Daniel Kahnemann, "Maps of Bounded Rationality: A Perspective on Intuitive Judgement and Choice," Nobel Peace Prize Lecture, December 8, 2002, http://nobelprize.org/nobel_prizes/economics/laureates/2002/kahneman-lecture.html (Accessed December 10, 2009); Daniel Kahnemann, *Thinking, Fast and Slow* (London: Penguin, 2011).

without any exception—can be contained and managed within the conventional system of beliefs. We tolerate the unexplained but not the unexplainable.[31]

It is in the nature of political projects to provide an explanation. It is expected of writers to provide an accurate representation of such projects, and that is one of the most difficult parts, because it is the meanings over which we struggle. For the cultural anthropologist Stuart Hall, representations, a concept similar to Goffman's frames, define "with whom do we belong." For Hall, "They define what is 'normal,' who belongs and therefore who is excluded."[32] Belongings, then, are not just declared, they require recognition. They emerge in the process of contestation of forces that lay claims on representation of polities. Mobilization of belongings more narrow than the cosmopolitan, including ethnic or regional, is also a form of struggle—to be on the map.[33]

Choosing to Be Eastern or Western, and Knowing Whether One Is an Orientalist or an Occidentalist

If belongings are not just *there*, but arise in specific interactions, how do we treat the dyad of the East and the West? *East* and *West* serve as more than a spatial orientation and we navigate with them in political and cultural terrains. They provide clarity to some, who use them for explaining the world.

They might be confusing to others, even become objects of resistance, if those others feel misrepresented by such clarity. East and West are not just geographic coordinates used politically—it is common to speak of global South and North, especially in developmental discourses.[34] In *Orientalism*, a book that became a key reference in postcolonial scholarship, Edward Said, reviewing mostly French, British, and American texts on Arabs and Islam, wrote that the chief problem in the system of knowledge about the Orient (East), created by writers he studied, is how self-referential these texts are:

> Not only is the Orient accommodated to the moral exigencies of Western Christianity; it is also circumscribed by a series of attitudes and judgements

---

[31] Goffman, *Frame Analysis*, 29–30.
[32] Stuart Hall, "Introduction," in S. Hall (ed.), *Representation: Cultural Representation and Signifying Practices* (London, Thousand Oaks and New Delhi: Sage Publications and Open University, 1997), 1–12.
[33] Craig Calhoun, "Belonging in the Cosmopolitan Imaginary," *Ethnicities* 3, no. 4 (2003): 531–53.
[34] In *Imagining the Balkans*, Todorova (citing Lawrence Wolff) notes that E/W replaced N/S as key division in Europe in the eighteenth century. I am not sure whether the East and the West are the dominant division at the time of writing. Many of the debates about economy and migration at the beginning of the twenty-first century have revolved around north-south axis, with east-west not really disappearing.

that send the Western mind, not first to Oriental sources for correction and verification, but rather to the Orientalist works.[35]

Said and the many writers he inspired critiqued what they saw as hegemonic nexus of power and knowledge about the East. Yet, which East, and when? Said himself calls them "supreme fictions."[36] Easts and Wests have not developed as organic political communities, and the lines of separation between them have been shifting across time, but also depending on who wrote about them. Much of what is celebrated today, in some accounts, as success of "Western civilization" has been borrowed, stolen, or imported from "the East."[37] As Goody reminds us, some of the "eastern" items that enabled "the rise of the West" include "printing, paper, porcelain, cotton, silk weaving, compass, gun powder."[38]

As (city) states and empires have encountered each other through trade, war, or science, and literature (think Arab translations of Greek thinkers), they changed each other's trajectories. Goody tells us that the non-West was understood as inferior in thought: "they" (the others) do not think like "us," which is why they did not "modernize."[39] It is paradoxical, that exactly in the period, when the West discovered "the reason," some of the most pervasive stereotypes and myths about the East were formed.[40] The problem in some narratives of easts and wests is perhaps exactly the question of destiny, teleology, and suggestion that things were always supposed to be this way.[41]

While there have been various writers throughout history who critiqued what we now call Orientalist frames,[42] it was Said's work that inspired a global audience of followers and critics.[43] Perhaps the controversy that it started suggests how important the theme of producing the other is, and the powerful

---

[35] Edward Said, *Orientalism*, 25th anniversary edn (New York: Vintage Books, 1994) [1979 orig.], 67.

[36] Said, *Orientalism*, xviii.

[37] Hobson, *The Eastern Origins of Western Civilization*; Goody, *The East in the West*.

[38] Jack Goody, *The Eurasian Miracle* (Cambridge: Polity Press, 2010), 49.

[39] Goody, *The East in the West*, 37.

[40] Nancy Bisaha, *Creating East and West: Renaissance Humanists and the Ottoman Turks* (Philadelphia: University of Pennsylvania Press, 2004).

[41] In *The Eurasian Miracle*, Goody holds, that East and West, or, various civilizations inhabiting Eurasia, were switching in periods of influence throughout history. He argues that "alteration automatically rejects essentialism and the notion of permanent advantage" and suggests that in the next decades the leadership might as well evade Europe.

[42] Jill Beaulieu and Mary Roberts(eds), *Orientalism's Interlocutors: Painting, Architecture, Photography* (Durham and London: Duke University Press, 2002).

[43] According to Yacinta O'Hagan, Said criticized Michel Foucault and Raymond Williams, on whose work he drew, for Euro-centrism, but he himself could not escape accusations of contradicting himself exactly because the "humanism, enlightenment and emancipation," to which he subscribed was seen by many as extension of Western imperialism—the very approach he criticized. O'Hagan, *Conceptualizing the West* Jacinta O'Hagan, *Conceptualizing the West in International Relations: From Spengler to Said* (Houndmills, Basingstoke, Hampshire and New York: Palgrave, 2002), 185-211.

response the motives of exoticism and fantasies of homogeneity generate. Said could not escape some of the same simplifications he criticized. As he later extended the analysis to current debate on the West and Islam, he invited even more criticism: Does not the very fact that he has produced much of his scholarship at a "Western" institution suggest that there indeed is a pluralism in "Western" thinking about the world?[44] His writing has been called reductionist[45] and, arguably, more detailed classifications of writing about the East have been produced since then. But, as Maria Todorova notes, with all the present knowledge, he "would not have written Orientalism."[46] While Said calls himself "an Oriental," he spent much of his academic career at an American institution. When a reporter asked him: "Where are you the happiest today?" he replied:

> I think probably on a plane. . . . I live in New York, I don't think I could live anywhere else. I find New York's anonymity and volatility terrifically energizing but I myself live a very quiet and sedentary life. I am a creature of the university.[47]

The author's location matters just as much as his work. It was the situation of displacement that offered the author both the torment of exile[48] and a unique vantage point from which to observe the East and the West. Said's message was carried by his personal story of displacement and the choice he made to use his liminal location to ask difficult questions.

In everyday conversations, easts and wests rarely appear with footnotes documenting who, how, and when they were used and what they meant. The cacophony of possible meanings has already led some analysts to call for abandonment of these categories, or, to use Varisco's words, to "move beyond the polemicized rhetoric of the binary blame game."[49] Yet it seems that easts and wests are still too entrenched as imaginaries of control and resistance to be dismissed, also in academic settings. Spencer notes that

> At a recent ASA Oxford conference on globalization, the most vociferous opposition to the analytic abolition of the West came, of course, from non-Western anthropologists, and the substance of their objection was compelling: if

---

[44] For influential debates on contributions and problems of *Orientalism*, see Daniel Martin Varisco, *Reading Orientalism: The Said and the Unsaid* (Seattle: University of Washington Press, 2017); O'Hagan, *Conceptualizing the West*; Todorova, *Imagining the Balkans*.

[45] Hobson, *The Eastern Origins*.

[46] Todorova, *Imagining the Balkans*, 12.

[47] Edward Said interviewed by the US TV station C-SPAN 2 (2000), https://www.youtube.com/watch?v=tvPHcU1T864.

[48] Edward Said, "Reflections on Exile," in Edward Said, *Reflections on Exile and Other Essays* (Boston, MA: Harvard University Press, 1984).

[49] Daniel Martin Varisco, *Reading Orientalism: The Said and the Unsaid* (Seattle: University of Washington Press, 2017).

it is not the West, what is it that swamps our domestic markets, fills our television and radio broadcasts, and sets our academic agendas?[50]

One reason analytic abolishment of the West (and therefore the East) would most probably be futile is that there is no centralized knowledge and understanding of what these two are. And perhaps more importantly, changing the nomenclature does not change the perceived reality.[51] They continue their lives as categories both questionable and unquestioned. Library shelves hold books that engage genealogies of these terms, but also books that assume their readers simply understand what easts and wests *are*. Scholars do not have a shared understanding of these terms. Take "Occidentalism," a term that often appears as a mirror to Orientalism. What for one author is a "fantasy about the West"[52] means for another a dehumanizing ideology—"the West in the eyes of its enemies."[53]

The political easts and wests have been shifting over time and space and so have intellectual projects that tried to describe them. For Spengler, for example, the Mediterranean is marginal, while many others refer to Greece as the "cradle of Western democracy."[54]Would Spengler, writing from Germany in the early twentieth century, be a Western author? Would he be an Orientalist or an Occidentalist? Which thinkers created a corpus of knowledge about the West? Is there a closed list? Where do they have to come from if we at the same time know that boundaries between the East and the West have been shifting and, even in the same time zone, there is no consensus on the exact border? Imaginaries of easts and wests have been translated into very tangible political institutions governing the lives of humans. But grasping what easts and wests *are*, trying to do this on a timeless continuum, is probably an exercise that leads to a labyrinth made up of mirrors. Because if belongings are relational, and easts and wests matter, one needs to take into account much more than an "easterners' image of the west" and vice versa. Lindstrom proposed terms such as "auto-orientalism" and "auto-occidentalism" to distinguish between how a person claiming eastern/western

---

[50] Jonathan Spencer, "Occidentalism in the East: The Uses of the West in Politics and Anthropology of South Asia," in J. G. Carrier (ed.), *Occidentalism: Images of the West* (Oxford: Clarendon Press, 1995), 234–57, 251.

[51] Fanon, *The Wretched of the Earth*.

[52] Meltem Ahıska, *Occidentalism in Turkey: Questions of Modernity and National Identity in Turkish Radio Broadcasts* (London: I.B. Tauris, 2010).

[53] Ian Buruma and Avishai Margalit, *Occidentalism: The West in the Eyes of Its Enemies* (London: Penguin, 2005).

[54] Discussed in detail by O'Hagan, *Conceptualizing the West in International Relations*.

belonging reflects not just "the other" but also their "self."[55] This would already bring us to a matrix with four squares—differentiating between easterners' and westerners' images of self and other. But should not the matrix have two more squares accounting for how we think the other sees us?[56] That would be a more complex matrix and yet still not a precise one. Humans speak from intersections of several belongings, and perceived easternness/westernness is just one of them. We would then need to expand the grid to include genders, religions, ethnicities, ages, and many other marks of sameness or difference. The simplicity of the first four to six squares disappears. But who would need the more complex table?

While easts and wests are too fuzzy to be used as analytics beyond geography, relationship to knowledge, as something frequently mobilized in arguments about the Orient and the Occident, should probably stay at the center of our inquiry. It has often been used as an important mark of differentiation between the Ottomans and the West Europeans. In her book exploring the period now known as the "European Age of Reason or Humanism," the historian Nancy Bisaha observed how, in this period, some medieval encounters between Ottomans and Western Europeans were rediscovered and employed to build a narrative placing the two in essential opposition. The Western European humanists, after the Ottoman conquest of Constantinople (now Istanbul), increasingly saw the Ottomans through the prism of their (assumed) disdain for learning. Bisaha concluded:

> This perception has more to do with narrow definitions of learning and culture prevalent in Renaissance Europe—definitions predicated on the classical canon. The unfamiliar was relegated to lower cultural categories. Regarding the Turks "barbarians" seemed an appropriate category for humanists who confused noninterest in "real" (that is, classical) culture with backwardness or simplicity.[57]

---

[55] Lamont Lindstrom, "Cargoism and Occidentalism," in J. G. Carrier (ed.), *Occidentalism: Images of the West* (Oxford: Clarendon Press, 1995), 33–60.

[56] This is how it would look:

	Frames of the East	Frames of the West	How "the other" sees "us"
Person "belonging" to the East	auto-Orientalism	Occidentalism	Believed? Lived? Experienced? Orientalism
Person "belonging" to the West	Orientalism	auto-Occidentalism	Believed? Lived? Experienced? Occidentalism

Terms "auto-orientalism" and "auto-occidentalism" were proposed by Lindstrom, "Cargoism and Occidentalism," 35..

[57] Bisaha, *Creating East and West*, 74.

Learning and Knowing (Who Gets to Write the Story?)

If knowledge lies at the heart of tensions that emerge in binary (and often oppositional) relationships let us now turn to what this could mean for people living at different ends of these binaries. Knowledge is patchy. Knowledge-making is standardized, with several procedures in place on what counts as good research. But the fact that something is *known*, or considered to be known in one milieu, regardless how prestigious that milieu is or how much work went into producing the research results, does not mean that it is going to be accepted or understood elsewhere. Arjun Appadurai's three observations written at the beginning of the present century provide guidance:

> The first is that there is a growing disjuncture between the globalization of knowledge and knowledge about globalization. The second is that there is an inherent temporal lag between the processes of globalization and our efforts to contain them conceptually. The third is that globalization as an uneven economic process creates a fragmented and uneven distribution of just those resources for learning, teaching, and cultural criticism [. . .] That is, globalization resists the possibility of just those forms of collaboration that might make it easier to understand or criticize.[58]

The emphasis then is not on materiality (as in wealth/poverty), although these of course matter, but on the possibility to comprehend and challenge the developments. Here we need to pay attention to Appadurai's take on research, an activity he proposes to think of beyond the production of scientific results. If research is "the systematic pursuit of the not-yet-known,"[59] then one needs to ask: Not yet known to whom? Some type of research is necessary for any human activity, beyond the university environment, especially with regard to the growing complexity of data infrastructures.[60] For Appadurai, to seek knowledge, one needs an aspiration and the tools to achieve it:

> Without aspiration, there is no pressure to know more. And without systematic tools for gaining relevant new knowledge, aspiration degenerates into fantasy or despair.[61]

---

[58] Arjun Appadurai, "Grassroots Globalization and the Research Imagination," *Public Culture* 12, no. 1 (2000): 4.
[59] Appadurai, "Grassroots Globalization," 9.
[60] David Chandler, "Digital Governance in the Anthropocene: The Rise of the Correlational Machine," in David Chandler and C. Fuchs (eds), *Digital Objects, Digital Subjects: Interdisciplinary Perspectives on Capitalism, Labour and Politics in the Age of Big Data* (London: University of Westminster, 2019).
[61] Appadurai, "The Right to Research," 176.

This translated to our context means that the possibility to learn is essential for shaping one's sense of belonging or being in the world. The emphasis is on accessibility, similar to the questions Dryzek asks about a "right to democracy,"[62] as something foundational to citizenship. The emphasis is not on advancing knowledge in general, but on creating conditions in which those who want to learn can do so. What matters is the purpose of gaining knowledge. This is to contrast it with current developments in field of knowledge, what Chandler calls "correlation machine"—a new digital governance in which data are collected for many other purposes (including control), but not really to address problems impacting human life.[63]

In 2017, a writer from Turkey visited Prague. As we were speaking, she noticed a book I left on the coffee table, Bilge Yesil's *Media in New Turkey*. She took it, briefly glanced through the pages, and wondered, where I got it. "The library," I said. "You can just get stuff like this in the library here?" she asked. She was not surprised by the fact that I had a book on Turkey, or the specific content of the book. It was the title, the year of publication, and the fact that a Prague library held a current volume on the subject. As we will see later in the present book, it is sometimes hoped that the only reason Prague is doing what it is doing is because it does not know the complexities of life further east. Books can be often found at places where one does not expect them. Such as when bookstores in Turkey offer books authored by writers in detention.

Putting names on places, finding orders, or establishing them where they seem to be missing is sometimes a product, sometimes a driving force, of curiosity. Writers do not just describe worlds they see, they create new ones. I am not so sure I opened a very new world for reading Turkey's European lives in this chapter, but perhaps that has not been the ambition. What I tried to do was to defend the crucial importance of *belonging*, as a lens and a sense, as something that always intervenes in the conversation on the topic, regardless of whether it is spelled out explicitly or hides under different words. No matter which attributes authors give to East—democracy, modernity, and their imagined and lived opposites—*belonging* is inescapable. Both as a human need or a desire and as a category imposed by others. The latter might linger even if one tries to resist.

---

[62] John Dryzek, "Can There Be a Human Right to an Essentially Contested Concept? The Case of Democracy," *The Journal of Politics* 78, no. 2 (2016).
[63] Chandler, "Digital Governance in the Anthropocene."

2

Europe Becoming an Institution

Welcoming new members was part of the plan from the beginning. The founding fathers were confident enough of their idea to leave the door open for other European countries to join.[1]

"European Union may be a response to history, but it can never be a substitute."[2]

The European Union means different things to different people, but there is little dispute though that it is a dominant actor in European politics. Its life can be narrated chronologically, referencing summits, treaties, and dates at which it grew wider, by admitting new members, and deeper, by adopting new federal regulations. It can also be told as a set of related stories, those of steel, fish, environment, trade, or science and many other common policies. Policy, as Cris Shore and Susan Wright tell us, "finds expression through sequences of events; it creates new social and semantic spaces, new sets of relations, new political subjects and new webs of meaning."[3] This chapter sketches out complexities of the EU as an institution and a set of policies by focusing upon notions of *unity*, *overcoming*, and *aid/help*. These categories offered themselves as the most suitable for interpretation of ethnographic material presented in later chapters and they are neither exhaustive nor separate. Importantly, all of them are contested. If we place them on a provisional linear timeline, unity could be what keeps the EU together today, the past is something that was overcome, and help/aid is something being done toward the future. Of course, there are cracks. The EU's motto stipulates "united in diversity"[4]—but it is up to discussion whether some type of sameness is not in fact preferred.[5] Overcoming can mean getting over the

---

EU Commission, Enlargement website, 2010.
Tony Judt, *Postwar* (London: William Heinemann, 2005), 831.
[3] Cris Shore and Susan Wright, "Conceptualizing Policy: Technologies of Governance and the Politics of Visibility," in Shore, Wright and Pero (eds), *Policy Worlds: Anthropology and the Analysis of Contemporary Power*, 12.
[4] https://europa.eu/european-union/about-eu/symbols/motto_en.
[5] The motto "unity in diversity" was also used by the Ottoman photographers Osman Hamdi and Marie De Launay, as noted by Zeynep Çelik and Edhem Eldem(eds), *Camera Ottomana: Photography and Modernity in the Ottoman Empire1840–1914* (Istanbul: Koc University, 2015), 240.

past, resolving disputes, but the past is far from settled, Europeans are far from united and whether the aid they provide, as a collective, is always helping is not that certain either. What follows is not a concise history of the EU—it is rather a sketch of its present complexity.

In official narratives, mobility of goods and citizens is often celebrated as a major achievement of the seven decades of integration. Yet there are movements that destabilize this narrative, such as travels between different pages of history. In one politics course taught around the middle of the past decade, I asked students to read excerpts from two texts. One was a newspaper article written at the peak of the 2013 protests in Ukraine, describing how its citizens demanded "realignment of the country away from Russia toward Europe."[6] The other was Frantz Fanon's manifesto[7] written during the Algerian war of independence in which the author appealed: "Come, then, comrades, the European game has finally ended; we must find something different." This was an introductory session, one in which syllabus and mutual expectations are discussed and work begins on making sense of key analytical lenses. At this stage, I did not expect anyone would be familiar with the Ukraine or Fanon, the point was to get us started on different framings of Europe, and how and why they are often conflicting. In the initial round of responses, one student commented that Fanon's "anti-Europeanism" reminded him of Nigel Farage, a British politician crucial in the Brexit campaign.

That comment—based on text solely and without knowledge of context in which it emerged—might seem startling at first but is in fact at the very core of the questions which present-day European integration invites. Critique of EU-rope is often dismissed as uncooperative nationalism or anti-Westernism. Moreover, putting, of all people, Fanon and Farage in the same box might raise eyebrows: one has experienced a violent colonial war and documented its atrocities; the other has used a comfortable seat in the European Parliament to unleash a hate campaign. A separate essay can be written on Farage and Fanon, what they did and witnessed, their specific relationships to Europe and what possibilities the time they lived in afforded and took away from them.[8] But if we zoom out of their life-stories, we may realize that this anecdote, in which Fanon's and Farage's messages are conflated, can also be read as an evidence of wider

---

6   David Herszenhorn, "Thousands Demand Resignation of Ukraine Leader," *The New York Times*, December 1, 2013, http://nyti.ms/ICFuS4.
7   Frantz Fanon, *The Wretched of the Earth* (Penguin: London, 2001 [1961]).
8   It is my observation from other contexts that a scholar of European politics has to be familiar with Farage, but not much happens if s/he has not read Fanon.

trend in current debates on European integration in which their participants are often asked to state whether they are for or against "Europe." Being *for* or *against* sometimes shouts louder than the details, such as what kind of Europe do we back or oppose.

Unity Is What Keeps Us Together

There are around five hundred million people today who can claim rights and are governed by a complex set of rules in the European Union. The number is probably much bigger—as we learn from scholars of EU's presence in the world, it has an "ideational force" which "consists in its ability to shape conceptions of 'normal' in international relations in line with its unique normative basis, which is rooted in its history."[9] It also has a "considerable regulatory capacity for externalizing internal policies and regulations."[10] But who and where is the EU? Futures of the Union are debated in parliaments, ministries, and TV screens of its twenty-seven (post-Brexit) member states and in various federal (often called "supranational") institutions. Over 700 members of the European Parliament migrate between working rooms and plenary halls in Brussels (Belgium) and Strasbourg (France) and their constituencies in towns and villages around the continent. The members of parliament, until the 1979 first direct election appointed by governments, have been gradually gaining more voice in making decisions on federal affairs. The ministers and other government representatives discuss European questions in national capitals, and national questions with their colleagues from the EU's twenty-seven member states on summits in various formations of Council of the European Union. The councils, together with the parliament, have to give a green light on all legislation that is to become binding in the Union. Such legislation can be proposed only by the European Commission, whose representatives are nominated by member states and approved by parliament. In addition, there are common courts, committees, funding bodies, and even a "citizens' initiative"—a possibility to petition the institutions directly. And while Europeans have found many ways of claiming or "enacting" their citizenship,[11]

---

[9] Ian Manners, "Normative Power Europe: A Contradiction in Terms?" *Journal of Common Market Studies* 40, no. 2 (2002): 235–58, 239.

[10] Chad Damro, "Market Power Europe," *Journal of European Public Policy* 19, no. 5 (2012): 682–99.

[11] Engin Isin and Michael Saward (eds), *Enacting European Citizenship* (Cambridge: Cambridge University Press, 2013).

the question of making one polity or demos preoccupies scholars as well as policy makers.[12]

A look at what started seven decades ago as a common market in coal and steel with six states and a minimum set of institutions involved shows a gradual rise in complexity. The EU is now a platform for debating agriculture, common currency, border-free travel, and antidiscrimination legislation, to name a few. There are more states, more institutions, more policies, more documents, more difficult navigation between who is who. Lecturers in European politics often joke that the EU has a wonderful online archive of documents but if one wants to find something, it is better to (insert the name of your search engine) it. Integration moved in different tempos, the adopted policies a result of many compromises between representatives of states and federal institutions.[13] An observation that also matters is how this happens in negotiation rooms. The political geographer Merje Kuus, who studied encounters between diplomats from "new" (postsocialist) and "old" (anyone who joined before 2004) member states, made an important point on processes of "blending in," in itself an exercise in building unity. Diplomats representing the older member states had greater confidence, easiness in presenting their positions, something that "new" diplomats were learning gradually.[14]

This complexity, the many avenues for counting in citizen preferences, has not delivered an uncontested legitimacy of the federal structures. In fact, campaigns against "Brussels dictate" are often led by *elected* representatives who commute between the many policy rooms and public spaces around the continent and have plentiful opportunities to see that while some policy approaches and actors might be more dominant, "Brussels" is not a singular actor and thus has very few possibilities to dictate anything to anyone.[15] The power distribution and its policy outputs, however, are not convincing for many citizens. Yet as "Europeans" they do not have many common means of collective mobilization.[16] Despite huge investments in marketing, in some states election participation

---

[12] Klaus Eder, "The EU in Search of its People: The Birth of Society Out of the Crisis of Europe," *European Journal of Social Theory* 17, no. 3 (2014): 219–37.

[13] In her book *The Life of the Law*, anthropologist Laura Nader proposes that "harmony ideology . . . a legal ideology characterized by the idea that agreement and conciliation are ipso facto better than conflict models minimized disruption to the civilizing processes" (Berkeley: University of California Press, 2002), 126. Nader's work is not situated in the EU-related discussions, but her observations are relevant for this context as well.

[14] Kuus, *Geopolitics and Expertise*, especially chapter six.

[15] After 2019 elections to European Parliament, when it took a while to elect its chairperson, one newly elected MEP informed his constituency that it is not "our [MEPs] fault"—it is the representatives of EU member state governments who first have to reach an agreement on nomination.

[16] Eder, "The EU in Search of its People."

remains very low. In Slovakia, a member state from the "class of 1989/2004," the highest turnout in the country's European Parliament elections did not reach even one quarter of eligible voters.[17]

Lack of legitimacy and concern about that lack has preoccupied EU-makers from early on. As the anthropologist Cris Shore vividly described in his seminal study *Building Europe*,[18] after a realization that integration of some parts of member states' economies did not deliver one European people, the leaders of the then Western European integration platforms took to manufacturing Europeans, in a similar vein as national leaders in earlier decades worked on creating the Germans or the French. While builders of the EU cultural policy used many of the tools common in creating nation-states, including symbols such as flag, anthem, competitions, and awards (Eurovision, Woman of the Year), there were limits in how far these could have gone. The EU might copy many of the things from the nation-state–making book, but it cannot take them all. Europeans do not pay direct federal tax and do not get federal pensions. True, part of the federal budget is used for what is called "cohesion," or bridging regional disparities, but this is a very negligible exercise in solidarity: EU common budget represents a marginal share of the GNP and much of taxing and income redistribution policies are in powers of member states.[19] What also deserves attention is the way in which cohesion is being made. National or regional authorities and NGOs submit projects for specific activities, and for a specific time duration.[20] Thus, the cohesion and regional development funds do not materialize as something to which citizens are entitled. They are more a result of a lottery and success in bidding. The North/South and East/West divides in incomes are notable and have regularly become subject of debates about solidarity. This perhaps explains why, in making of the narratives about a united Union, it seemed convenient to rely on motives from earlier times, such as ideas of Europe or Western civilization.

In debating futures of Europe and its various reform projects, two keywords are commonly floated: substance and narrative. Should we change the way *we do* Europe or the way we *talk* about it? Should the EU be different, or should it tell a different story about itself? In his essay *Europe's True Stories*, historian

---

[17] For summary of European Parliament election turnout since 1979, see https://www.election-results.eu/turnout/.

[18] Shore, *Building Europe*.

[19] At the time of writing there are discussions on deeper fiscal integration.

[20] There are repeated calls, especially from the leftist/progressive intellectuals and politicians to "return" to social-democratic origins. A recent volume: Ernst Hillebrand and Anna M. Kellner (eds), *Shaping a Different Europe* (Bonn: Dietzt, 2014).

Timothy Garton Ash calls for Europe to compare itself not with "others" but with its own past. It is here, that the new narrative should emerge.[21] Yet, while Ash dismisses what he calls "one size fits all" narratives of European history, adding that stories have to be adjusted to audiences, even a text about narratives cannot avoid substances. Ash praises the amount of funds provided to southern Europe before it joined the EU and laments that a similar program has not been offered for eastern Europe after the 1989. Narratives and substances cannot be separated—stories after all make sense to their audiences if the characters are situated in material world, and, importantly, if readers can identify with some of the protagonists.

We can think about narratives of unity as an effort to establish relations—or bring to forefront some not noticed relations. On one level, the narratives of unity are efficient and appealing—the Turkish leadership has repeatedly expressed the wish to see more "family pictures" with their EU counterparts. We, however, need to ask, whether such narratives reflect actual relationships of Europeans. Campaigning for Europe (a cooperation) often happens along the lines of *we're all one big family, therefore it is important to carry out patriotic duties*. We are related, therefore, we have to work together. But while resources have been invested into what Shore calls "symbolic integration," some of the actually existing relatedness has been downplayed in dominant narratives of unity. That is not lost on EU citizens, as attempts to unify them through storytelling and info campaigns have not really *made* Europeans. Debate about austerity policies is a case in point.[22] Commenting on the eurozone crisis, often called the "Greek crisis," toward the end of the first decade of the present century, anthropologist Michael Herzfeld, who has conducted many years of research in rural Greece, argued that the "morality tale" of lazy Greeks and responsible Germans conveniently overlooked that there have been other villains in the story.[23] Herzfeld writes:

> The accusations launched against Greece by German and other Western European observers, ring particularly hollow when we consider that the political establishment thus accused of corruption has long served the interests of these sanctimonious critics.[24]

---

[21] Timothy Garton Ash, "Europe's True Stories," *The Prospect Magazine*, Issue 131, http://www.prospect-magazine.co.uk/article_details.php?id=8214.

[22] In introduction to a recent theme volume on anthropologies of austerity Theodore Powers and Theodoros Rakopoulos discuss relatedness of wider European economic policies and austerity and its impacts outside of Europe. "The Anthropology of Austerity: An Introduction," *Focaal: Journal of Global and Historical Anthropology* 29, no. 83 (2019): 1–12.

[23] Michael Herzfeld, "The Hypocrisy of European Moralism," *Anthropology Today* 32, no. 2 (2016): 10–13.

[24] Herzfeld, "Hypocrisy," 11.

We may add to Herzfeld's point that the figure of lazy Greek featured also in East European debates—Slovak or Czech politicians and commentators were rising up against expectations to help solve Greek debt, noting that the average wage in these countries is lower than in Greece, and lectured Greeks about importance of hard work. Hungarian political economist Zoltán Pogátsa, who has been researching wider European context of the debt crisis wrote an open letter to what he called "anti-Greek Eastern European bloc," in which he, among others, reminded his regional milieu that "It is not that Greek wages were too high, but your wages are too low."[25]

Moreover, various developments in and out of the EU, including Brexit, Russia's annexation of Crimea and intervention in east Ukraine,[26] as well as the debate about refugees have renewed efforts to defend what is often called the "European project." What specifically was to be defended? Unity might be difficult to oppose in principle, because why not unite? It is the particulars in which differentiation arises. Some of the mentioned *threats* have paradoxically strengthened the EU as an institutional platform, one that needs to stick closer together to address what is happening and prevent other attacks. As one analyst suggested, Greek crisis has been a "catalytic moment,"[27] another concludes that both Ukraine and Greek crises have enhanced more unity-focus and "return of politics."[28] For some EU outsiders, including Turkey, this has meant that they suddenly had to face an even thicker wall separating them from the EU. Unity, in debates about the Greek debt, has been invoked to save the future (and to make investors trust the markets). But knowledge of how related things have been before the crisis broke out has not made many headlines.[29]

---

[25] Zoltán Pogátsa, "Open Letter to Anti-Greek Eastern European Bloc," July 8, 2015, https://www.sigmalive.com/en/news/greece/131867/open-letter-to-antigreek-eastern-european-bloc.

[26] The debates about Russian intervention in Ukraine and about EUs approach to migration have also led to renewed polarization around the east/west axis.

[27] Amelie Kutter, "A Catalytic Moment: The Greek Crisis in the German Financial Press," *Discourse and Society* 25, no. 4 (2014): 446–66.

[28] Luuk Van Middelaar, "The Return of Politics – The European Union after the Crises in the Eurozone and Ukraine," *Journal of Common Market Studies* 54, no. 3 (2016): 495–507.

[29] To underline the complexity of debating European politics, let us also keep in mind that much of it is mediated via national frameworks and representatives. Given the over twenty national languages in the EU, when federal representatives address the EU citizens, their statements are refracted in interpretations of commentators who translate them for national audiences. The federal developments are read through lenses of issues resonating in national debates—and there are also differences in the depth of coverage. A Czech member of the European Parliament recently shared, in discussion with students, his concern about lack of nuanced reporting on European issues in the Czech media. The parliamentarian said that as he drives home from the Brussels or Strasburg sessions through Germany, he listens to the radio. While the German broadcasts immediately address how a specific norm discussed in the parliament was going to matter for Germany, he rarely hears such detailed debate in the Czech media. My point here is not to suggest that the Czechs or others do not discuss developments in other member states and in federal institutions. On the

Unity seems to be both a way and a goal for establishing difference. It is a subject of curiosity, of desire. It is something requested that the EU gets itself a better PR. What we perhaps do not discuss enough is that some forms of doing unity may reinforce differences between EU citizens and their neighbors. Themes such as tax policy, migration, or environmental protection matter at both sides of the EU border. And while there are nuances in how they are discussed by Europe's many communities, it would be hard to argue that there is an essential EU vs. neighborhood difference between ideological positions on these questions.

But what is to be protected in the united Europe? Shore, writing at the beginning of the present century, makes an important point that European citizenship has gradually become "an identity forged around and through an ideal of the European consumer."[30] While it of course cannot be said for all instances in which citizenship is discussed in the many European debates, the right to consume in peace can be traced in much of current public communication of federal institutions. A case in point is the recent promotional video announcing the Union's 2016 Global strategy. In this simple guide to peaceful shopping, which I warmly recommend to the reader to enjoy with its full visual and sound elements, a young man and a woman walk us through the animation showing seas, deserts, EU buildings, builders, and a flag. In its book form we have to do with a transcript of the message read by a narrator:

> Europe's foreign policy matters to you. Yes, I *am* talking to you. When Europe's region is unstable, terrorist groups can spread, our economies get weaker and many people around Europe are forced to flee their homes. A strong European foreign policy can help our region's stability and provide Europeans with great opportunities. Entrepreneurs can expand their activities, our goods can be exported to new markets and we can keep enjoying the freedom to travel and to learn. Isolation is not the answer to the challenges of our times. The European Union needs to engage outside our borders, working with our partners on common solutions to common challenges. Our investments create new opportunities for growth. We support human rights, education and good governance and our servicemen are helping to make our region more secure. This is the Union we are building with the global strategy for foreign

---

contrary, they do, and leaders and events from other states often become symbols in debates of their neighbors. The point is that these discussions, when wider audiences are engaged, are often more about symbols than the actual detailed sequence of events. In immediate interactions, such as everyday proceedings in the Brussels institutions, the participants have the opportunity to revise their earlier expectations.

[30] Shore, *Building Europe*, 85.

and security policy. This is what Europe can achieve when we act together, the European way.[31]

We can close this section with an epilogue. The European Commission that assumed office in the fall of 2019 introduced a new portfolio—a vice president for the protection of the European way of life. There is a heated debate on what this means but it seems that the primary impetus was not similar to demands heard on environmental Fridays for Future demonstrations. The policy makers who objected to framing of this portfolio highlighted that it is playing into the hands of xenophobic movements.[32] Looking at complexities of Europe-making in its first seven decades, it is indeed hard to argue that there is something distinctly *European,* separating Europeans from their neighbors, other than the separation itself, and the borders demarcating it.

A Story of Overcoming: The Past That Unites Us

When, after the Second World War, some Europeans started laying the foundation of what later became the European Union, colonialism was not yet a past and a new reification of East and West was just emerging. In the Cold War, freedom was the line of separation between the two.[33] In western European quarters, some older versions of connection between the West and civilization were picked up and constituted, to use Samuel Moyn's expression, a "usable past."[34] After the demise of the Cold War, the narrative of the EU as a defender of rights perhaps could rely on stronger evidence. After all, incorporating the eastern states was another moment when the EU could lay claims to "uniting the continent."[35] A widely cited academic book on the subject authored by international relations professor Milada Vachudova was titled *Europe Undivided.*[36]

[31] EEAS, "EU Foreign Policy Matters to You," http://europa.eu/globalstrategy/en/global-strategy-fore ign-and-security-policy-european-union.
[32] Alice Tidley, "What's the European Way of Life? EU Chief's New Commission Portfolio Draws Criticisms," *Euronews,* September 12, 2019, https://www.euronews.com/2019/09/10/what-s-the-eur opean-way-of-life-eu-chief-s-new-commission-portfolio-draws-criticism.
    Sophie In't Veld, "Threat to European Way of Life is Not Migrants. It's Populists," *Politico,* September 13, 2019, https://www.politico.eu/article/populist-threat-to-european-way-of-life-sop hie-int-veld-ursula-von-der-leyen/.
[33] Jan Nederveen Pieterse, "Globalisation Goes in Circles: Hybridities East and West," in D. Schirmer, G. Saalman and C. Kessler (eds), *Hybridising East and West* (Munster: LIT Verlag, 2006).
[34] Samuel Moyn, *Last Utopia: Human Rights in History* (Boston: Harvard University Press, 2012), 21.
[35] This is a common trope in reports produced by EU institutions.
[36] Milada A. Vachudova, *Europe Undivided: Democracy, Leverage and Integration after Communism* (Oxford: Oxford University Press, 2005).

The seven decades of European integration are sometimes told as a story of overcoming.[37] In the more optimistic accounts, available in EU promo brochures but also in several academic texts, Europeans have succeeded in memory politics since the membership in the Union has provided opportunities for reconciliation.[38] Peaceful resolving of disputes with neighbors, putting the past *behind* is considered one of the successes and cornerstones, reasons for the existence of the European project. Entering the EU means escaping the past and taking a step toward the future, a time which is nicer than the past. Such logic has underpinned the Union's eastern enlargement, but also the southern, before the 1989. Also Greece, Portugal, and Spain were expecting (and expected) to become more prosperous and better governed by adopting the standards of the north/west. For all of the above, joining the EU was a path *away from* authoritarian past.

A peace narrative then became something like a tradition. As Renée Jeffery notes, what matters is not just the way new tradition is constructed, it is also the purpose, the *why* of something becoming a tradition.[39] It may seem so that that ideas about the past seem to be a more functional glue for bringing Europeans closer together than views on the present. Yet it has been mainly the Second World War experience that shaped official memory of common points of departure, with the colonial past being the "less convenient memory," as Nicolaïdis, Sèbe and Maas put it.[40] There have been differences in how the pasts figured in understanding the present. Anthropologist Ann Laura Stoler speaks about "colonial aphasia"—an inability to understand the connection between what happened in the past and present-day situation of former colonial subjects in France.[41] Renato Rosaldo writes about "mourning for what one has destroyed" and shows connection between gazes into older past and the realization that a certain idea of progress has reached its limits; longing for the lost past also comes with ignoring or not seeing causal connections with the present.[42]

[37] Judt in *Postwar* speaks of forgetting and "collective amnesia" as building blocks of the early postwar Europe.

[38] Some authors provide very optimistic accounts of how memory is "uniting" the Europeans, for example, Peter J. Verovšek, "Expanding Europe through Memory: The Shifting Content of the Ever-Salient Past," *Millennium: Journal of International Studies* 43, no. 2 (2015): 531–50.

[39] Renée Jeffery, "Tradition as Invention: The 'Traditions Tradition' and the History of Ideas in International Relations," *Millenium: Journal of International Relations* 34, no. 1 (2005): 57–84.

[40] Kalypso Nicolaïdis, Berny Sèbe and Gabrielle Maas (eds), *Echoes of Empire: Memory, Identity and Colonial Legacies* (London: I.B. Tauris, 2015), 1.

[41] Ann Laura Stoler, "Colonial Aphasia: Race and Disabled Histories in France," *Public Culture* 23, no. 1 (2011): 121–56.

[42] Renato Rosaldo, "Imperialist Nostalgia," *Representations* 26 (1989): 107–22.

That more benevolent look into the past though does not seem to be the case when colonial pasts of others are at stake. In relation to Turkey, the past does not appear only in the more general notions of "backwardness" as a mix of underdevelopment and cultural difference referenced in the previous chapter. There are also very specific issues on which the country is expected to take a stand if it wants to be more European. A prominent case is the mass murders/ genocide[43] of Ottoman Armenians during the First World War. By now the European Parliament and several national legislatures have passed bills that ask Turkey to adopt specific policies on the issue.[44] The resolutions vary in their content and expectations, they have been adopted with different strength and rarely without dissenting voices. In some cases, Cyprus and Germany, for example, which passed more than one of these resolutions speak as much about bilateral relations and unresolved issues with Turkey as they do about the Ottoman past. The connection of this memory politics to present-day concerns is obvious also more broadly—about half of European resolutions on the issue were adopted at the time when the Council and the Commission discussed Turkey's application for membership.[45] In the eyes of many lawmakers in the EU, Turkey's possibility to become a member and the relevance its pre-republican past are indivisible.

In Turkey, however, the demands from European parliaments are perceived as neither helpful nor benign. On the contrary, they stand for a mechanism of exclusion. The government recalls ambassadors, pledges to cancel trade bids.[46] *Lies, lies*—is one of the responses. The EU parliamentarians have made this all up to weaken Turkey. *Irresponsibility*—as in "why do you do this, when it only helps our nationalists?" is another critique. *Confusion*—"why can't people say what they think? Does not the EU protect free speech?" *Not enough*—the latter, however, is only a minority opinion. This is what needs to be emphasized. In the plethora of voices commenting on the "genocide resolutions," very few suggest that this is a good step, something of which the European Union should do

---

[43] What seems to be contested is not so much that a violent act happened, as the question of how that act is going to be labeled today. Putting a name on what happened is one of the most contested parts of the story and subject to present-day political struggle both in Turkey and between various actors in Turkey and the EU. Even recent academic volumes on the issue walk carefully in titles—for example Suny, Ronald G., Fatma M. Göçek and Norman M. Naimark, *A Question of Genocide: Armenians and Turks at the End of Ottoman Empire* (Oxford: Oxford University Press, 2011); Thomas De Waal, *Great Catastrophe: Armenians and Turks in the Shadow of Genocide* (Oxford: Oxford University Press, 2015).

[44] I discuss this in more detail in a manuscript under preparation "Spectacles in the Anthropocene: 'Armenian genocide resolutions' of European parliaments."

[45] Counting correct in 2016.

[46] David L. Philips, *Diplomatic History: The Turkey-Armenia Protocols* (New York: Columbia University, 2012).

more. Even those who *are* curious and ready to reread history are either careful about the resolutions or outright against them. The late Hrant Dink, Turkish-Armenian journalist and one of the campaigners at the forefront of addressing this painful past, spoke out frequently and courageously against such memory laws.[47]

Several observers have noted that in recent decades we have seen not just a European but a wider, global trend to remember, which often presents itself as "acting out, having an effect."[48] The growing interest in the past has been evident in building memorials and museums displaying records of past violence. Tony Judt remarked: "If we must have Memorials, then people should at least be encouraged to visit the Historials first."[49] We can thus read the resolutions addressing the fate of Ottoman Armenians as part of a wider trend. At the same time, not everyone in the European Union wants to touch all pasts. Some pasts are better to be dealt with ambiguously, for the preservation of unity and peace. Even when the Armenian past is at stake, there is no unanimity—not all parliaments (or all parliamentarians) would say a resolute *yes, you have to recognize*. That this is a diplomatically sensitive issue is obvious also in reports the European Commission publishes on candidate's progress on the accession track. In one of them, the Commission notes that Turkey-US relations "have been marked by tensions [...]after the Foreign Relations Committee of the House of Representatives adopted a resolution recognizing the killings of Armenians in 1915 as genocide."[50] In March that same year as covered by the report, the parliament of an EU member state, Sweden, passed a similar resolution and this has caused diplomatic tensions. The report does not say a word on Sweden.

The role of the past in Europe-making is ambiguous. There is no binding policy manual determining which past has to matter in the present decision-making. There, however, is a lot of evidence showing that some pasts matter more than other. Moreover, how much they matter depends on who speaks about them. Merje Kuus, in her ethnography of expertise in post-2004 Brussels, makes several important observations on the role of history in the everyday business of negotiations.[51] One of those that matter for our story is that there is an effort, among policy makers, not to take a stand on other's pasts, because then

[47] Hrant Dink, *Two Close Peoples, Two Distant Neighbors* (Istanbul: Hrant Dink Foundation, 2014).
[48] Ann Rigney, "Reconciliation and Remembering: (How) Does It Work?" *Memory Studies* 5, no. 3 (2012): 251–8.
[49] Tony Judt (with Timothy Snyder), *Thinking the Twentieth Century* (London: William Heinemann, 2012), 283.
[50] European Commission, "Turkey Progress Report 2010," SEC (2010) 1327, Brussels, November 19, 96.
[51] Kuus, Geopolitics and Expertise, especially chapter seven.

one could not get anything done. There is a tendency, the author notes, to tread carefully around historical legacies because they might destabilize consensus-building on questions of today. And then there are the paradoxes, when the new eastern members want to speak on politics that relates to their past and geography, the representatives of the older member states stop listening. Kuus writes:

> Ironically, it is precisely the region in which the new states claim most expertise—the EU's eastern neighborhood—where their expertise is in question most.[52]

The EU does and does not have a common narrative of the past. There are notions that have made it into narratives reproduced and endorsed by federal institutions. But one cannot speak of a strictly federal versus national divide. Some narratives of Europe are employed by some representatives of national political forces in everyday battles. Pasts are an important source of mobilization—and it is not just the "national" pasts. When several Eastern European diplomacies suggested that they should not be obliged to receive refugees from the Middle East during the 2015 "crisis," a justification they often used was "we did not colonize." In other words, Middle Eastern refugees are a product of the Western European past.

The question, however, is not whether Europeans do or do not have a common *past*. The European states and societies have been meeting well before the EU was founded. The question is of the common *narrative*—of what it is that happened in that past. The search for common narrative goes hand in hand with building common institutions (just like it was in the case of nation-states). The cracks in that narrative, the nonexistence of a singular reading of history in the EU, and, in parallel, demands for specific memory politics from a candidate country clearly shows that these appeals are a mechanism of strengthening solidarity within the EU.

United in Help/Helping We Are More United

In debates about the European Union, *unity* is often demanded and lamented as existing only in name. When the present does not offer success, the past becomes a rich source of common roots. If the past does not help sufficiently, the world at large, and neighbors specifically, and their assumed expectations of wanting

---

[52] Kuus, *Geopolitics and Expertise*, 175–8.

to be European can fill in the blanks. Aid or helping are important keywords in discussing the EU as the institution it is today and the process that made it. Leaflets and brochures explaining the EU contain lists of things the Union is doing for others and highlight the size of its aid contribution in comparison to the rest of the world—such as "The EU provides 60% of the world's development assistance and helps the world's most needy countries to fight poverty, feed their people, avoid natural disasters, access drinking water and fight disease."[53] In the EU constitution, helping goes under the word *solidarity*, a sense or a relationship of obligation to each other.[54] Helping matters for unity, it is also a step toward a better future.

Aid and helping is inscribed already in the first years of European Union, it underpins the past, the process of EU becoming an institution. The Marshall Plan provided a package of loans, grants, and investment from the United States from which only West European states benefited—Judt notes that Greece and Turkey became "honorary west Europeans."[55] This help was not received with unanimous gratitude: many questioned its contribution and the growing influence of the United States in European politics.[56] The plan helped shape geography—the Soviet bloc did not participate and some of its members joined the "transatlantic partnership" established (and strengthened with NATO) only after 1989.

Already the founding text of European integration, the May 9, 1950, Schuman declaration, which outlined the framework of cooperation on coal and steel contains a pledge to assist the "development of the African continent," deemed as one of Europe's "essential tasks." Considering the changing meanings and definitions of help, it might be problematic to come up with a precise balance sheet of who provided what to whom since the beginning of the EU story. But it is probably not far from the truth to say that in contemporary dominant narratives it is the EU helping others. Thus, guest workers invited to western European countries from Spain or Portugal (current but not the founding members) or Turkey are not commonly referenced in the aid stories featuring

---

[53] Oscar La Fontaine, *EU in 12 Lessons*, 2014, https://publications.europa.eu/en/publication-detail/-/publication/2d85274b-0093-4e38-896a-12518d629057, 35. See also Shore, *Building Europe*.

[54] Article Two, Treaty on the European Union.

[55] Judt, *Postwar*, 91.

[56] The Marshall Plan and the USEU partnership have been transformative in many ways, but that is beyond the scope of the present manuscript. Let me just briefly reference Timothy Mitchell's work in which he argues that this partnership increased Western Europe's dependence on oil. The relevance of this goes beyond environmental impacts—Mitchell also argues that oil replaced coal and that also limited democratic politics—previously striking coal workers could paralyze economy. Timothy Mitchell, *Carbon Democracy: Political Power in the Age of Oil* (London: Verso, 2013), 29–31.

in info brochures produced by EU Institutions, nor are they a common part of European integration curricula. What also has to be considered is the changing meaning of inside and outside—when Europe-building began, parts of Africa were still considered Europe, so it was not outside. After all, the very fact that decolonization has had such a transformative effect on former colonial centers is a testimony of this. As Judt notes, the importance of European space for some of the founding members, France namely, increased and Europe became a new space for projection of influence.[57] Later, in the wake of twenty-first-century refugee crises, the Union adopted "migration compacts" that would build on its "special relationship" with African countries.[58] The lack of better terminology than "special relationship" shows continued discomfort with colonialities.

Aiding and helping has been instrumental in the creation of a European narrative, in fostering unity, a sense of *us*. This is well evidenced in new member states confirmations of their belonging to the Union by developing programs for working with states further east and south.[59] Because in parallel to EU common budgets and programs, member states run their own separate aid programs. Several states that joined the Union in 2004 prioritized so-called "transition know-how" sharing with countries perceived to have a similar past and wanting a similar future, such as Eastern Europe and the western Balkans. While providing aid is a formal obligation for members of the EU and the Organization for economic cooperation and development (OECD), there is much more at play. Aid is a form of visibility for the donor country and also a way of wielding leverage—both in the "recipient" country and among EU counterparts. There are sets of national funding schemes, annual reports, and pictures of success stories of what a former high-level representative of one of these new states called "sticking a flag,"[60] aka, marking a territory.

And yet, while there are so many fragmented narratives supported by national foreign policy strategies, there is a content, there is a drive, there is a beating heart behind the federal aid. Part of the fuel that pumps that heart is fear—and aid is also a defense strategy. That aid (as a defense) is a support

---

[57] Judt, *Postwar*.

[58] European Commission, "Communication on Establishing a New Partnership Framework with Third Countries under the European Agenda on Migration," COM (2016) 385 final, Strasbourg, June 7, 2016, https://ec.europa.eu/home-affairs/sites/homeaffairs/files/what-we-do/policies/eu ropean-agenda-migration/proposal-implementation-package/docs/20160607/communication_e xternal_aspects_eam_towards_new_migration_ompact_en.pdf.

[59] For overview of "emerging donor" strategies, see Ondrej Horky and Simon Lightfoot, "From Aid Recipients to Aid Donors? Development policies of Central and Eastern European States," *Perspectives on European Politics and Society* 13, no. 1 (2012): 1–16 (intro to special issue).

[60] Lucia Najslova, "Slovakia in the East: Pragmatic Follower, Occasional Leader," *Perspectives: Review of International Affairs* 19, no. 2 (2011): 101–22.

ground of common European intervention can be also seen by the numbers of staff allocated to Turkey. Ankara is now one of the biggest (the most staffed) EU representations abroad. As one diplomat who served at the mission noted—"It is not because we can do too much there, politically speaking. It is good for learning, otherwise, frustrating." The aid component has significantly expanded with the arrival of Syrian refugees.

By the end of the second decade of the twenty-first century, the EU consisted of a complex network of committees, voting procedures, consultation fora, and public engagement activities. It has a huge online archive with detailed reports tracing all its common policies. Diplomats and various communications officials attend or organize panels, every capital has a "European house" in which seminars are held on regular basis. The EU flags wave on national ministries, alongside with national flags. The list of places and issues with federal presence is long but so is the list of absences. Federal decision-making is complex, it is not the same as in nation-states, yet some things are shared, such as the community-building: the appeal to past and future when constructing present policies. The present chapter described the Europe-making processes via three threads: unity-building, overcoming the past, and helping others. These threads are overlapping and mutually constitutive, and can be found in discussions about past, present, and future of the Union. They are certainly not the only threads through which European history can be narrated, nor do they tell the whole story. But they have hopefully been sufficiently disruptive and thus convincingly illustrate the complexity of the structure with which Turkey is negotiating.

3

Turkey

Reflections on Learning (Fast Version)

When Turkish think-tankers, journalists, and academics came to conference rooms of their more western neighbors in the middle of the first decade of the present century, some would often note in their presentations "We were always part of Europe." A variation of the line would be used also by their hosts. Let us note it was not "we/they were always part of the *world*." It is Europe that matters here. Such statements were offered as one of many pieces of evidence that the process is worthy of continuation and that having being there all along constitutes grounds for becoming closer. There is nothing strange about this suggestion when one considers it in light of wider narratives of European integration, in which being there, sharing one space, is a convincing ground to deepen the bond, instead of cutting it or keeping it where it is. Moreover, appeals to shared past fit well with invented traditions[1] of nations, East(s), West(s), and Europe for that matter, as perennial entities. But when I heard for the first time the "argument by the past," I often wondered: Why justify things by the past when *future* is at stake? Why reach for the past, when in many European textbooks it is not a heyday of peaceful coexistence? In many European countries, the school curricula included texts on national liberation struggles against "the Turk."[2] In the wider public debates in Eastern and Central Europe, the very word "Turk" has meant something very different than it does in Turkey. From the benefit of hindsight, I realize how precious little I knew about the many other pasts of relationships between Turkey and western Europe when proposing to "talk about the future" instead.

How does one briefly tell the very complex story of how much "Europe" and "the West" mattered in the process of Turkey becoming the state it is today? In

---

[1] Eric Hobsbawm and Terence Ranger (eds.), *The Invention of Tradition* (Cambridge: Cambridge University Press, 1983).

[2] The question was recently addressed by Gabriel Pirický, "The Ottoman Age on Southern Central Europe as Represented in Secondary School History Textbooks in the Czech Republic, Hungary, Poland and Slovakia," *Journal of Educational Media, Memory & Society* 5, no. 1 (2013): 108–29.

some such short accounts, Turkey's recent history has been a linear progress toward the West, with occasional interruptions. The Ottoman Empire was losing power,[3] reformers took the opportunity and modernized the country, walking in shoes of those who started this process in the nineteenth century. In this narrative, Western meant better. That is after all why the transition was embarked upon.[4] Understanding of what constitutes history and whose voices matter in it has gradually widened. The burgeoning research on what is sometimes called "history from below"[5] has populated books with a diverse set of characters, beyond sultans, kings, and prime ministers, and other members of elite.[6] It also showed a more multifarious account of relations between Ottomans and Western European societies. None of these have been monoliths, and while the official regimes have not always been open to dissenting opinions and often punished them, there is a growing library documenting the plurality of views on a range of public affairs in various periods.

This chapter shows some of the formative moments and angles in which Europe/the West was discussed in Turkey before the accession negotiations started. Just like the Western Europeans talked about Turkey/Turks to get a better sense of who their own communities are,[7] for Ottomans/Turks ideas about the former were an important reference in planning their own society. But while a mirror metaphor offers itself as an easy simplification, and hence a good entry into the pasts of the relationship, it is just an entry—Western Europe was not trying to "catch up with" Turkey, or become like Turkey.[8] Moreover, political geographies of the West have been changing and its institutional membership recently expanded to countries which do not feature among those that the

[3] For a concise account of problems with writing about the end of the Ottomans, see Farouqhi, *Approaching Ottoman History*; also Finkel, *Osman's Dream*; Goffman, *The Ottoman Empire* referenced in the first chapter of the present book. For discussions of the most current work in Ottoman historiography, the Ottoman History Podcast http://www.ottomanhistorypodcast.com/ is a very valuable resource.

[4] Bernard Lewis, *Emergence of Modern Turkey*, would perhaps be the best scholarly example of this type of writing. Review of key milestones of westernization with emphasis on this being a good and natural thing is also a common part of policy-oriented writing in which researchers often have very little space for providing "background" before getting to the "core," which usually focuses on "today/tomorrow."

[5] This recent volume provides a valuable collection of research articles and personal reflections of historians doing "history from below": Selim Karahasanoğlu and Deniz Cenk Demir (eds), *History from Below: A Tribute in Memory of Donald Quataert* (Istanbul: Istanbul Bilgi University Press, 2016).

[6] Erik J. Zürcher, *The Young Turk Legacy and Nation Building: From the Ottoman Empire to Atatürk's Turkey* (London: I.B. Tauris, 2010), 47.

[7] Levin, *European Union and Turkey*.

[8] For discussion of images of the West in Turkey, see Ahıska, *Occidentalism in Turkey*.

Ottoman/Turkish reformers wanted to emulate.[9] A look into the readings of the
past also helps to establish that catching up or competing with the West has
not been just an abstract reference in government declarations or intellectual
manifestos. Westernization has been lived by people not familiar with (or not
interested in) the many academic classifications of social change. It has cut
across political spectrum and socioeconomic background; it mattered to those
who admired the West or its parts and to those who criticized it. This chapter
should help us understand why there have been recently so many frequent
allusions to fatigue in the relationship and why many of the debates held at the
stage of accession talks revolved around speed and urgency. Because if one is
not considered "Western" or "European" by the virtue of discussing their past,
present, and future in these terms, could they ever be?

A Rupture, or Not: Reading Histories

The historian Erik Jan Zürcher, reflecting on Bernard Lewis's *Emergence of
Modern Turkey*, a work he considers foundational although not undisputed,
recently wrote: "What does 'emergence' really mean? [. . .] the word surely
suggests that we are faced with a spontaneous and gradual process, through
which modern Turkey hatches like a chick from its egg."[10] The establishment
of the republic and the reforms that accompanied it often appear as a new
page in history. In fact, Turkey did literally enter into new times—it adopted
the Gregorian calendar, thus making a shift of several centuries, and moved the
weekly resting day from Friday to Sunday. This meant reorganization of how
time is measured and how it is counted. It also meant closer attention to that
time. Hayri, a protagonist in Ahmet Hamdi Tanpınar's novel *Saatleri Ayarlama
Enstitüsü* (Time Regulation Institute), recalls "a system of fines [. . .] for every
clock or watch not synchronized with any other clock in view."[11] This is a
fictional account of the early republican era, yet it offers a wealth of observations
startlingly similar to nonfiction histories. A short walk through this era shows
reformers abolishing sultanate and caliphate, introducing female suffrage,
embarking upon rapid industrialization, and building of new transportation
corridors. The republican leadership moved the political center from Istanbul to

[9] Some of my Turkish interlocutors often noted with offended disbelief that "even Romania and
   Bulgaria got in" or wondered "Why should I explain myself to Slovakia."
[10] Zürcher, *The Young Turk Legacy*, 41.
[11] Ahmet Hamdi Tanpınar, *The Time Regulation Institute* (London: Penguin, 2013). Trans. Maureen
   Freely and Alexander Dawe, 11.

Ankara and introduced a range of new institutions, including laws that decreed particular dress codes and banned others. Politics was discussed in a literally new language—Ottoman was "purified" from Arabic and Persian elements and the script changed from Arabic to Latin.[12]

In the process of building the new state, many categories from the cosmopolitan book of belongings were mobilized, including gender, religion, ethnicity, and socioeconomic and urban/rural background. As many of the reforms were measured against what was believed to be a more advanced "Western" standard, nation-building and westernization are hard to separate. Sources of political legitimacy in the new state were *the people*, citizens of the new republic, and a narrative of who these people are was one of the things that was being built in the 1920s. Scholars of nation-building often use dichotomies such as civic/ethnic, political/cultural to describe what holds communities together.[13] In a state established for all of its citizens, everyone was expected to pledge allegiance to constitutional values, yet historians of this period remind that access to rights had been selective. Some of the preferred markers have been ethno-religious. Membership in the only party that could legally exist until opening up to multiparty competition in the 1950s was restricted to only those considered ethnic Turks, and constraints were placed on use of languages other than Turkish and on rights of non-Muslims.[14] Gender roles have been another important site for flagging westernness and new Turkishness. The introduction of female suffrage in 1934 is often presented as a symbol of cutting ties with the old and becoming more progressive than some Western European countries at that time. Already in 1929, the newspaper *Cumhuriyet* held a Miss Turkey contest, and in 1952 a Turkish contestant won "Miss Europe title."[15] For the sociologist Nilüfer Göle, the emphasis on women underlines uniqueness of Turkish transformation:[16]

---

[12] The introduction of the new script went hand in hand with mass literacy campaigns. For the nuances see, Hale Yılmaz, "Learning to Read (Again): The Social Experiences of Turkey's 1928 Alphabet Reform," *International Journal of Middle East Studies* 43, no. 4 (2011): 677–97.

[13] While in the civic, sometimes called constitutional, the members pledge allegiance to a set of agreed norms, the ethnic, sometimes called cultural, is somehow more exclusive, in the sense that it is more difficult to join. Yet this dichotomy is confusing as the two types basically never exist in their "ideal" forms. Rogers Brubaker, "Myths and Misconceptions in the Study of Nationalism," in J. A. Hall (ed.), *The State of the Nation: Ernest Gellner and the Theory of Nationalism* (Cambridge: Cambridge University Press, 1998); Roger Brubaker, "Categories of Analysis and Categories of Practice: A Note on the Study of Muslims in European Countries of Immigration," *Ethnic and Racial Studies* 36, no. 1 (2013); Billig, *Banal Nationalism*.

[14] Söner Çagaptay, *Islam, Secularism and Nationalism in Modern Turkey: Who is a Turk?* (New York: Routledge, 2006).

[15] Feroz Ahmad, *The Making of Modern Turkey* (London and New York: Routledge, 1996). Halis won Miss Universe 1932.

[16] The new generation of gender researchers would perhaps disagree; the fact that women do not appear in some (earlier) accounts of other revolutions might mean that the writers "forgot" about them. In state-socialist Eastern Europe, women were also important part of national symbolism.

Unlike most national revolutions, which redefine the attributes of an "ideal man," the Kemalist revolution celebrated an "ideal woman." Within the emerging Kemalist paradigm, women became bearers of Westernization and carriers of secularism. . . . Among the cast of characters of the new republic, the serious, hardworking, professional women devoted to national progress, appeared as a touchstone set apart from a "superficial" and mannered claim for Europeanness.[17]

Importantly, nation-building did not happen in monologue. The Turkish republic, like many others, has been celebrated as a victory of a national project, and, like many others, needed an approval of wider international community. The first version of borders of the post-Ottoman state was negotiated at a conference in Sèvres, but the resulting 1920 treaty never entered into force. Such treaty would, in the view of founders of the new Turkish state, make any such state unviable. Thus the Turkish war of Independence had to follow. What some call "Sevresphobia" continues to be a reference point in debates about the West, and in some narratives, ethno-religious minorities are "pawns of foreign powers," as the latter's foreign policies, including those on minority protection of select minorities, have been viewed as weakening the late Ottoman state.[18] It is, however, one thing to point out problems of ethno-nationalism and quite another to pay attention to actual western policies, critique of which should not be dismissed. The main contours of the present borders of Turkey were recognized with the 1923 Treaty of Lausanne.[19] As Lerna Ekmekçioğlu writes in her study on early republican period, while the Turkish state did not follow thoroughly stipulations on protection of minorities, the notions of minority protection in the treaty were rather distant from what Western European countries enforced in their own lands.[20] As Ekmekçioğlu observes, the guiding idea was mainly to establish order:

> To accommodate the near unattainability of one state for one nation, the concept of "minorities" was engraved in the national and international legal order. According to this mentality, if minorities were protected and given room to express their differences, they would not forge extraterritorial alliances and act as a fifth column.[21]

---

[17] For a recent comprehensive discussion on meanings of the Sèvres in later decades of Turkish political life, see Fatma Müge Göçek, *The Transformation of Turkey: Redefining State and Society from the Ottoman Empire to Modern Era* (London: I.B. Tauris, 2011).

[18] Göçek, *The Transformation of Turkey*.

[19] One later change of borders was brought with referendum on Hatay, formerly a French mandate in Syria, currently a province in southeastern Turkey.

[20] Lerna Ekmekçioğlu, *Recovering Armenia: The Limits of Belonging in Post-genocide Turkey* (Stanford: Stanford University Press, 2016), 94–5.

[21] Ekmekçioğlu, *Recovering Armenia*, 93.

As we already know, belongings and minorities or majorities emerge through a variety of markers. Narrating the early years of modern Turkey history through a story of *Hay Gin*, an Armenian journal briefly published in this period, Ekmekçioğlu opens a window into complexities of loyalties, including those to ethnic kin, the nation of citizenship, and fissures within the feminist movement. Some Armenians were courting Western European allies with notions of shared Christian civilization and women faced difficult choices between emancipation and loyalty to their expected roles as mothers, as the ones tasked with the survival of Armenians.[22] Her book might be read as a study of a small community of survivors. It can also be a story of the nation-states on which they depended.

Belongings are complex. People rarely define themselves *only* by gender, religion, or ethnicity. In nation-building narratives and related policy making, some markers often matter more than the others. The historian Kader Konuk observed that when some German scholars expelled by or fleeing from Nazis were invited to work at Turkish educational institutions, "the scholars were greeted as Europeans, not as Jews."[23] Selectiveness of markers of belonging mattered for determining who is a legitimate citizen, one that deserves rights and protection. Contesting dominant narratives was often punished.[24] Nation-building came with reinforcement of desirable values and restrictions on what can and should be said in public.

It also came with literal moving of people. As noted in the previous chapter, mass deportations and killings of Ottoman Armenians during the First World War are a recurring theme in Western European policy rooms when Turkey is on agenda. A related subject, which to my knowledge appears less frequently in these debates, is the Greek-Turkish "population exchange" shortly after the end of that war. Perhaps the most important for the subject of the present book is the assumption underpinning the "internationally sanctioned" deportations: social peace cannot be maintained in societies that are not culturally (here ethnically/religiously) homogeneous.[25] The exchange has had repercussions for the individuals and families, who have first lived as a minority in one state only to

---

[22] Ekmekçioğlu, *Recovering Armenia*, esp. 67, 118–19.

[23] Kader Konuk, *East-West Mimesis: Auerbach in Turkey* (Stanford: Stanford University Press, 2014), 84.

[24] A case in point would be expulsion from the public discourse of some perspectives related to different nationalities/ethnicities. Media, public or private, the latter often being part of bigger companies with interests in various sectors of the economy, often toed the state discourse in order to not lose access to state contracts. (Bilge Yesil, *Media in New Turkey: The Origins of an Authoritarian Neoliberal State* (Champaign, IL: University of Illinois Press, 2016), 68). The article 301 of Penal Code remains, even after it was softened in the early 2000s, a tool for prosecution of writers whose work is considered "insulting" to the nation.

[25] Yıldırım, *Diplomacy and Displacement*.

be sent to become a minority in the second one. The journalist Bruce Clark titled a book about their experience as *Twice a Stranger*.[26] It also had ramifications for Turkey's social and economic structure—as Onur Yıldırım's research shows, it is not just *how many* left, but also *who* left and came. Of no less importance, as Yıldırım vividly described, is how the exchange was later reproduced in many other European contexts.[27] The protests of the directly impacted communities mattered little to organizers of the exchange, and so did their immediate needs, the latter provided for by spontaneous actions of individuals and charities, as the state authorities were ill prepared to manage the task.[28] A century later precisely this question—why is it private charities or ad hoc collectives of individuals who seem to be more ready to think of the well-being of refugees than the states that are bound by international treaties—remains unresolved in many European capitals. Also familiar are the suggestions of many around Europe that migrants from non-European or non-Christian lands should not be allowed in.[29]

While the early republican reforms seem like sudden breaks with the past, especially from the vantage point of the present, historians caution that transformations are not singular events. New codes can express reformers' ambition for the future; they can also reorder ways of remembering the past. But societies and individuals do not immediately switch to different ways. Some laws are more enforced (and enforceable) than others, some can be subject to resistance. Take generational cohorts—as young children entered school, their lessons came already in a new language, and heritage even from a very recent past remained to be discovered only in later decades.[30]

In the century since the establishment of the republic, social relations were reordered in many other ways. Various development plans, infrastructure projects, and national education strategies have created cities and citizens that residents from the beginning of the century might find hard to recognize. Until 1945, Turkish voters could choose only one political party. Military coups in 1960, 1971, and 1980, as well as the removal from office of the *Refah* (Welfare Party, predecessor to the AKP) government in 1997 and the most recent coup attempt in 2016 have all reframed avenues for who can shape the public sphere and under what conditions. The coups including the failed one came with

---

[26] Bruce Clark, *Twice a Stranger: How Mass Expulsions Forged Modern Greece and Turkey* (London: Granta Books, 2006). The book opens with an eponymous (*Iki kere yabancı*, Twice a stranger) recollection by Professor Ayşe Lahur Kırtunç.

[27] Yıldırım, *Diplomacy and Displacement*.

[28] Clark, *Twice a Stranger*.

[29] This is discussed in more detail in Part Three of this book.

[30] Faroqhi, *Approaching Ottoman History*.

shock, fear, the dead, and the wounded. They brought trauma, arrests, and bans on political participation for specific individuals and groups.[31] Whichever new development or reform was on agenda, the foundation of the republic, the rupture of the 1920s, has served as an important lens through which new developments were analyzed; it will thus remain our narrative focal point for the rest of the chapter.

Some weeks after the 2016 coup attempt, we were sitting in a café with a friend, Bilge. We were both confused by everything that happened in that period. Like many others, we also tried to navigate the everyday, discussing life and the world in their broad contours. An important part of our complaints were the stifling heat and humidity of the Istanbul summer, something residents of the city, be they temporal or perennial, can talk about for hours and how deep this concern goes is often beyond the comprehension to anyone who has not experienced it. At one point, Bilge wondered: "And have you noticed, that they [the government] are going to add a new national holiday?" At that time, I was reading a lot of texts on memory and memorials, and thus asked, casually: "Why could not a new national holiday be added?" only to realize that all national holidays, with the exception of two religious feasts and a May (Labor) Day, have commemorated events of the 1920s Independence war.[32] When the "Democracy and National Unity Day," was eventually introduced to the calendar, this was the first time a national holiday was not explicitly referring to foundation of the republic. For comparison, the public holidays in the current Czech calendar commemorate events spanning centuries.[33] In Turkey's official calendar, the early republican period remains the key symbol through which achievements and problems of westernization (and nation-building) are narrated.[34]

---

[31] The 1980 coup has often been referenced as bringing stillness to political participation for many years. That has briefly changed in the 2013 Gezi protests—for a number of interlocutors this was "the moment when your mother would join you at the protest."

[32] In 2019, there were eight days to celebrate the Feast of Ramadan and the Feast of Sacrifice and four days of *milli bayramlar* (national public holidays) commemorating events from the Independence war.

[33] In 2019, the Czech calendar lists fourteen days of national holidays. Five of these are related to Christmas and Easter. New Year's Day is a national holiday as well, yet it is also a day in which another political holiday is celebrated, so I am not listing it separately. That leaves nine days referring to various periods of Czech history. I am listing them in sequence in which they are commemorated (i.e., starting in January and ending in December) and indicate name of the holiday and the year of the event which is being commemorated: Day of Renewal of Independent Czech statehood (1993); Labor Day (1890); Victory Day (1945); Day of Apostles of the Slavs (ninth century); Day of Burning of Jan Hus (1415); Day of Czech statehood (935); Day of establishment of independent Czechoslovak state (1918); Day of Struggle for Freedom and Democracy (1939 and 1989). The list with short explanations (in Czech) is available, for example, at http://svatky.centrum.cz/svatky/sta tni-svatky/.

[34] Turkey voted in the April 2017 referendum to switch to presidential system. At the time of writing, Turkey is approaching centennial of the establishment of the 1923 republic. Some writers have

The past is not just what happened, it is here, and those who live today keep rediscovering it, forgetting it, making satire of it, and are concerned about that satire. A short movie *Mutlu Ol! Bu Bir Emirdir* (Be Happy! It's an Order) takes us to a house in which a group of people of several generations sing and play *türkü* (folk songs), with obvious joy.[35] Just as we are tuning in to their melody, the camera turns to a different part of the room and shows a line-up of policemen with guns. The police scold the group for singing *türkü* and provide instead a list of Western composers. They remind the musicians that "batılı olacagız, mutlu olacagiz" (we are going to become Western, we are going to become happy) and force them to smile. The villagers indeed start playing Mozart and Beethoven, with a reed, and as the police start dancing, one of them wonders why he actually likes this "Western" song.[36] The film does not hide its desire to reject imposition of cultural norms. As we watch the villagers playing Beethoven's "Ode to joy," the EU official anthem although many of EU citizens are not familiar with it, police become a bit more relaxed. The closing text reads: "The political authority which bans peoples' music, culture, lifestyle has always been caught strange against life."[37] Ertuğrul Özkök, former editor of *Hürriyet*, one of the country's biggest newspaper, penned a column titled *Çok güldüm, ama* (I had a good laugh, but).[38] In the text, he cautioned against going too far in questioning founding principles of the republic. He thus expressed concerns of many, who feared that the incumbent government might dismantle checks and balances including those protecting secularism. The title of the movie alludes to one of the most oft-referenced sayings of Mustafa Kemal, the founding president: *Ne mutlu Türküm diyene* (How happy is the one who can say "I am a Turk"). The movie aired five years into the AKP tenure in government and three years into the interrupted accession talks with the EU.

There are variations in how we encounter events and symbols from the more distant pasts when browsing the pages of the present. A crucial work in this realm has been undertaken by the anthropologist Esra Özyürek, who, in one of her texts, observed that newspapers tend to select different photographs of the founding president depending on their political leaning, and thus, Mustafa

---

suggested that after the recent failed coup attempt and the 2017 switch to presidential system, the country is in its "second" or the "third republic."

[35] A movie by director Sinan Çetin, *Mutlu Ol! Bu Bir Emirdir* was screened in 2008. I thank Dr. Tunç Aybak of Middlesex University for bringing it to my attention.

[36] The short film shows the law enforcers at one point being more uneasy than the musicians, who seem to be relaxed most of the time.

[37] This is the English translation.

[38] Ertuğrul Özkök, "Çok güldüm ama," *Hürriyet*, March 9, 2008.

Kemal might be portrayed praying or doing something more "modern."[39] A similar point has been raised about selective remembering of pre-republican times.[40] The republic's rush to adopt Western ways has been celebrated, as an achievement, and decried, as an act of violence. In the decades since its establishment, it has been an important topic in many spaces—from political rallies, to cafes, and *meyhane* through cultural journals and films. As Gönül Dönmez-Colin notes, in cinema, this theme has been so widely portrayed that it became "almost obsolete."[41] This intensity, sometimes to the point of weariness, tells us that while the republican reforms did launch new institutions and regrouped hierarchies of preferable cultural codes, they have not stopped the discussion on alternative solidarities. At the time of reordering of the empire there have been more imaginaries of possible future, including the pan-Islamic and pan-Turanist projects.[42] Regardless of which type of solidarity has been advocated for, Western Europe, or parts of it, have been a frequent reference in intellectual reflection and political mobilization. In the 1990s, as Iğsız notes, smaller presses started publishing accounts of people who were affected by displacement, a theme later picked up by mainstream outlets and even receiving public funds.[43] A whole new window opened into challenging earlier hegemonic narratives. Elif Şafak, one of Turkey's most popular novelists, wrote recently about the joy of discovering Arab writers, after a childhood spent mostly with Western and Russian literature.[44] Reading beyond conventional ruptures can lead one to see commonalities that have been cut off. The past can make one curious or sad, it can also appear as a fashion trend. *Ottomania* has been widely noted in pop culture, including telenovelas and special sultan's menus at fast-food chains.[45] Pasts can be also be sold in political campaign. In the second decade of the twenty-first century, several AKP candidates for parliamentary seats smiled from billboards dressed up in Ottoman-style costumes. To some

[39] Esra Özyürek (ed.), *The Politics of Public Memory in Turkey* (New York: Syracuse University Press, 2007).
[40] Fisher Onar, "Echoes of a Universalism Lost: Rival Representations of the Ottomans in Today's Turkey," *Middle Eastern Studies* 45, no. 2 (2009).
[41] Gönül Dönmez-Colin, *Turkish Cinema: Identity, Distance and Belonging* (London: Reaktion Books, 2008).
[42] See Çagaptay for discussion.
[43] Aslı Iğsız, "Polyphony and Geographic Kinship in Anatolia," in Esra Özyürek (ed.), *The Politics of Public Memory in Turkey* (New York: Syracuse University Press, 2007), 162–90.
[44] Elif Şafak, "Finally Turkey Looks East," *The New York Times*, February 23, 2011.
[45] This is an admirable collection of artefacts and observations on many things including living internationally since the 1980s: Meltem Ahıska, *The Person You Have Called Cannot Be Reached at the Moment: Representations of Lifestyles in Turkey 1980–2005* (Istanbul: Ottoman Bank Archives and Research Centre, 2006). See also: Deniz Kandiyoti and Ayşe Saktanber (ed.), *Fragments of Culture: The Everyday of Modern Turkey* (London: I.B. Tauris, 2002).

the past is threatening, to others it provides a form of reassurance. When in 2010 Istanbul became a "European Capital of Culture," a traveling selection of cities initiated by the EU to strengthen cultural tourism, the bulletin prepared by the local organizing committee referred with easiness to Turkish, Greek, Armenian, and Sephardic cultural milieus as sources of the city's present pride. Rediscovery and reconstruction of multicultural past(s) and monuments were part of the agenda offered to visitors.

Travels between the past and the present and categories in which we think about them might sometimes be disorienting. As Istanbul was celebrating its diverse pasts and multicultural encounters, perspectives on such encounters in the present were less optimistic. To illustrate concerns of many, let us hear from one leader of a human rights NGO, with whom I was discussing meanings of EU-rope and expectations from it:

> Well, I am happy that we have all kinds of exchange and cooperation. But I sometimes wonder, when the discussion comes to women rights, why do they act like everything has been resolved in the West? This is an issue which does not really work anywhere.

There is a well-documented tendency in approaches from "outside" of Muslim majority countries to focus on women rights.[46] Women rights are often *the* lens through which modernity is interpreted and they are one of the sites in which we can see the messiness of spatial and temporal boundaries. The interlocutor cited in the foregoing quote did not object to discussion of women's rights in principle. This is a question very relevant in Turkey. But a friction emerges when these rights are brought up *by Westerners* in a way which suggests they have a solution that they often do not. As we will see later in this book, it is one thing to value certain standards of human rights, it is quite another to know how to improve them. Values, wishes, and knowledge of course take different contours depending on whether one does or does not *belong* to the society they wish to improve. But again, this is not a conversation between monolithic Turkey and the West. A plumber with whom I was discussing basic things related to laundry machines, around the time I spoke to the NGO director cited earlier, told me that his main concern about the EU was that it "forces our women to work." When I recounted the conversation to acquaintances and friends working in middle-class professions, some would note *off köylü* (oh, a villager) or *darkafalı* (narrow-minded), or *tipik Türk erkeği* (a typical Turkish man). A conversation would

---

[46] Lila Abu Lughod, "Do Muslim Women Really Need Saving? Anthropological Reflections on Cultural Relativism and its Others," *American Anthropologist* 104, no. 3 (2002): 783–90.

often ensue on how and why "the people" need to be educated. Yet there was not much in the words of this Turkish plumber that a more western European would not say. Perhaps more importantly, as this is a book about knowledge and understanding, we also need to keep in mind that the plumber, although he did not have access to the finest institutions of higher learning, voiced his opinions in a way more respectful than many college graduates.

The difficulty of making sense of classification in how we relate to segments of history and groups of people could well be demonstrated viewing Tunç Okan's 1977 movie *Otobüs* (The Bus). Here, a group of Anatolian villagers embarks on a journey to Europe. Their smuggler abandons them in the center of Stockholm, the capital of Sweden. We witness their shock, surprise, and embarrassment, as they discover this new place, walking past shop windows displaying naked figurines and ending up in a club in which drinks are sold. For some, Okan's film may well be read as an account of a clash of two systems guiding gender relations; others might be startled at the portrayal of Stockholm as a very decadent place. I have first learned about the existence of the movie when browsing a repository of migration research center of the Koç University. After watching the movie, I reached for Dönmez-Colin's *Turkish Cinema* to learn more about its background. In this book, the film is also listed in migration section, yet, as the author tells us, it has many more layers. The director's choice not to include dialogues helps to deliver an important message: that understanding "the other" can be a difficult task, even an impossible one. Moreover, it is not just a story of encounters of classes, cultures, or nationalities. Dönmez-Colin citing an older interview with the film director shows that the problem that needs to be addressed is not located in one particular geography:

> The film does not blame the developed countries, he pointed out, but questions if the development model of the consumer society of the West, copied by the whole world, even the communist, is a solution for happiness.[47]

We do not need to cross frontiers of the nation-state to see the problems of understanding. In another movie, *Iki dil bir bavul* (On the way to school),[48] we meet Emre from Izmir, a city in western Turkey. Emre is a fresh graduate sent to teach at an elementary school in the southeast of the country. He came to teach, which he does, but he also ends up learning. We could say he is *there*

---

[47] Dönmez-Colin, *Turkish Cinema*, 69–71.
[48] A movie of directors Özgür Doğan and Orhan Eskiköy screened in 2008. The literal translation of the name would be *Two languages, One Suitcase*.

all alone. Most of the verbal dialogue happens on the phone, in conversations with his mother. The only people physically around are his pupils and their parents, whose first (and main) language is Kurdish. For a fresh graduate of a national education system this is a very different country. The "big history" of what is often called "the Kurdish question" is often narrated through the optics of violence, pain, and death (including civilian) suffered in battles between the state military and outlawed groups. And yet here we are, invited to read the story from different angles, such as when a young man in his twenties finds himself spending a year with no one of his own (age) generation present.[49]

Modernity as a Battle between Convergence and Resistance?

In a seminal study of the first two decades of Association Agreement with the EU, Mehmet Döşemeci suggests that debates about Turkish politics were shaped by two overlapping logics: civilizational and nationalist.[50] While one looked to Europe for aid and inspiration, the other was more protective and focused on internal state-building. These two were of course overlapping. As the author shows, the Western model was *invited* by Turkey's own reformers.[51] Döşemeci argues that one of the reasons why historical and cultural arguments were dominant in Turkish government justification of the European Economic Community's (EEC) importance is the lack of staff with technical or economic expertise who could match the EEC skills and knowledge.[52] This is a crucial point on production of expertise—to know what is beneficial for us, we need tools and resources that help us find out. At the same time, the importance of "being civilized" in EU policy practice has been well-documented by other authors.[53] While the common cultural and foreign policies were established in later phases of the Union's life, individual members did pursue them separately also before. As we saw in previous chapter of the present book, notions of civilization and culture discourse mattered for Western Europeans from the very beginning

---

[49] To meet "a different country" within one's own one does not need to leave the European Union. In Slovakia for example, "the East" has only recently been rediscovered by journalists.
[50] Döşemeci, *Debating Turkey's Modernity*.
[51] Döşemeci's work, although centered on the first two decades of the Association Agreement, is to my knowledge the most eloquent account of relationship between the *invitational logic* and the EU process. The author makes many points relevant for present EU-Turkey relations, including the observation that "nationalist narratives" are often treated as "primary sources" in discussions of TR-EU relationship, and rarely engaged with as intellectual points on their merits.
[52] Döşemeci, *Debating Turkish Modernity*, 88.
[53] This is briefly discussed in previous chapter.

of establishment of the European communities.[54] In fact, it is these individual cultural pasts that fed creation of the EU common cultural policies and their export further to neighbors via enlargement and neighborhood policies. In other words, even before the EEC/EU came up with a corpus of "civilizing" policy instruments, ideas about cultural supremacy of a "European" model, or its specific iterations, such as French, Italian, or other (western European) variation, shaped decision-making and public opinion. Needless to say, cultural hegemony often passes as expertise.

In Ahmet Evin's and Nora Fisher Onar's reading, the intellectuals discussing Turkey's relationship with the West faced a *dilemma of convergence and resistance*.[55] But once we know that Europe has never been a homogeneous entity, and there has been a gap between its self-representation and actual conduct, the aporia of convergence and resistance becomes more blurred, and perhaps also more easily reconciled. Doubts about Europe and westernization could well be articulated in the following way: Can the model (western states, later the EU) answer the aspiration? One could well be inspired by ways of social organization as they exist in EU-rope or its parts but could consider policies and cultural codes of those entities toward Turkey as unfriendly or unsupportive. Furthermore, it is one thing to be inspired by declared ideals of the model and quite another to realize that its self-narratives do not always match real life. Thus, if what the "model" is doing and how they live is disassembled from the aspiration, convergence and resistance can be perfectly reconciled. In other words: one may try to converge with the ideal but resist the practices of those who claim to "own" that ideal.[56]

And while Europe mattered tremendously for Turkish debates, it was not the only Western reference, nor the only external reference or potential model. Alliance with the United States and their growing presence on international stage after the Second World War also meant that American lifestyle became more visible in Turkey. At the beginning of the Cold War, in 1952, Turkey joined NATO, a transatlantic alliance establishing a partnership between North America and Western Europe, one that went way beyond military cooperation. In the 1980s, during reforms under Prime Minister Turgut Özal, notions of

[54] As discussed by Shore in *Building Europe*, see previous chapter.
[55] Ahmet Evin and Nora Fisher Onar, "Convergence and Resistance: The European Dilemma of Turkish Intellectuals," in Justine Lacroix and Kalypso Nicolaïdis (eds), *European Stories: Intellectual Debates on Europe in National Contexts* (Oxford: Oxford University Press, 2010).
[56] There is a well-documented anger at being wrongly/incorrectly represented by the Western writers. See for example, chapter by Zeynep Çelik, "Speaking Back to Orientalist Discourse," in Beaulieu and Roberts, *Orientalism's Interlocutors*.

Turkey as "little America" were proposed as an alternative to the European models.[57] In pop culture, North America and its products became unavoidable. Contemporaries remember how natural it seemed then. An acquaintance, a man in his fifties, who grew up in Turkey and then spent some two decades in the United States and came back "home" in the late 2000s shared this story to illustrate how highly valued new products were:

> Imagine a well-off Turkish family, they have their fancy evening meal at home, or maybe in a restaurant. Everybody dressed up, robes, women in high heels. Then they go to 7-Eleven to grab a midnight hot-dog. 7-Eleven was a place to be, since it was new and came from the West.

As he was sharing the observation, we both laughed. There was something comic about the situation. I told him about the arrival of McDonald's to Slovakia in the 1990s. For similar reasons, it was a place to go for reward, a special occasion, people would save money to buy a milkshake or fries. I added how to my great surprise, when actually going to America, I found restaurants of this chain were often empty. We briefly discussed other fast-food chains and quality of fries and burgers. When drafting this chapter and engaging this memory, I visited that same McDonald's in Bratislava again. There was nothing festive about it—a man next to me was on the phone, telling someone that he had to grab a quick meal before returning home from a teacher-training seminar. A group of teenagers at the opposite table were planning a party and busily instructed everyone that "no pictures be taken"—an adjustment to the digital age. Places may keep the same names, but their meanings and roles change.

Models and Copies: On Possibility and Necessity of Authenticity and Strategic Choices

In the many debates about westernization, a theme that comes to the forefront with a particular urgency is that of authenticity, as genuineness and as something worthy of respect. Thousands of pages have been written about the travails of catching up and whether this goal can be accomplished. This theme weaves together several related questions: *Should we have a model? Is the West the model? Can we ever catch up?* Here the assumptions of model moving at the exact same speed (or faster) makes catching up a futile endeavor and what remains is lament.

---

[57] See Ahıska, *The Person You Have Called*; and Kandiyoti and Saktanber, *Fragments of Culture*.

Tropes of movement versus stillness are common in reflections of dialogue with the West.[58] Imitation opened lively debates and these included frustration. As Ahmet Evin described in the first English-language work on Turkish novel, the genre was introduced by people trained in the art of government, with three goals:

> [T]o disseminate their ideas among a wider audience, to attract the attention of the public to current issues and to borrow from Europe those institutions that were deemed worthy of being adopted.[59]

Yet, Evin argues, when writers started adopting European styles, it often sounded artificial. Novels as specific art forms and tools of education gradually became also channels for critique of pretentiousness of some forms of westernization.[60] If something is pretentious, then, the dictionary tells us it is not genuine. But if we think a bit more about the "whys" of pretense and imitation, we get to basic questions of respect and recognition. As the author Nurdan Gürbilek pointed out, a commonly asked question in intellectual circles has been the following: Will Westerners respect us for imitating them?[61] Responding to voices who suggest there is something lacking in Turkey, Gürbilek writes:

> The criticism of lack is in fact torn between two extremes. The first one assumes that what is original is elsewhere ("outside," namely in the West) while the second insists that we do have an authentic literature and a genuine native thought but in order to appreciate it we have to leave aside all those lifeless imitations and snobbish efforts related with the West.[62]

Meltem Ahıska, author of a nuanced account of images of Occident in the early radio broadcasts in republican Turkey suggests that "the impact of the West . . . was a performance for the imagined western audience."[63] From this perspective, we can think of certain type of reforms as being done more for *the other*, than for *the self*. These and other critiques then do not focus so much on actions

---

[58] One of the most well-known collections of essays on the topic, authored by Tarik Zafer Tunaya, is titled *Medeniyetin bekleme odasında* (In civilization's waiting room).

[59] Ahmet Evin, *Origins and Development of Turkish Novel* (Minneapolis: Bibliotheca Islamica, 1983), 18.

[60] Evin, *Origins and Development*.

[61] Nurdan Gürbilek, *The New Cultural Climate in Turkey: Living in a Shop Window* (London: Zed Books, 2011). This question has been addressed more extensively in writings of Ahmet Hamdi Tanpınar, the author of, prominently, *Time Regulation Institute* and *Inner Peace*, with whose work Gürbilek extensively engages.

[62] Nurdan Gürbilek, "Dandies and Originals: Authenticity, Belatedness, and the Turkish Novel," *The South Atlantic Quarterly* 102, nos. 2/3 (2003): 599–628.

[63] Meltem Ahıska, "Occidentalism: The Historical Fantasy of the Modern," *The South Atlantic Quarterly* 102, nos. 2/3 (2003): 351–79. Performative aspects are also core part of Gürbilek's work.

and rhetoric of the Westerners, but problematize what Ahıska calls *fantasies* of the West that drove actions of Turkish elites, walking between selecting parts from institutions established by the French and other Europeans, and calling for genuinely Turkish ways of doing things. For Gürbilek, longing for that genuineness and sense of being late is not a consequence of norms imposed by outsiders, it is an act of self-denial:

> One can't return; for what is known as the self emerges as otherwise through always changing lenses, sometimes as a defensive reflex, and usually coalesced with the will to power. . . . For as long as "our self" is not problematically defined, it remains a past effect merely for show, a few Ottoman motifs, an Eastern atmosphere. It is always too late to return to oneself. And more: the call to return is itself an expression of that belatedness.[64]

In the 1990s, Turkey started cultivating its own *model*.[65] This did not really mean giving up debates about becoming more similar to the West—the aspirations to be an example for countries further east and south coexisted with debates about its place in Europe. As we saw in the previous chapter, the effort to position oneself as a model after all is not too different from what other East European countries started doing once they joined the EU.[66] It is also not too different from what the West European states have been doing before they joined or founded the EU. It is common for EU states to run various bilateral cooperation programs with other partners, often focusing on sharing their "experience." One's particular positioning in temporalities of development and not being able to match the models might be a source of regret. An inter*national* framework can be an invitation to brand one's own model.

Pasts in the Books and Those Happening as We Are Speaking

Relationship with the West, whether this meant a lifestyle or a form of governance, has been felt at all stages of Turkish history, in all kinds of recording of that history, be they scholarly accounts or pursuits of everyday curiosity. There are of course many wests, but Europe is spatially present. There is no reason why

[64] Gürbilek, *The New Cultural Climate in Turkey*, 184.
[65] For critique of the model, see Cihan Tuğal, *The Fall of the Turkish Model: How the Arab Uprisings Brought Down Islamic Liberalism* (London: Verso, 2016).
[66] Discussed in "Identity and Solidarity in Foreign Policy: Investigating East Central European Relations with Eastern Neighborhood," a special issue of *Perspectives: Review of International Affairs* 19, no. 2 (2011), see especially the editorial introduction by Elsa Tulmets.

these pasts should not be re-entering discussions as Turkey and the EU switched to accession talks mode in the first years of the twenty-first century. As we will see in the following chapters of this book, new times brought new events, but did little to revamp the oppositional foundation of the relationship. They did provide new scripts and channels in which the old suddenly appeared or was picked up for convenience.

Often, when I visited Turkey, or made a new acquaintance, my interlocutors would remark that it must be interesting to visit, *because these are historic times*. What they usually meant was that too many things were happening at the same time, too many meaningful things. I often found it difficult to catch up with news headlines and soon realized that this has not been just my imperfect attention or a consequence of appearing from a different geography and not being able to follow all the references. It was also Turkish friends and interlocutors who often found it difficult to keep on pace with events in the country and its immediate surroundings. But these were not just dry statements, such comments were also invitations and urgent questions—*What do you think? Where are these times going to lead us? What is going to happen? How do you see what we are doing?* During one summer stay in Istanbul I decided not to follow the news and my interlocutors were surprised and rushed to fill me in. Being "out of the loop" was a thing to be corrected. I *had to* become synced. I sometimes wondered, after such conversations, whether there could be anything more *historic* than the changes Turkey experienced at the time of establishment of the republic. And it has been conversations like these that made me realize the many meanings of ruptures and how we learn about them. Because any time people referred to "historic times," it was in relation to events happening or reported at the time of our conversation. Historic times thus meant times in which history is being written or made. While such conversations often reference past events or personalities, these were not the key. It sometimes seemed that anything I have read about the Ottomans or the Kemalists did not matter. Awareness of history is just as much related to being *in* on the current events as to those that have already passed, those about which one learns from books. In the former case, novelty is happening right now, it has a potential to reshape future; in the latter, we already know how they have reshaped the world. In a recent article,[67] and one which shaped thinking on the present book, anthropologist Rebecca Bryant writes about moments when we are acutely aware of the present, because we

---

[67] Rebecca Bryant, "On Critical Times: Return, Repetition, and the Uncanny Present," *History and Anthropology* 27, no. 1 (2017): 19–31.

cannot know what the future might bring. There is an element of anxiety in such "critical times", and we will engage with this angle in the next part of the present book. In "these are historic times" as described in the present chapter, the emphasis is not on anxiety about the future, but on curiosity and awareness of "history," which emerges in the conversation not just in relation to events that are unfolding, but also in the situation in which people meet someone from the "outside." The emphasis then is not on the impending change, but on the search for feedback. History can be something in books, monuments, it is also something that we are living—but not always shaping. The latter could also be read through current debates on relationship between humans and natural disasters. In the latter, we sometimes do not do anything. Sometimes we try to exercise our agency, such as when people try to cut down on flying or go zero waste. It is not clear whether similar agency is possible in relation to earthquakes.

Part Two

Recognitions and Realisms

When novelists structure their work into chapters, they have many things in mind. A chapter can be named or numbered. It can focus on individual protagonists or sketch out complex situations. It can suddenly make a detour, only to be followed up by another chapter that returns us to the main plot line. Chapters do not have to tell the events as they unfold. It can well happen that only the last pages of the book reveal something important about the lives of the protagonists before we met them; something we need to know for the story to make sense. Novelists often spend a lot of time figuring out the best sequence in which the reader should learn all they need to know. A novelist then perhaps would not want us to read a chapter twenty-seven before we have read a chapter four. But then, novels tell stories that have already seen some closure—or at least the author has seen enough to tell a story that they serve us, chapter by chapter.

Chapters as we know them in the diplomatic communication of Turkey-EU relationships do a very different type of work. To be sure, one also needs to "read" them all but that is one of the very few similarities with novels. Chapters are packages of EU law that the candidate needs to adopt. Once a formal accession process starts, as it did in 2005, diplomats, journalists, and other participants of Turkey-EU diplomatic relationships use this word very often. They count the chapters—x have been open, y have been closed, and, in case of Turkey, z have been blocked. The numbers are indicators of progress—how close the candidate is to becoming a member. The sequence is not linear—there is no need to start with number one and end with number thirty-five. They can be opened and closed in a random order, everything depends on agreement between the member states and the candidate. If one state disagrees and the others are not convincing enough, then no one gets to read the chapter, or, at least not in a way that would matter. A chapter can be blocked. Participants in the process may have different opinions on importance of individual chapters. But membership does not *happen* unless everyone has read and signed everything.

Turkey is not an EU member state. When we discuss whether it could be, a yes or no answer is often requested and offered. Casual observers of the relationship sometimes say "yes" and "no" depending on how compatible they see Turkey and the EU at the moment of speaking. Long-time students of Turkey-EU relations might find it difficult to use one of these short words. They often reach for a counter-question to explain that the path toward a membership is a process, in which many things should, could, and hopefully will change. At the end of the process, both the EU and Turkey will be different compared to their present. Decision-makers who sign diplomatic agreements often cannot do a "yes, but". They have to opt for a yes or no.

Organization of the relationship into chapters was a novelty introduced by the launch of the formal accession talks. What else was new? In the diplomatic phase we call accession talks, new milestones opened. The switch from being associated country to a negotiating country brought different opportunities for rejection or validation. As we will see, some of the anxieties that later surfaced in the conversation about the relationship have been caused exactly by the ambiguity of proximity of the moment of accession that the new framework offered. It might seem that the step from associated to accession country has increased Turkey's chance to become a member. It might also be proposed that it revealed how deep some of the earlier misunderstandings have been. The past conflicts and misunderstanding did not disappear. The interlocutors are delegated by the same institutions. While a "civil society dialogue" was added, the main decisions are adopted by the governments and parliaments. The compositions of cabinets and legislatures has altered in the fifteen years of talks, but perhaps more in the EU than in Turkey, where throughout this period one party has been a dominant actor, although it underwent a number of internal transformations. And while the European Union has been gradually moving toward more coordination in foreign policy, and its 2009 constitutional reform was designed to bring it closer to having "one voice," the national governments and parliaments have the last word on decisions whether to admit a candidate. They are also very unpredictable in whether they will uphold commitments of their predecessors. Diplomats, journalists, aid workers navigate this complex inter*national* relationship, and sometimes feel that their main job is to make "the other" understand their position. That labor of understanding, as we already know, can sometimes become too demanding.

The chapters in this part take us through experience of participants of this new format. Chapter 4 explores confusions and disappointments that transpired once the accession talks were suspended shortly after their opening; once Turkey was told that it still should try but perhaps there will be no result. Chapter 5 pays closer attention to "state-civil society relations," a dichotomy inside a (Turkey-EU) dichotomy. In Chapter 6 we travel to a place which is neither in Turkey nor in the EU, but is foundational to their relationship. Geographically, that place is Northern Cyprus. Conceptually, that place is timing of democracy. Wait a moment—is there such a thing as "timing" of democracy? Maybe there is, if we consider that EU accession is supposed to deliver precisely this—more democracy for the candidate state. But then, only a democratic state can become a member. The central theme guiding these chapters is recognition, something often locked in discourses of borders and international law but in fact a theme much wider as it connects profoundly to belongings. In the inter*national* world, recognition is central to belonging. It is not sufficient to proclaim that one feels part of something. If the others do not validate this claim, one is left in limbo.

4

Yes, Still Talking about Accession

That moment when, from a certain perspective, accession did seem realistic, came at the beginning of the present century, in 2004, when Turkey and all twenty-five[1] member states of the EU agreed to move their dialogue to a new setting: *talks about accession*, sometimes referred to as *accession negotiations*.[2] This meant the introduction of a new language, scripts, and tasks. Turkey was now subject to "screening" procedures in which the EU diplomats reviewed Turkish legislation to see which parts already corresponded with the EU law and which parts still needed to be harmonized. For the purposes of enlargement, the EU law is divided into thirty-five chapters covering policy areas. Only when all of them are discussed and voted as closed a candidate *could* become a member. Emphasis on a possibility rather than a certainty matters here because a membership has to be approved by elected representatives of all member states and the candidate country. None of the politicians are obliged to follow conclusions of the diplomats or legal services.

The policy-oriented literature on EU enlargement widely acknowledges that there is very little to negotiate in accession negotiations—the candidate has to adopt the EU law.[3] After all, the EU sets the rules and the candidate has to follow them. But let us look at *negotiations* from a bit different angle: while Turkey's duty to adopt the EU law might not be negotiable, the setting established by this new format has opened space for the renegotiation of some of the key moral

---

[1] Romania, Bulgaria, and Croatia joined the bloc after 2004.
[2] From a certain perspective, this stage opened earlier, in 1999, when Turkey was given a "candidate status." The 1999–2004 period is considered, by many scholars of the relationship, a hey-day of reform. See for example, Mehmet Uğur, "Open-Ended Membership Prospect and Commitment Credibility: Explaining the Deadlock in EU-Turkey Accession Negotiations," *Journal of Common Market Studies* 48, no. 4 (2010): 967–91; Paul Kubicek, "Political Conditionality and European Union's Cultivation of Democracy in Turkey," *Democratization* 18, no. 4 (2011): 910–31. For a perspective suggesting a double look at the role of EU conditionality in the process, see Kıvanç Ulusoy, "Turkey's Reform Effort Reconsidered, 1987–2004," *EUI Working Paper RSCAS* 28 (2005).
[3] For a general overview of accession process, see Helen Wallace, Mark A. Pollack and Alasdair Young. Eds. *Policy-Making in the European Union.* 6th edn (Oxford: Oxford University Press, 2010).

categories in European integration. Participants of the process often ask: "How will/would the EU look with Turkey as a member state?" As they search for answers, and imagine the future, they employ fragments of the pasts, including Ottoman-European encounters. The new format requested more meetings between diplomats, politicians, and what is often referred to as "civil society." This novel phase in the *process of becoming* has also meant different forms of presence of the EU and Turkey in media debates and political campaigns. I am cautious to say "more presence," because historians tell us of quite close encounters in earlier times.[4]

In discussions within the accession format, microscopic attention is dedicated to various items from the long list of standards the candidate needs to adopt—from minority protection to specific rules of collecting statistical data. EU-rope has not arrived only to parliamentary and conference rooms—it has made subtle appearances in places not formally tasked with the process of integration. In one of the episodes of *Behzat Ç*, a *polisiye* (crime) TV series, the policemen half-jokingly complain that the EU anti-torture legislation prevents them from doing their jobs right. In another series, a family drama unconcerned with international politics, a Turkish character, who has lived some time in Germany moves back to Turkey and finds herself questioned by a policeman. When she objects to being interrogated without her lawyer, the officer wonders whether she is now going to teach him law, adding "you came from the EU, you know your rights, right?" and continues, undisturbed, in his earlier style.[5] Such utterances take only a few seconds on the screen, the scriptwriter does not need to provide deeper explanation of the context. The viewer is expected to get the hint, EU-rope is a household item in Turkey, it has, very organically, become a part of everyday.

Rights and EU-rope go hand in hand, in serious demands and ironic remarks. Yet, while the EU law might provide very specific answers to a long list of questions including treatment of detainees and quality of vegetables and meat on the market, it remains notoriously ambiguous on the big question of whether Turkey is a "European state." The EU constitution[6] stipulates that "any European state" can apply for membership. But while it provides detail on how such

---

[4] Konuk, *East West Mimesis*, 46. Bisaha, *Creating East and West*; Karahasanoğlu and Demir, *History from Below*.
[5] *Bir Çocuk Sevdim*, TMC film, 2011–12, Episode 13.
[6] Treaty on the European Union, Article 49. I use the term "constitution" with lowercase c to indicate "a body of fundamental principles" (*OED*). The EU states discussed adoption of a constitution with a capital C, for now though the process has been put on hold due to several factors. One of them was rejection of such document in referenda in France and the Netherlands. Yet, regardless of how the main treaty is called, the EU does have a constitution. Treaty on the European Union establishes

application will be processed, it does not come with a list of countries recognized as European.[7] Legally binding decisions about "being European" are then given on the go, by representatives of the member states and the EU institutions, who happen to be in office at critical moments in the application process. The way Europeanness is negotiated in debates that lead to those votes resembles the way anthropologist Marilyn Strathern proposed thinking about gender:

> [T]he many ways in which people think about interaction between the sexes, and the many ways in which this interaction is used to talk about, becomes an idiom for, *other things*. (italics mine)[8]

Translated for our discussion, we could think about Europe, or being European, as a synonym for democracy, modernity, culture—or their lack. (Not) being European is then best understood as a short-cut for a "mode of differentiation"[9] in which other differences are at stake. While opening of the accession talks has not settled the question of whether Turkey is or could be European, it has reframed some of the ways in which the question is asked. It has also opened a way for a different experience of time. Rebecca Bryant, in her ethnography of Cyprus, proposed to think about *now* as the moment in which decisions about the future are taken. Studying "the particular experience of temporality that people express when they use the term 'crisis,'"[10] Bryant proposes the term "critical thresholds" as moments in which

> We acquire a sense that what we do in the present will be decisive for both the past and the future, giving to the presence a status of a threshold.[11]

Debates held within accession talks, or, a process of becoming, have provided a number of moments of such intense awareness of the *now*. The future that is being made in the *now* might have many faces, including one which is apocalyptic, or one which is simply uncertain. Bryant's suggestion to "bracket the philosophy of history" is also productive in the sense that it opens more room for focus on the many different angles from which the *now* is lived from different positionalities.[12]

---

the most important principles on which the member states agreed and to which other laws are subordinate.

[7] To date, only Morocco's application was rejected on the grounds that this is not a "European" state.

[8] Strathern, *Before and After Gender*, 53.

[9] Bahar Rumelili, "Constructing Identity and Relating to Difference: Understanding the EU's Mode of Differentiation," *Review of International Studies* 30 (2004): 27–47.

[10] Rebecca Bryant, "On Critical Times," *History and Anthropology* 27, no. 1 (2017): 19–31.

[11] Bryant, "On Critical Times," 20.

[12] Bryant, "On Critical Times."

European integration is often discussed in a language of wishes. In that case, it does not only matter where and how Turkey is *now*. The possibility and desirability of future changes in this or that direction is also equally important. Many texts on relations between the EU and the candidates engage in the notions of the Union's power to transform its neighbors. This literature has burgeoned with the 2004 "big bang" enlargement and there are a number of overlaps between academic texts and the EU institutional narratives of self.[13] It is thus fair to argue that a candidate is offered a promise that following the EU path brings benefits. But while there is a general enlargement framework, it is also clear that not all candidates are considered willing or capable of following that path. The future-making happens *now* and, as Helen Sjursen has showed, the decisions about who to include are often driven by "kinship-based duty" rather than cost-benefit calculations or cosmopolitan all-embracing approach.[14] Moreover, the present state of affairs in the candidate country is often projected on the future screen. Voices skeptical about Turkey's possibility of becoming suggest that either *Turkey will always be Turkey—it will not move forward*, or, if it does, it is bound to be moving in a certain distance from EU-rope. In such logic, Turkey not only cannot become a member but also cannot become similar, democratic, prosperous—it cannot become "like Europe."

The EU documents explaining why this new format of relationship has been introduced, repeatedly express hope that the process would facilitate reform in Turkey. Yet, it is a very cautious hope, as already stipulated in the oft-cited 2004 Council conclusions, which gave green light to opening of the talks: "These negotiations are an open-ended process, the outcome of which cannot be guaranteed beforehand."[15]

Writing a few years before the talks were open, Mehmet Uğur provided a convincing and, to my knowledge, yet unrefuted explanation of problems of the lukewarm commitment.[16] A framework without guarantees leads to what he called an "anchor-credibility dilemma," a situation in which both diplomacies, locked down by their respective domestic debates, take advantage of the ambiguity of rules and, eventually, no convergence happens. The question of EU

---

[13] Klinke, "European Integration Studies."

[14] Helen Sjursen, "Why Expand? The Question of Legitimacy and Justification in the EU's Enlargement Policy," *Journal of Common Market Studies* 40, no. 3 (2011): 491–513. See also: Helen Sjursen (ed.), *Questioning the EU Enlargement: Europe in Search of Identity* (London and New York: Routledge, 2006).

[15] Council of the European Union, Brussels European Council 16/17 December 2004, Presidency Conclusions.

[16] Uğur, *The European Union and Turkey*. It of course later transpired, that for some protagonists, this setup has not led to dilemmas but rather a convenient way of achieving political objectives.

credibility became one of the key words in writing about EU-Turkey relations. There is one more point Uğur emphasized, one which sometimes escapes in analyses striving to grasp the complexity and speed of changes in Turkey, the EU, and global politics: the recurring *crises* in their relations happen exactly because of the institutional setup, not so much due to external factors or the changing configurations of parliaments at home. In a related point, Bahar Rumelili, comparing EU relations with Turkey to those with Morocco argued:

> In this case, the absence of a relationship of Othering is again dependent on the continued recognition by Morocco of the construction of its identity as inherently different from the EU.[17]

Even without a set deadline, time in the relationship is carefully measured. The European Commission annually publishes *progress* reports on Turkey's alignment with the EU law.[18] Had the talks been only a process of harmonization of law, one might have expected a more or less rhythmic opening and closing. Any hope for regularity was thwarted a mere year later, in 2006, when the member states put a pause on the process, since, shortly before opening of the talks with Turkey, a divided Cyprus entered the Union.[19] The diplomatic justification for this rupture could be summed up as follows: Turkey refused to recognize the (Greek) Cypriot government as a legitimate representative of all Cypriots, and the EU refused to continue full version of the talks with a state that does not recognize one of its members. The member states decided that until the issue is resolved, eight chapters cannot be opened and no chapter can be closed.[20]

During the following decade, virtually every academic paper on the relationship noted that this decision has alienated Turkish society from the EU. Observers of the relationship, academics, and commentators have, since that 2006 decision, increasingly questioned whether the EU could still aspire to encourage better governance, democracy, or access to rights. The incomprehensibility of blocking chapters of the law directly related to civic freedoms was pointed out especially

---

[17] Rumelili, "Constructing Identity," 46.

[18] A very insightful account of importance of these documents for politics of the relationship was provided by Bilge Firat, "Political Documents and Bureaucratic Entrepreneurs: Lobbying the European Parliament During Turkey's EU Integration," *Political and Legal Anthropology Review* 39, no. 2 (2016): 190–205.

[19] For EU's role in the Cyprus conflict prior to 2004, see Nathalie Tocci, *EU Accession Dynamics and Conflict Resolution: Catalysing Peace or Consolidating Partition in Cyprus?* (Ashgate: Aldershot, 2004); Thomas Diez (ed.), *The European Union and the Cyprus Conflict* (Manchester: Manchester University Press, 2002).

[20] Cyprus has since then been referenced as an obstacle in EU-Turkey relations. As we will see in Chapter 6, it can also be thought of as analogical case, as far as the debate on recognitions and realisms is concerned.

during moments of upheaval, such as the Gezi protests in 2013 or, perhaps even more intensely after the 2016 failed coup, which left many dead and wounded. After the coup attempt, the government declared a state of emergency and passed several rounds of decrees leading to large-scale dismissals from work and imprisonment.[21] Suspension of the accession talks is neither in the distant past nor a singular event that has simply happened while life coincidentally brought other concerns.[22]

In the memories of some, Turkey's accession is not realistic because its policies on civic freedoms are incompatible with those in the EU. In fact, it is common to hear that it has never really been realistic—and the present-day situation is offered as evidence that those who have been against membership ten years ago were in fact right.[23] In the memories of others, especially those who followed the process closely and whose lives were directly impacted by this process, the EU has resigned to the possibility to shape Turkey's institutional setup, or more precisely, to let Turkey become a part of European "we." As the Commission continued publishing its progress reports, gradually noting more regress than progress, some started asking, "why, if Turkey is serious about becoming an EU member, does it not adopt the EU law regardless of the Union's position on its accession?" The Turkish government *did* rename the EU Copenhagen criteria[24] as the "Ankara criteria" and even proposed several deadlines for accession, but the alignment with the EU law has been patchy. The suggestion that a candidate could become like the EU without the EU being directly involved contravenes the logic of the accession process and buries much of the epistemology of "EU as a democratizing power." It also disregards the political and relational, as opposed to purely legal, or, as is sometimes suggested, "technical," nature of the process.[25] The politics, the contestation, does not happen only *within* the national polities involved in the diplomatic framework, it also happens *between* them.

---

[21] It is perhaps an irony, considering the growing concern with state of academic freedom in Turkey, that the only chapter which has been provisionally closed, is the one named "Science and Research."

[22] In *Mohawk Interruptus*, an ethnography of North American First Nation, Audra Simpson writes about Mohawk "refusal to forget" events that led to their current position in the United States and Canada.

[23] This is connected to debates on intentionality that emerged already when a government with religious leanings came to power shortly before opening of the accession talks. For the reasons of space, I do not go into details of intentionality at this point and will address the question in the last part of the book focusing on the 2016 "refugee deal."

[24] A set of criteria adopted by the 1993 Copenhagen meeting of EU leaders (EU Council) specifying conditions a candidate should meet.

[25] "Technical" can rarely be separated from "the political." Reuben Rose-Redwood, "With Numbers in Place: Security, Territory, and the Production of Calculable Space," *Annals of Association of American Geographers* 102, no. 2 (2012): 295–319.

Calls for a Referee

Thousands of pages have been covered by explaining the dynamics in the EU, that led to the suspension of accession talks so shortly after their opening. None of those explanations provide a reassurance to a Turk (or, an EU supporter of the accession), who would like to take the EU constitutional values literally, and who has seen the EU decision of exclusion as an act difficult to comprehend. In the milieu of the defenders of the merits of the accession process, a sense of injustice has been the dominant emotion. Various tools were mobilized, and appeals were penned, engaging EU's own narratives, in an effort to correct the double standards. In a widely cited report published at a critical time, Senem Aydin Düzgit argued that

> [T]he increasingly discriminatory practices towards Turkey violate the Enlightenment principles upon which Europe itself is founded and endanger the formation of a Europe governed by Kantian ideals.[26]

Düzgit, whose report has been endorsed by several high-level EU politicians, recounts a number of areas in which more has been requested of Turkey, a candidate, than from actual members. In a similar argument, journalist Semih Idiz challenged the EU countries' critique of Turkey's notorious Article 301 criminalizing offence of "Turkishness" when their legal systems carry similar articles.[27] Many more illustrations could be listed to demonstrate both the depth of a sense of injustice and the wide array of evidence amassed to convince the EU decision-makers that the process of becoming should not be blocked. Those who campaigned for continuation of accession talks were not asking for special concessions for Turkey, nor were they contesting the rule that Turkey should adjust its legislation to EU norms. They merely expected the EU not to demand more from Turkey than it does from its own members.

This sense of injustice invited a search for a referee. To be sure, on the one hand, the accession process already has an arbiter—the public opinion in the EU, in Turkey, but also elsewhere.[28] But the referee that has been invoked is both an impartial and an intimate one. Some authors have suggested that there

---

[26] Senem Aydin Düzgit, *Seeing Kant in the EU's Relations with Turkey* (Istanbul: TESEV, 2006). Note: In Part One of this book, I reference historians' work showing that Enlightenment, or Age of Reason and Humanism has also been the period in which "othering" of Ottomans played a significant role in construction of European narratives of the self.

[27] Semih Idiz, "Article 301 and its European Cousins," *Turkish Daily News*, October 19, 2006.

[28] As Turkey's dominant religion has been often considered one of its most distinctive marks, it perhaps no surprise that the talks have been widely followed in media in Muslim majority countries. The question has also attracted significant attention in the US policy circles.

is no such a thing as a "right" to membership. This, however, is a perspective, which applies the EU law to the rule outside of the EU. In fact, it is perfectly in line with the wider contours of the EU engagement abroad. It is true that the EU constitution does not guarantee a right to membership for states outside the Union. The question of who guarantees rights in this relationship is in fact the essence of the conflict and the call for cosmopolitan justice has resonated in the newspaper commentaries and academic discussions. In one such article, Fuat Keyman and Feyzi Baban write:

> [T]he progress reports written on Turkey and decisions made about Turkey's success in full accession negotiations should be universal and impartial. *Universality* means that the EU should treat Turkey not as a special case, but as one of the countries for full membership status. *Impartiality* means that the EU's distance from Turkey's full membership should be the same as its distance from full membership of other candidate countries.[29]

This call for impartiality has been a direct response to atmosphere in conference rooms at that particular time. The conclusions from the EU 2004 summit that gave green light to opening of the talks refer to various transitional periods, safeguards, and derogations.[30] In parallel with opening of the talks, many in the EU have promoted options such as "privileged partnership."[31] There is no authority to tell the EU how to report on candidates, and all authority in the Union comes from national elections. But if avid supporters of Turkey's EU membership request and demand such an authority, their call cannot be dismissed as naïve or insufficiently informed of how the EU works.

While the membership started becoming elusive almost immediately after the hopes were raised and it became difficult for Turkey's political parties to campaign on this goal, the Union did not disappear from the domestic debate all of a sudden. In fact, the setup of the accession process, together with wider discussions on the changing role of (and expectations from) "the West" in international politics, offered the possibility for role reversals and simulations. Helle Malmvig has studied the dynamics between the EU and its Mediterranean Arab neighbors, which are part of similar policy frameworks although, unlike enlargement policy, the neighborhood framework does not offer even a theoretical possibility of membership. Based in epistemological hierarchy, the EU offers good practices

---

[29] Feyzi Baban and Fuat Keyman, "Turkey and Postnational Europe: Challenges for the Cosmopolitan Political Community," *European Journal of Social Theory* 11, no. 1 (2008): 107–24.

[30] Peter Ludlow, *Dealing with Turkey: The European Council of 16–17 December 2004* (Brussels: Eurocomment, 2005).

[31] Metaphors of love/divorce/break-up, through which the relationship is often viewed, are a theme for a separate chapter.

and the neighbors accept them.[32] Malmvig suggests that while none of these states openly question the importance of reform, in their actual conduct they fake it no less than the EU fakes its support for them:

> Political reform seemingly indicates a direction and a telos (toward democracy), but this direction might also be a "transition to nowhere," the very meaning and truth of political reform blurring. Yet for European Reform managers, the reality principle must of course be saved. If not, then the very promotion of democratic reform would itself become meaningless and subverted.[33]

While "reform" also belongs to key words in the vocabulary of the EU-Turkey talks, perhaps the more important avenue for our further discussion is the notion of fairness. Fairness is one of the signal words in the many Commission documents on the progress in Turkey-EU talks. To quote one of recent strategies: "Enlargement is a strict but fair process built on established criteria and lessons learned from the past."[34] The question then is: What does this stark contrast between the Commission's reporting of the relationship and how the latter is seen in Turkey, mean? Flagging of fairness, in this case, resembles the survival strategies in the state-socialist Czechoslovakia described by Václav Havel. The late playwright, dissident, and president, Havel, in his well-known essay "The Power of the Powerless," talks about a green-grocer, who, in order to protect himself from potential persecution by the then authoritarian regime in Czechoslovakia, displayed a slogan "Workers of the World Unite" in his shopwindow. That slogan has been often used by the pre-1989 government to differentiate the Eastern bloc from the West. The latter was frequently portrayed through markers of imperialism and ignorance of workers' rights. For the greengrocer, Havel writes, this has been a relatively harmless way of showing compliance with the regime, while not really violating his beliefs, as there is nothing essentially wrong with an international worker unity.[35] The Commission, a body in charge of reporting on the candidate's progress, is in a complicated situation. It should provide opinions on the candidate's progress, and dance carefully amidst shifting and often contradictory demands of member states and candidate governments. *Fairness* then is a principle, which it has to, by its role description, champion. It does not defend itself against an authoritarian regime, but it defends its positionality in an atmosphere in which it is expected to be fair.

---

[32] Helle Malmvig, "Free Us from Power: Governmentality, Counter-conduct, and Simulation in European Democracy and Reform Promotion in the Arab World," *International Political Sociology* 8, no. 3 (2014): 293–310.

[33] Malmvig, "Free Us from Power," 307.

[34] European Commission, "EU Enlargement Strategy," COM 2015 (611final).

[35] Václav Havel, *The Power of the Powerless*, 1978, http://www.vaclavhavel.cz/showtrans.php?cat=e seje&val=2_aj_eseje.html&typ=HTML.

While the Commission cannot ignore the perspectives from Turkey, its legitimacy comes primarily from the EU polities. Thus, while drawing analogies between the positionality of a high-level EU institution, with a huge apparatus of bureaucrats who supply knowledge, and a small shop-owner trying to survive in an authoritarian state might seem as a too-creative nonfiction, the exercise is helpful in showing the actual limits of the Commission as an impartial arbiter. I wish to emphasize that the limits are shaped by the sources of legitimacy of the institution, not so much by intentionality of its individual members, while the latter, of course, also matters.[36] The Commission is, first of all, accountable to EU citizens and while it can solicit views of the neighbors, through public opinion polls and informal consultations, the latter do not have formal means of holding it accountable.

The absence of an impartial referee opened a room for role reversals. In one such step, Turkish diplomacy published, in 2012 and 2013, its own progress reports, similar in structure to those produced by the Commission. In the EU circles, this was met with surprise—after all, no candidate had previously done such a thing. Yet some of the wording has won Turkey few friends. The press release accompanying this first Turkish report quoted the then minister for EU Affairs Egemen Bağış: "Turkey's self-confidence is a challenge to the skewed mentality in Europe," continuing with "The "sick man" of yesterday is writing prescriptions for Europe today."[37] The wording goes further than mocking earlier orientalist paradigms, it reverses their language, this time Western "mentality" is commented upon by "the East." Language of triumphalism, even Schadenfreude, also responds to the context in which the report was published. These were the years when the "Greek (eurozone) crisis" began. Turkish media commentators chastised EU for its lack of solidarity and gave coverage of Turkish politicians travelling to Greece to offer advice to a neighbor in need. While some in Turkey criticized the language as well as the act of self-reporting as nothing more than a spectacle, the EU's handling of the "Greek crisis" had been one more indication of EU-rope's problems with solidarity.

---

[36] Journalist Aslı Aydintaşbaş recently noted that Turkish leaders tend to speak with respect about European people but use much harsher language when referring to European leaders. She found this fascinating, because it is the governments in EU who tend to be supportive of working with Turkey, while populations are skeptical or ambivalent. The 2018 interview with Aydintaşbaş is available here: https://turkeybooktalk.podbean.com/e/asli-aydintasbas-on-turkey-and-europe-beyond-hypocrisy/; see also the tellingly titled report published by a prominent EU think-tank Aydintaşbaş, Aslı. "The Discreet Charm of Hypocrisy: An EU-Turkey Power Audit," European Council on Foreign Relations, March 2018, https://www.ecfr.eu/page/-/EU_TURKEY_POWER_AUDIT.pdf.

[37] Ministry for EU Affairs of the Republic of Turkey, Press Statement by H. E. Egemen Bağış on Turkey's Progress Report, December 31, 2012.

The act of making one's own progress reports, with their emphasis on confidence and the suggestion that this is a challenge for Europe, touches the core script of accession process in which the candidate is mostly expected to accept the rules set by the EU. In that same statement, Bağış went further and dismissed the legitimacy of the reports published by the Commission: "only our people have the mandate to judge and evaluate our Government."[38] Similar calls have repeatedly been heard at different stages in the relationship. When in early 2018, the European Parliament passed a resolution criticizing the human rights situation in Turkey, the government said it was "null and void."[39] The mutual nonrecognition conferred upon many representatives of EU and Turkey had, however, different sources (origins) and manifestations. In the near fifteen years of accession talks, polities in and out of the EU had undergone a number of transformations. Turkey had hardly converged with the EU expectations regarding freedom of speech and association and it is common to note gradual regress. At the same time, the language of national sovereignty and emphasis on "the will of the people" as something at odds with European integration has become mainstream in EU's own polities. This became perhaps more obvious and widely commented upon when the EU was, post-2014, forced to debate more intensely on responsibility-sharing in migration and refugee affairs. At the same time, it had to face its own limited ability to respond to authoritarian politics in several member states, starting with Hungary. The Hungarian government has slowly been walking toward its own interpretation of European values, without much effective opposition from the EU members and institutions.[40] By fall of 2018, the government felt confident enough to criminalize assistance to refugees and disallow gender courses at universities.[41] It justified many of its steps by "love for Europe" and the need to defend the sovereign right of its people to protect their cultural heritage from destructive ideas coming from Brussels or the Soros network.[42] In other words, at a time when the notions of sovereignty

---

[38] Ministry for EU Affairs of the Republic of Turkey, Press Statement by H. E. Egemen Bağış on Turkey's Progress Report, December 31, 2012.

[39] Bia News, "EP Passes Resolution Condemning Turkey, Ankara Declares it Null and Void," February 9, 2018, https://bianet.org/english/politics/194175-ep-passes-resolution-condemning-turkey-ank ara-declares-it-null-and-void.

[40] Only in September 2018 the European Parliament voted for Article 7 procedure, which, if initiated, could mean Hungary loses its voting rights in the EU.

[41] For gender studies "reform" see Andrea Pető, "Attack on freedom of education in Hungary: the case of gender studies." *Engenderings*, September 24, 2018, https://blogs.lse.ac.uk/gender/2018/09/24/att ack-on-freedom-of-education-in-hungary-the-case-of-gender-studies/

[42] PM Orban's "Declaration of Love for Europe" as well as many other texts explaining the new ideology have been assembled in a recent volume with a telling title: Márton Bekes (ed.), *The Future of Europe: Hungary – Brave and Free* (Budapest: Public Endowment for Research on Central and Eastern European History and Society, 2018).

are being recast in the EU itself, and the states that have only recently undergone "Europeanization" are especially loud in requesting "Europe, yes, but on our terms," the older paradigms of sovereignty and agency in the EU accession processes are coming under increasing pressure.

It is now an established knowledge that the relationship has been in an emergency mode since its new beginning, or to quote Nathalie Tocci, its leading chronicler, "Since the opening of Turkey's accession negotiations in 2005, storm clouds have darkened EU-Turkey skies,"[43] and include repeated demands for withdrawal from talks and vetoing their individual chapters by EU states.[44] In Turkey, these acts rarely go without response of government and commentators. And (some of) Turkey's responses are not lost on commentators in the EU. After one such suggestion to end the talks, this time made by an Austrian minister, a former Czech ambassador to Turkey, Václav Hubinger, wrote that suggesting the end of accession talks is a "gift" to Turkey's president.[45] The Austrian diplomat should have kept quiet, the commentator writes, because it is all too clear what response from Turkey would follow. Hubinger's point is not unique—similar observations were heard around many European conference rooms. Such cautions for restraint are as much a part of accession negotiations, as are the official diplomatic statements. The conversation is very transparent. The commentator is not secretly strategizing, his blog can be read by anyone. I reference it to highlight that in the abundance of texts on the relationship, it has become commonplace to reflect on the relationship as a set of acts that will elicit an expected response. The research presented in this book, however, shows that we are often unable to understand the distinction and the relationship between expressions of grievance and exploitation thereof.

It is certainly tempting to think of the diplomatic conflicts in Turkey-EU relations as a series of scenes in which the "two sides" search for each other's flaws, take them out of context and exaggerate some aspects to score points with their respective electoral constituencies. On several occasions when discussing earlier drafts of this manuscript, colleagues suggested the author clarifies whether

[43] Nathalie Tocci, "The Baffling Short-sightedness in the EU-Turkey-Cyprus Triangle," Documenti IAI 1021 (2010), http://www.iai.it/sites/default/files/iai1021.pdf.
[44] In December 2016 the European Parliament has passed a resolution, supported by majority of its members, that the talks should be put to a halt. While political atmosphere in the country (and in the relationship) has been different from the more hopeful optimism of a decade ago, few in Turkey saw this as an act of supporting democracy and care for well-being of Turkish society—exactly because, repeatedly, calls for blocking of the talks have been made also at more optimistic moments in the relationship, when it was believed that "Europeanization" was progressing.
[45] Václav Hubinger, "Rakouská hra s tureckým míčkem na evropský účet [Austrians play with a Turkish ball, Europeans will pay the bill]," 2016, http://blog.aktualne.cz/blogy/vaclav-hubinger.php?itemid=27787.

the main concern is "belonging" or how the belonging is *used* by participants of the relationship. But this distinction is difficult to make. One can speak about belongings as instrumental, as means to an end, but one cannot omit the actual rejection and a related sense of injustice. Focus on instrumentalization, and on what Robert Putnam called two-level games[46] in which different things are said to domestic[47] and international audiences, might easily switch the conversation to an endless bibliography of two parties responding to each other. In reading politics essentially as a fight between strategies on public relations it is tempting to put genuine grievance into a footnote, as something exploited but not necessary to be engaged with on its own merits.

In Turkey, the government clearly has access to the information that the country cannot become a member without the approval of all member states and EU institutions. The Commission's monitoring is part of the accession partnership, rules of the game to which (that same) government committed at the beginning of the process. In the EU, governments clearly know that certain steps they take are contradictory to the spirit of the many documents on cooperation in Europe ratified by parliaments that give legitimacy to those very same governments. It has become commonplace to think about the relationship in "transactional"[48] terms, as a pool of potential projects or interests that both parties can pick up and elaborate on more deeply, while disregarding the less convenient ones. Such suggestions can hardly be considered as specific to Turkey—after all, debates about "multi-speed Europe" or "variable geometry"[49] have been around for a while. In the EU capitals, relations with Turkey have been only one of many considerations in thinking about Europe's future. The 2004 enlargement, in which the EU doubled its geography, has brought a new angle to the discussions about the integration and some politicians called for realistic assessment of the Union's "absorption capacity," a suggestion critically examined by a number of policy analysts.[50] But what can get lost in the

---

[46] Putnam's work has been adapted by Andrew Moravcsik for EU context. For its contextualization in European integration theories and further references, see Ian Bache, "Theories of European Integration," in Ian Bache, Stephen George and Simon Bulmer (eds), *Politics in the European Union* (Oxford: Oxford University Press, 2011), 3–20.

[47] It would certainly be worthwhile to explore whether in times when, say, a campaign event in a small Turkish town can be broadcast live in Germany, local audiences are still what they used to be.

[48] A recent report has cautioned against such viewing of the relationship, suggesting "transactionalism... confuses realism with short-termism." Emiliano Alessandri, Ian Lesser and Kadri Tastan, "EU-Turkey Relations: Steering in Stormy Seas," GMF US, Turkey, Europe and Global Issues Report No. 31 (2018), http://www.gmfus.org/sites/default/files/publications/pdf/EU-Turkey%20Relations-%20Steering%20in%20Stormy%20Seas_July%2031.pdf.

[49] For a recent contribution, see for example, Yves Bertoncini, "Differentiated Integration and the EU: A Variable Geometry Legitimacy," Instituto Affari Internazionali, March 2017.

[50] Senem Aydin, Gergana Noutcheva, Michael Emerson, and Julia De Clerck-Sachsse, "Just What is This 'Absorption Capacity' of the European Union?" CEPS Policy Brief No. 113 (2006), https://www.ceps.eu/publications/just-what-absorption-capacity-european-union.

various modes of thinking "differentiated integration"[51] is the very simple notion that being inside and outside of the registry of decisions and scenario-building is not the same thing. The Turkish society as a collective, by the virtue of being *outside*, does not have the same legitimacy to contest and co-shape the EU as is the case with EU societies. It does not have the same tools and access: if we take the visa process as a metaphor, then permission to speak and defend one's case has to be regularly requested.

The Right to Ask, to Be a Member, to Be Understood

Rights, freedoms, and quality of life are things frequently associated with living in the EU. While the EU does not offer as many rights for noncitizens, it still is an important source of inspiration outside of its geography and jurisdiction. The rupture between inside and outside is intimately experienced by those who have approached the boundary of differentiation. A young woman, who has engaged in various human rights campaigns and journalistic collaborations with Western colleagues, shared her disappointment in words that echo the experience of many other interlocutors:

> I am fed up with hearing that the EU did this, and that. It is us who struggle and fight. The EU did not invent human rights. Sometimes I think it [the EU] is even making the situation worse. The way in which it pushes certain themes, it just strengthens our nationalists. *Maybe we were doing better before the EU came.* (emphasis mine)[52]

The *arrival* of the European Union *has* meant more opportunities to know what the other is doing and why, and these have not always led to pleasant discoveries. Statements similar to the foregoing quote are not a sign of instrumentalization. After all, they come from people who have no electoral audience to cultivate. In over a decade of accession talks, the debate has moved from an emphasis on the double standards and Turkey's uniqueness to an emphasis on rights. Turkey's uniqueness has featured in many of the arguments presented by the defenders of membership who emphasized that this was a country with specific features that might be complementary, yet not harmful to EU-rope.[53] In the duration of the

---

[51] Bertoncini, "Differentiated Integration."
[52] This observation comes from 2010, a time when the overall framework of the relationship was in considerably better shape than today.
[53] In addition, Turkey has clearly won its case in EU think-tanks, as many of the top policy centers have consistently advocated continuation of the accession talks despite or even because of Turkey's "difference."

accession talks, it perhaps transpired that every candidate's relationship with the Union had been shaped by specific histories, ethnic/religious maps, and other particular exigencies of political constellations.[54]

While in principle, some mode of differentiation in the process might be understandable, it is more difficult, if possible, to comprehend that for some, the possibility to belong is outright rejected. These concerns shaped a shifting emphasis on justice and rights: they are not only something on which the EU provides guidance or best practices, although that would be still welcome by many. Rights, however, should also be considered in relation to position of interlocutors in the process of becoming. How represented can they be? Perhaps we could approach the question through democratic theory and ask, together with John Dryzek: Do they have a "right to speech that matters"?[55]

The right to be taken seriously or the right for one's aspiration to be heard has become an important part of Turkey-EU conversations. It is then a dialogue about recognition—and maybe less about the formal recognition of the right to membership than a quest for understanding why one wants that membership. This sense of not being understood and "known" properly emerges often after interacting with the people who represent EU-rope. As one young NGO worker put it diplomatically—"many people mean well, but they simply do not have capacity to learn everything about Turkey before they come and give advice." The process of seeking understanding is exhaustive perhaps exactly because it happens between people who have already invested effort into knowing and defending the "other side." When they are faced with the reality of that other side, what often follows is a sense of betrayal. My Turkish interlocutors have often asked me a variation of the following question: *If the Europeans know the consequences of their actions, why do they keep doing the same thing? Such questions has, however, been asked by many in the EU as well.* It is not a question that emerges when one crosses the state border—it comes naturally when one participates in the relationship.

Within this "symbolic universe"[56] of EU-Turkey relation(ships) it is difficult to make believable the notion that the Union's actions are designed to support rights or democracy. The Union as a collective has not been able to legitimate itself as an actor who does such things to others. Part of the problem certainly is the lack

---

54 There are limits to our ability to compare conditions placed on candidates in successive waves of EU enlargement, as the volume of EU law has been growing over the course of time.

55 John Dryzek, "Can There Be a Human Right to an Essentially Contested Concept? The Case of Democracy," *The Journal of Politics* 78, no. 2 (2016): 357–67.

56 Peter Berger and Thomas Luckmann, *The Social Construction of Reality: A Treatise in the Sociology of Knowledge* (London: Penguin, 1991).

of comfort offered by the possibility that relying on those whom we decide to trust will be there not just in this particular moment but also tomorrow and in more distant future.[57] If time is an "object of power relations,"[58] the critique of the EU by someone campaigning to get elected might be partly explained as political instrumentalization. But it startles many EU observers when the critique comes from someone who is expected to be in the pool of "rights defenders," hence, someone who should "back the EU." For instance, shortly after the 2016 coup attempt, a decision to temporarily suspend Jean Monnet grants (EU scheme for higher education funding) was announced. Several friends and interlocutors, including those who teach/study European integration, were quick to "thank" the EU for one more gesture of abandonment. It later turned out that it has been the decision of Turkish government to suspend the program.

With accession talks not moving in the direction of membership, it is politically more beneficial for many to point out each other's problems rather than invest in genuine belief that common grounds can be found. While the European Union has entered the accession talks with an upper hand in terms of democratic credentials, it has been gradually losing it. Perhaps the more "known" it became to Europe-makers in Turkey, the less believable it was to them. Then, a Turkish supporter of European integration feels less loyal, less committed to defending the Union. That is not an exploitation of weakness— that is an expression of being left out, abandoned, and betrayed.

---

[57] In a recent contribution (and a succinct review of anthropological/sociological theorizing on trust and its temporality), Carey proposes to think deeper about mistrust—as a "general attitude rooted in the idea that familiarity is insufficient ground for trust" (p. 8). Matthew Carey, *Mistrust: An Ethnographic Theory* (Chicago: HAU Books, 2017).

[58] H. J. Rutz, *The Politics of Time* (American Ethnological Society Monograph Series, 1992).

5

Your Comment Is Not Relevant

Turkey is not a member, but neither is it outside. It is not ready yet to become a part of the EU and the latter is not ready to receive it. Meanwhile, the logic of the accession process tells us that until it becomes a member, it is to be helped. What kinds of relationships emerge in this specific setup? While the country does not have formal voting rights, many of its citizens do have some say in EU politics via diaspora links or academic and cultural exchanges. These happen on a temporary basis, in which Turks are often in position of guests rather than rightful inhabitants of the space.[1] Often they appear in the EU discourses without physically being there or asking to be there, such as when the Brexit campaign looked for votes threatening that if the UK does not leave, it may have to deal with Turkey in. Turkey is already *in* and more of it can be allowed, albeit in incremental, controlled numbers and images.

The chapter builds on conversations with commuters through the EU-Turkey frontiers, including civil society workers and participants of exchanges with West European counterparts, as well as on a study of EU archives. We learn that aid has gradually become a major policy framework, the "not ready" seems to be postponed ad infinitum and helping became a new site of contestation. Turkey is no more a country that can be "included" but one to be, maybe, helped. While aid is often appreciated, even invited, it also deepens hierarchical relationships.[2] Maybe this could change one day—once Turkey is sufficiently *aided* to earn the right of entry. But even that is not uncontested, as we see in repeated suggestions in European Parliament and elsewhere that aid should be cut. Aid and helping is not a new consensus, but another site, perhaps a more relevant nexus of the debate about Turkey than its membership itself. Imagine a group of actors improvising a scene and realizing after a while that it is not

---

[1] The same can be said about other Europeans in Turkey—but this is not a book about EU accession to Turkey.

[2] In *Bureaucratic Intimacies*, Babül shows reconfiguration of hierarchies within Turkish state institutions and how they relate to Western Europeans. The present book is more interested in the general questions of legitimacy and the difference between "aided" subject and one who can claim rights.

really leading anywhere. After a short break, they opt for an experiment with dialogues structured around different keywords. But even in this new attempt, they cannot really escape a gravity-like flow toward discussing differences. There is something essentially different between the two protagonists and maybe one could help the other to bridge some of the difference. Some of the viewers of the scene feel that it represents the reality well. Others can relate to what they see but it seems to them that the scriptwriter has not read the news recently. Some of what is portrayed as "different" is, in the life as they know it, in fact similar. Moreover, it is becoming less certain who is helping whom.

Everything Is Growing

In the documentary *Ekümenopolis—Ucu Olmayan Şehir* (Ecumenical City Without Limits), the director Imre Azem takes us through the consequences of Istanbul's rapid expansion on its environment and social fabric. In one scene, the camera stops on a writing on the wall that asks: "Will we enter the EU by exploiting the poor?"[3] In the past decades, the city has multiplied its population several times. Urban interventions and recent construction boom have brought jobs, but also displacement, moving many poor communities to the outskirts. This is often justified on the grounds of renovation or "earthquake preparedness."[4] Transformation, such as the third bridge over the Bosporus, the airport, the plan for digging a new channel to connect the Marmara and the Black Sea as well as many other projects around the country have been subject to critique and resistance. That resistance can well be seen as "environmentalism of the malcontent,"[5] a term coined by Arsel, Akbulut, and Adaman to describe a specific type of protest that picks up on environmental and social issues to make a wider statement on frustration with state (development) policy and exclusion of parts of society from having a say in shaping it.

Growth, building, and development have been indicators of success for several consecutive governments. In its *Vision 2023* manifesto, the AKP party,

---

[3]   *Ekumenopolis*, 2011, a film by director Imre Azem, 25 minute, original text on the building (copied here with language mistakes): "Avrupa birliğine mağdur hakı yiyerek mı katılacağiz," subtitle translates this as stated, perhaps the alternative would be: "Are we going to join the EU by doing injustice?"

[4]   Çağlar Keyder, "Capital City Resurgent: Istanbul since the 1980s," *New Perspectives on Turkey* 43 (2010): 177–86.

[5]   Murat Arsel, Bengi Akbulut and Fikret Adaman, "Environmentalism of the Malcontent: Anti-Coal Power Plant Struggle in Turkey," *Journal of Peasant Studies* 42, no. 2 (2015): 371–95. Note: in pre-1989 Czechoslovakia, environmental movements were delivering similar messages.

a dominant political actor throughout the accession period, pledged to make Turkey one of the ten biggest economies by the centennial of the republic in 2023.[6] Economist Mustafa Sönmez estimated that the number of people working in the construction sector in 2004–14 has more than doubled. While growth meant jobs, it also meant political benefits for the government.[7] Such a policy was presented as a continuity with the foundational values of the republic. It indeed was, as the government would often remind the critics who suggested that it was taking the country away from republican values. Growth was communicated as a way of not just catching up with but also surpassing the West.[8]

The architect Constantinos A. Doxiadis used the term "ecumenopolis" to describe "the coming city that, together with the corresponding open land which is indispensable for man, will cover the entire earth as a continuous system forming a universal settlement."[9] His argument engages with wider human community, the "coming city" in Doxiadis's imagination is not just a place in which roads, buildings, and sewage plants are constructed. He foresees a certain impending connectivity and wonders on what terms it would be reached. City-making is a site in which plans for the future are made. We may take this as one more invitation to reflect on what is growing (and how) in the architecture of the many Turkey-EU relationships. New cooperation schemes provided opportunities for plentiful encounters. The aid, cultural and academic exchanges, projects on harmonization with the EU law, funds and more reporting on those funds are more possibilities to meet each other or to read about each other. As we zoom on the particulars, unsettling observations come to forefront, on human experience between the new objects.

Sitting on the Fence

It is the pressure, one difficult to escape, regardless whether one sets out to mend fences or not. After I heard a few such stories, I started asking others

[6] AKP, *Political Vision of AK Parti (Justice and Development Party) 2023: Politics, Society and the World*. 2012, http://www.akparti.org.tr/english/akparti/2023-political-vision#bolum_.

[7] Mustafa Sönmez, "The Political Gain of the Construction Boom," *Hurriyet Daily News*, January 19, 2015, http://mustafasonmez.net/?p=4768; Mustafa Sönmez, "Too Many Payroll Workers, but Too Few Unions in Turkey," *Hurriyet Daily News*, February 9, 2015, 10.

[8] In the "West" itself, ideas about "degrowth" have circulated, although they certainly have not been dominant. See Nadia Johanisova and Stephan Wolf, "Economic Democracy: A Path for the Future?" *Futures* 44 (2012): 562–70; Serge Latouche, *Farewell to Growth* (Cambridge: Polity Press, 2009).

[9] Constantinos A. Doxiadis, "Ecumenopolis: Tomorrow's City," from *Britannica Book of the Year* 1968, *Encyclopaedia Britannica*, 32, http://www.doxiadis.org.

whether they have ever experienced something similar. When asked directly, the first response would almost always be "I have it all the time." A Turkish woman went to study Arabic to a neighboring country. She was surprised to find out how many new belongings this trip brought. "Westerners thought I was one of them—maybe because I looked white . . . Sure I could not, just like them, understand some of the things about the culture in Jordan but some I could, exactly because I am from Turkey." A young Turkish man, dividing his life between Turkey and Austria, recounted a moment when he was sitting with his friends in a Viennese restaurant. The service was taking longer than expected and he was getting "hangry," and said "The services in this country are terrible." An immediate response from one of the companions at the table was "Well, is it better in Istanbul?" The way he remembers the story is that the question was not so much an open-ended curiosity, but more of a suggestion or a statement, as in *don't tell me it's better*. Because why otherwise should one be asked to make that comparison? A young Turkish woman studied in the Netherlands. One evening she went for drinks with her schoolmates. One of them asked: "Does your family allow you to go out?" The way she recounts the situation is that the schoolmate was automatically assuming that as a Turkish woman she has to ask for permission. She was not happy at the situation, recounting later:

> I explain. I am sometimes very patient. I believe in education. Yes, people cannot know everything. But sometimes it is too much. I feel like exploding. I feel like— why should I explain myself all the time?

One does not need to be an activist or a determined mediator to experience moments like these. They just happen. Explaining the nuances can sometimes be fun. But it stops being a fun-learning exercise once it becomes a rule that one is by default placed in a box from which they perpetually *have to* walk out, prove themselves as not belonging there, and ask to be categorized elsewhere. Or nowhere. So it might be five, fifteen, or many explanations and teaching moments before one closes off or just snaps. When it happens, it is both frustrating and liberating. Eventually, belongings can be situational.

The EU-Turkey conversations happen in diplomatic premises but also in academic and activist projects. Often, they happen without projects. Dialogue is supposed to *correct* the differences, bring people and societies closer. In its everyday, this is not always the case. There are joys, friendships are formed, learning is done. But there is a price—the meeting and talking does not always lead to better comprehension, to emergence of the common *we*. In fact, those who seek out these dialogues perhaps feel a more intense state of the internal exile. People who engage in international conversation, who explain Turkey in the EU, and the EU in Turkey often feel not heard, not being counted. It is not a 24/7 feeling—it switches on, when it is being challenged.[10]

One does not have this feeling constantly, but there are moments when it comes up viscerally. And then, once it happens, it seems like it has always been there. It provokes a verbal, emotional response, or silence. It often does not come with words—one has had it so many times that it turns into angry helplessness. One can enjoy a breakfast, or family time, and then something happens, such as a thought of the upcoming visa process. One realizes that they constantly need to convince, there is no free pass, one needs to repeatedly provide evidence that they should be let in. It is not that all the participants of such conversations would believe in open borders. It is that they often feel structurally excluded from the possibility of shaping their future. It is after all a shared experience— many western European defenders of Turkey's EU path are after all, in their "home" societies, often considered as coming from different planets.

Moments like these are comparable to exile, without having to relocate homes. They are also comparable to the work of diplomacy, albeit without its usual protections and immunities. Edward Said in his *Reflections on Exile* invited us to think about this condition beyond the romance of discovery: "Exile is strangely compelling to think about but terrible to experience. [. . .] Exiles cross borders, break the barriers of thought and experience."[11] In this essay, Said talks about people who had to leave their original territorial home, but their experience speaks well also to the observations of those who did not move homes physically, but commute between diverse ethnic, national, or opinion groups. Whether one is thrown that way or makes a conscious choice in that direction, this is a life of diplomacy, one that involves meticulous attention to differences and translation of those differences in a way that a common ground is possible, or at least in sight. For such diplomats, hoping that more participants of the conversation will see the similarities, rather than differences, is the main driver. It can also be the main paralyzer when the overall discourse in the relationship is one of difference, not similarity.[12] In

---

[10] It is very similar to what nationalism scholars say about "national identity"—it switches on at certain moments. Billig, *Banal Nationalism*.

[11] Said, *Reflections on Exile*, 137 and 147.

[12] It is common for practitioners of dialogue in conflict settings to experience dilemmas of loyalty. Rebecca Bryant's *The Past in Pieces: Belonging in the New Cyprus* (Philadelphia: University of Pennsylvania Press, 2010) is to my knowledge one of the most insightful works on dilemmas of research in contexts of conflict.

such a case, they might find themselves in the position of traitors to at least one of the narratives of communities to which they travel.

Two Sides, Again

The European Union has built up and funded various types of discussion and cooperation formats with candidates and neighbors. These include diplomatic, academic, and civil society dialogues. The latter are built on the assumption that in less democratic states people working outside of the government institutions can come up with ideas to improve functioning of these institutions. To support this work, the EU offers the possibility to apply for funding from its common budgets or for grants provided by individual member states. By the second decade of the twenty-first century, some type of civil society dialogues has been an integral part of relationships with almost all of the neighboring states. Such dialogues pledge to encourage more exchange between the state and "nonstate" sphere *within* the candidate state(society), as well as more exchange *between* the EU and the candidate. In an ideal scenario, the result should be better cooperation and awareness of one's specific challenges. The participants of these dialogues are, however, subject to different policy regimes; they do not envision the same social order and there are also differences in the expectations about who the partners (allies) are on the EU side.

The year accession talks opened, the EU announced a new framework of civil society dialogue. Turkey and Croatia were the first two candidates.[13] The Commission document outlining the principles notes that "the dialogue with regard to Croatia may be of somewhat different nature from that on Turkey."[14] This is further specified as: "the dialogue will encourage a discussion on perceptions regarding everyday culture and values expressed by society and the State on both sides."[15]

Let us make sense of the foregoing quote: it will be the states and societies talking, those in the EU are different from those in Turkey, and everyone is different from Croatia. The notion of the "two sides" suggests that there is something essentially different between the two, and something common within

---

[13] This is a new structured framework, but Turkey and Croatia are not the first countries with whom the EU has had civil society cooperation, although it previously happened in different formats.

[14] European Commission, "Civil Society Dialogue between EU and the Candidate Countries", p. 3 (Note: State is capitalized in the original text).

[15] European Commission, Civil Society Dialogue between EU and the Candidate Countries, Brussels June 29, 2005, COM (2005) 290 final, p. 3 (Note: State is capitalized in the original text).

each of them. The neat boxes do little to capture the heterogeneities within. Take "civil society": depending who you ask it could be religious charities, unions, sports clubs, loose movements like the Gezi, migrant rights solidarity networks, or more institutionalized NGOs with offices and management boards. It could include political parties, labor unions, and universities. It could provide food, campaign for the rights, or represent in court clients who cannot afford a commercial lawyer. But where is the difference between the state institutions and civil society (often called nonstate)? Just like the governments, citizen groups also have ambitions to bring about change, to make a difference, but they can never make a change without the said governments. The civil society can do many things, including propose change of legal frameworks, but only parliaments can pass laws including those that regulate the existence of nonstate organizations. As Fisher's insightful review showed, it is the interactions and specific contexts in which it emerges that tell us more.[16]

Very often the two are discussed as monoliths and that might lead to confusion. Alexei Yurchak, in his ethnography of the recent Soviet past, discusses problems of speaking about "binary socialism," the oft-made distinctions between official and unofficial that come with suggestions that whatever happened in the official or permissible realm was somehow fake and failed.[17] This accent on different legitimacies of the official and unofficial sphere might help us better understand nuances of discussing the state-civil society cooperation. Political theorists often underline that the possibility of citizens to do something together, including via common civic associations, is an essential part of democratic governance. Yet such associations do not exist in a vacuum—and their work/acts happen in interaction with state structures.

Scholars studying civil society in Turkey have brought up extensive evidence of concerns of civil society workers involved in EU-related projects.[18] These include doubts whether what the Union is supporting should serve the Turkish society or whether the goals might be more beneficial to of the EU. It is also contested that the EU is *the* driver of the reform—as it is the locals who do

---

[16] William Fisher, "Doing Good? The Politics and Antipolitics of NGO Practices," *Annual Review of Anthropology* 26 (1997): 439–64.

[17] Alexei Yurchak, *Everything Was Forever Until it Was No More* (Princeton: Princeton University Press, 2005), 7–8.

[18] Büke Boşnak, "Europeanisation and De-Europeanisation Dynamics in Turkey: The Case of Environmental Organisations," *South European Society and Politics* 21, no. 1 (2016): 75–90; Selcen Öner, "Internal Factors in the EU's Transformative Power Over Turkey: The Role of Turkish Civil Society," *Southeast European and Black Sea Studies* 14, no. 1 (2014); Gözde Yılmaz, "EU Conditionality Is Not the Only Game in Town! Domestic Drivers of Turkey's Europeanization," *Turkish Studies* 15, no. 2 (2014); Nora Fisher Onar and Hande Paker, "Towards Cosmopolitan Citizenship? Women's Rights in Divided Turkey," *Theory and Society* 41 (2012).

the everyday work. Perhaps most importantly: whatever happens in the bigger diplomatic framework of the EU-Turkey relationship constrains the civil society work and, as Büke Boşnak put it, "there are fewer references to the EU, and in some cases such references may actually be counterproductive."[19]

Once, following a particularly sad period of Turkey-EU official (televised) diplomatic stand-offs, I wondered what really kept the cooperation ticking. With a friend who had a long track-record in activism and various cooperation projects between the state institutions and international agencies, we were discussing the "mess of the international." This was not our first conversation on the topic. Now, referring to various disappointments voiced by the civil society in Turkey, I asked, in a somewhat clumsy way, what is the worst about the betrayal of the EU. My interlocutor offered a perfectly consolidated answer:

> Wrong question. In this game, we cannot say everybody is good or bad. Some locals cannot see the big picture, some foreigners cannot see the local problems . . . If you ask specifically about the international NGOs, well, it seems that they are coming with a particular goal in mind, and maybe it would be good if they gave more thought to how they want to achieve it.

In one of our earlier conversations, this interlocutor mentioned that even people, who come informed by "post-colonial theory," often underestimate the importance of being on the same page, creating mutual understanding with local partners. It is up for further debate how far the misunderstandings are products of intentionality or insufficient personal preparation, and how far they are a result of institutional setup of aid programs. Moreover, and this is part of the argument conveyed in the present book, success of aid depends on the setup of diplomatic relations between states which are home to recipients and sponsors. Aid certainly cannot be a replacement of a rules-based diplomatic framework.

It is the specific case-by-case interactions between the state and civil society that allow us understand the actual dynamics of the relationship. Turkey is involved in a diverse set of projects, ranging from education, NGO exchanges, and various types of trainings. Elif Babül in her outstanding ethnography of the EU-sponsored training programs for Turkish state representatives vividly describes the perhaps unexpected (by planners) dynamics of aid:

> In order to maintain their accustomed superiority and governmental legitimacy, government workers have to transition from distinction based on universal claims in the local and national realm to one rooted in claims to local knowledge in a transnational realm. [. . .] Depicted as theoretical, abstract, ungrounded

---

[19] Boşnak, "Europeanisation and De-Europeanisation," 87.

or decontextualized, transnational standards of good governance and human rights acquire the status of imposed fantasies.[20]

While Babül emphasizes that the programs brought about a very different type of change than alignment with universal human rights standards, and thus, her argument is more concerned with how the state institutions in Turkey resisted the very goals the programs were supposed to bring, the angle of the present chapter is a bit different. I am not so much interested in compliance with "universal standards" as in the specific constellation of Turkey-EU inter-*national* relationship, a one that seems to foreclose some futures. The EU aid is not dismissed outright —it is considered a contribution—the problem comes with the process in which participants cannot shape all the frameworks they are subject to and have to follow. The problems in aid-related encounters are a symptom of a wider uncertainty of Turkey's future in the EU. And we already know that future-making happens *now*. The question is not whether to engage with the EU. It is rather on what terms *can one* engage? Moreover, who gets to choose the terms? The civil society groups in the EU often voice precisely the same type of critique of EU programs as do the groups on the other side of the border. At the same time, the whole network of institutions (state and civil society) in a candidate country has limited possibility of shaping EU's policy towards the candidate.

What Money Tells Us

One object appears travels in these conversations is money. There are many ways how such object makes a difference, many ways that tell us that a difference is being made. Wherever we look for money, we encounter other connections. The anthropologist Erica Caple James in her ethnography of international presence in Haiti speaks of "compassion economies":

> the finite flows of beneficent material resources, knowledge and expertise, technologies, therapies, and other forms of exchange circulating between the aid apparatus and its clients and the aid apparatus and its donors.[21]

Let us take the few avenues through which money can lead us. A friend in his late thirties with many years of experience in the EU but also with UN-funded projects, when asked about the biggest transformation since such projects began, looked back nostalgically:

[20] Babül, *Bureaucratic Intimacies*, 57–8.
[21] Erica Caple James, *Democratic Insecurities* (Berkeley, Los Angeles and London: University of California Press, 2010), 104.

End of volunteering. When we were younger, we were happy to do things out of the joy, and did not really want money. It was nice if someone paid lunches and travel money. Now, the young people are getting directly professional. On the one hand, it is good, when they get paid. On the other, it is difficult to find volunteers. In environmental theme, we cannot find volunteers, not even fresh graduates. They either go to public sector, at a ministry they get five thousand lira as a starting wage, or to private sector, to work at CSR.[22]

It can be comparisons with the past that make a difference, it can also be geographies. Discomfort with professionalization (although this has been something longed for) goes hand in hand with uneasiness about bureaucratization. The need to report things in charts and figures and write reports for undetermined audience is a frequent complaint of many interlocutors working in civil society organizations and applying for EU funding. It was one of the things that felt very familiar to experience for recent graduates of accession process, the new member states. In the fifteen years of cooperation with various NGOs in the more western part of Europe, I have never met anyone who would not feel defeated by growing administrative and reporting demands which often come at the expense of substance, the dialogue that cooperation programs should support. Thus, high administrative demands are not something the EU "does to the candidates." Also insiders have to cope with them.

Some geographies though do not seem to be crossable easily. If we take advantage of the rich archive of reports produced by European Commission, we notice that collaborations flourish in different directions and that the EU frontier is not the dominant differentiating line. One map of research and academic collaboration can serve as good illustration. According to a recent report on such cooperation funded by the Union in 2007–13, a framework intended to produce good science but also to bring Europeans together, there is a considerable inequity in the distribution of EU funds for research cooperation between member states.[23] The top ranks of projects awarded are populated by institutions from northwest. Five of the top ten academic institutions with highest participation in grant agreements were based in the UK and none in eastern countries that joined after 1989. A list of top ten research organizations (where primary task is research, not teaching) also does not include any of the eastern states—three are from France, three from Germany, and one each from Spain, Italy, Netherlands, and Finland. Academic or research institutions from the eastern member states did not make it even into the first fifty in both categories. That same report also shows the

[22] CSR stands for Corporate social responsibility.
[23] European Commission, "Seventh FP7 Monitoring Report. Directorate General for Research and Innovation 2015 – Evaluation," March 11, 2015, 15–16. (Note: FP7 program was an EU-wide funding instrument that ran in the period 2007–13).

intensity of collaboration between the EU and candidate countries.[24] The web of connectivity is the densest within north-western Europe—that is where the chart shows thickest patchwork of lines. And EU's northwest is also the region with most connections to Turkish academic and research institutions—these are connected especially with counterparts in Germany, France, and Italy.[25]

It may seem that science and research is secondary to the accession process; after all, scientists' recommendations not to derail Turkey's path to membership have not been accepted by policy makers. It is somehow ironic that the Science and Research chapter is the only one of the thirty-five sectors of EU law which has been provisionally closed. Yet the screening report that provided a roadmap to closing of the chapter notes: "Turkey will need to ensure and demonstrate scientific freedom regarding all relevant scientific institutions."[26] Turkey's track-record of scientific freedom has been repeatedly questioned—by citizens and institutions from "both sides."

Money matters, not just in terms of *how much*, but also who provides it and where it flows. Money matters, perhaps not in terms of gross disbursements, but as indication of where exactly the links and connections happen. Turkey is not connected to all states. Moreover, the disharmonies in approaching the candidate are similar to disharmonies within the group that is already inside. From the main budget line for candidate countries, Instrument of Pre-accession Assistance, Turkey is receiving the biggest "total," but when the numbers are broken into per capita contribution, it is the last of all candidates.[27] In addition, the funds provided by the EU do not constitute a significant portion of the country's annual budget. To illustrate—in 2015, Turkey's budget was estimated at 520.4 billion TL (187 billion EUR), while the EU allocation for that year was 626.4 million EUR—less than 1 percent of the national budget.[28]

---

[24] Turkey participated in 4th and 5th framework programs for support of science and research and since the 6th is associated country.

[25] Annex B, table B2 of the above report European Commission "Seventh FP7 Monitoring Report." Directorate General for Research and Innovation 2015 – Evaluation, March 11, 2015, 100.

[26] European Commission, "Screening Report Turkey – Chapter 25 – Science and Research," February 3, 2006.
The report though is mostly focused on networking, budgetary capacities, mobility, need to cooperate with industry. Turkey was already eligible for some support before this chapter was closed.

[27] Helen Sjursen, in "Why Expand" cites Asa Lundgren (1998—PhD Thesis at Uppsala, the thesis is in Swedish), compared EU funding for Turkey and Poland. Lundgren noted that if Turkish democracy mattered for EU, it would have received more funding. My own calculations for the 2007–20 period based on available EU records show the lowest (and significantly lower) per capita disbursements. For validation, see the following sources: European Commission, "Transformative Power of Enlargement," 2016, https://op.europa.eu/en/publication-detail/-/publication/18a7ff84-fbba-11e5 -b713-01aa75ed71a1/language-en; European Commission, "EU Accession Western Balkans," 2019, https://ec.europa.eu/neighbourhood-enlargement/sites/near/files/eu-accession-process-western-ba kans_0.pdf; Population statistics provided by Eurostat.

[28] Reference for budget size: "Turkish Parliament OKs General Budget for 2015," *Hurriyet Daily News*, December 23, 2014, http://www.hurriyetdailynews.com/turkish-parliament-oks-general-budget -for-2015.aspx?pageID=238&nID=75997&NewsCatID=344.

Discussions on aid sometimes run into the problem of "foreignness" of the funding. When Czechia and Slovakia started receiving pre-accession aid from the EU before they joined it in 2004, participants of civil society projects from that era often noted that it was difficult to convince the relevant authorities that EU funds should flow not only to the state institutions but also to civil society. Eventually, what proved convincing was that much greater share of EU funds allocated for candidates was managed by the state institutions.[29] Fifteen years into EU membership, NGOs working on human rights issues are often accused of being "Western agents," acting on others' behalf. While "civil society dialogue" might have the ambition to encourage pluralism and connectivity between the various "sides," in the absence of possibility of becoming (real membership), it is also a platform where many of the interlocutors become more aware of the difficulties in imagining the "common we" of Turkey and the EU. Moreover, while civil society is often expected to be the mediator, its individual members are liminal subjects, sitting on the fence, often in precarious position and the very effort to explain "the other side" puts them in a position of traitors. Civil society dialogue can be thought of as a form of nonrecognition of other's right to politics and replacement of rights-based solidarity by aid.

Dialogues That Matter and Objects Left Hanging In There

There are many dialogues between the EU and Turkey, both official and unofficial. There are also dialogues about the principles on which those dialogues should be held. Before publishing its revised guidelines on civil society dialogue, the EU delegation in Ankara held a series of online and offline consultations with participants around the country. The collected responses are published online, divided neatly into the following categories:[30]

Category I—Comments which support the Guiding Principles

Category II—Relevant comments to be introduced in the revised version of the Guiding Principles

Category III—Relevant comments but too detailed to be introduced in the revised version of the Guiding Principles and that could be considered in the future while designing programs and projects

---

[29] Lucia Najslova, *Foreign Funding* (Madrid: FRIDE Working paper, 2013).
[30] Annex II—Table of Categorised Comments—Civil Society Consultation, 2010.

Category IV—Comments received that were not considered relevant to be
introduced in the revised Guiding Principles

It is the last category (comments not relevant) that caught my attention. I had
to reread these comments several times. I printed the document and started
underlining parts that seemed the most perplexing. Eventually, I realized that
what is the most perplexing is that a category IV exists. Let us read a few entries
categorized as irrelevant:

> EU is totally ignorant about the realities of Turkey. Documents are prepared
> somewhere, however, they have nothing to do with our reality and impossible to
> implement. (Consultation location: Eskisehir)
>
> CSOs should definitely operate on the basis of voluntariness; otherwise, they
> may have a company profile rather than a CSO. (e-consultation)
>
> Today what brings us together is the fact that we all stand close to the EU
> process so while pluralism is important, it has to be inclusive. And even today,
> the meeting is not inclusive because only we are here. (Consultation location:
> Ankara)
>
> We do not even know how the EU could support us; how can we reply to your
> question. (Consultation location: Trabzon)
>
> EU's dialogue approach and this consultation meetings are appreciated.
> However, the Guiding Principles should have been prepared together with CSO.
> (Consultation location: Eskisehir)[31]

What eventually is the purpose of a consultation, if such comments make it into
"irrelevant" folder? Are there indeed any comments that *could* be dismissed
in such type of consultation? Perhaps yes—perhaps if someone suggested that
the Guiding Principles should include a commitment for the EU to make the
planet Saturn inhabitable by 2050. But the "irrelevant" passages did not include
anything like that. The excerpts and some other comments listed in this category
were similar to observations I have heard repeatedly from several interlocutors
and seen in academic research findings documenting experience of civil society
in Turkey and the EU. Moreover, Turkish civil society is not alone in this
critique—any of these comments could have been written by an NGO based in
the EU.

What might come as a surprise is that the comments are left hanging in
there. Anyone who browses the EU archives can read the comments and the
(non)response. They are not a part of any secret file—they are part of the official

---

[31] These are direct quotes; I did not correct the grammar or spelling.

record of the relationship. Would it change the overall tone of the relationship had the particular officer in charge of producing this document taken the time to respond to these comments? Would it change the substance of the relationship had not these comments been put into this category? Can we say that the EU image would be better served if the category IV did not exist? Regardless of the answers to these questions, category IV is an object that both co-shapes the relationship and tells us something about it.[32] But we have already established that the Commission, the EU body that manages aid projects, does not have ultimate say over Turkey's membership. It is the member states who get to decide.

Permissions and Flourishing Fatigue

In order to travel for a workshop in the EU, one needs permission. This permission includes visa form issued by an EU member state upon the presentation of invitation or purpose of travel and several additional documents and on paying the processing fee. The work they come to present clearly benefits EU citizens and policy makers also. Here is an excerpt from one recent call inviting submissions for an academic conference:

> We are particularly but not only interested in recent, robust quantitative studies, and also in the methods and field experiences in studying hard to reach/hidden populations in Turkey. . . . For all submissions travel expenses will be covered and for up to four international participants accommodation will also be covered [but not visa expenses]."

This is a standard wording of calls for papers circulated in academic settings. There is a variety of possibilities regarding what gets funded—sometimes the convener has a budget to cover all of the presenters' expenses, sometimes none. I received this call when finishing up a section of this book dealing with permissions and categories, and could not help but notice the obvious paradox in which researchers are asked to present findings on hard to reach populations, yet their own visa expenses were not to be covered. Thus, for a non-EU researcher, the EU becomes a "hard to reach population."

Consider a recent experience of a Turkish scholar of European integration, a person well read in the histories and cultures of several EU states. She really

[32] Meltem Ahıska in *Occidentalism in Turkey* notes her initial surprise when starting research at the archives of TRT (public broadcaster) at how much material seemed to have been thrown out/discarded, while for example the BBC would keep potentially embarrassing materials also.

likes Europe, she is curious about it and she is disappointed by it. In the past five years, she had to go through the process of getting Schengen visa five times. That means five times the effort of proving one's credentials and trustworthiness. One must show they plan no harm to Europe and also that they do not plan to stay, that they have reasons to return home. One is permitted to show love for Europe by proving their willingness and readiness by not overstaying the welcome. Once she was asked to provide a copy of a travel license of the bus driver who was going to take the tour from one city to another in the country of her destination. Another time the administrators needed to see the booking reference in English, not in Turkish. Another time the email invitation for a conference was not accepted—they asked for one with signature. She was very angry: "It's just that thing that when I am a professor of European studies, this all is so unnecessary. Like why?" Yes, of course, the Turkish state also requires one to do a lot of paperwork—this is not "against" the EU. But just how much more does one need to prove to Europe considering the unpleasantness of the time to be spent in generating new evidence, filling out new forms? The anger and discourse directed at the *system* (or, how the system works) are not exclusively targeting the EU or member state institutions—after all, these are not the only bodies that would present what is often deemed as unnecessary paperwork. But being rejected or burdened with extra administrative work *by Europe* if one's day-to-day work is focused on building dialogues *about Europe* gives that frustration another angle.

6

For Turkish Cypriots, the Summit Will Be Web-streamed

Let us now travel to a place which is somewhere between Turkey and the European Union, one which is part of neither yet is very important for their relationship. If we think territorially, the place would be called Northern Cyprus, whose residents live in "areas not under effective control of the Republic of Cyprus," at least that is how the EU law sees them. If we use ethno-national marker, we will speak about Turkish Cypriots. Conceptually, the place we will travel to is democratic legitimacy and its timing. In 2006, the representatives of the EU member states voted on an aid package for the Turkish Cypriot community, declaring it should bring it "closer to the Union."[1] The Commission website that carried basic information about the aid was, until recently, illustrated with a photoshopped picture of a young man reaching for the stars on the EU flag. On a closer look we see that the stars are merely a window reflection—even if the man could extend his hand farther, he could never really touch them. This image, just like its location, is a telling snapshot of the Turkish Cypriots' status in the European Union. *Asymptotic* might be the best word in English language that describes their collective condition—they are approaching, but not really able to get in. While they became citizens in 2004, until the resolution of the Cyprus dispute they are, officially, a community to be helped. Shortly after the aid regulation was discussed, a Turkish Cypriot politician asked a senior European Commission official whether Northern Cyprus is an EU member or a neighbor. He received an enigmatic answer: "It is up to you to decide." The politician was entertained but unsurprised. He, just like many other Turkish Cypriots would strongly object to such an understanding of their situation.[2]

---

[1] EU Council regulation 389/2006 of February 27, 2006, https://eur-lex.europa.eu/legal-content/EN/TXT/?uri=CELEX:32006R0389.
[2] Part of the research in this chapter was presented at the PRIO Cyprus Centre Annual Conference 26–27 October 2012 in Nicosia. The work is informed by the author's interviews in Nicosia, Brussels, Bratislava and Prague, 2006–13.

In conversations regarding Turkey's European path, Cyprus is often referenced as an obstacle as well as an evidence of fragility of Europe's beginnings and ends. This is for a good reason: when the EU members suspended the accession talks in 2006, they justified it by Turkey's reluctance to comply with the EU law on this specific issue. Considering the wider developments in EU-Turkey relations, many participants of the relationship concluded that such a legalistic approach has somehow been a more convenient way of not letting Turkey too close. Moreover, discursive exercises on Turkey's proximity to Europe often start with a geographic argument: only 3 percent of Turkey's territory is in Europe, the rest is in Asia. Case closed. But Cyprus is further from EU-rope than most of Turkey. On maps of the continent, which include the Mediterranean Sea and parts of Africa and Asia, Cyprus appears at the upper right corner of the sea, almost at the very end of Turkey.

The Turkish Cypriots are EU citizens. However, for the EU law to apply in the north, a solution to the Cyprus problem has to be found. This situation suggests some parallels with the positionality of Turkey as a candidate and opens new avenues for thinking about wider questions of legitimacy and democracy in European integration. There is no real consensus in Turkey on how to approach Cyprus: for some it is a valued national cause; for others, a waste of resources.[3] In what follows, I propose that the experience of polities that do not have a stamp of official approval (recognition) provides a different perspective on the positionality of Turkey. As we learn from the abundant literature on the topic, for Cypriots, Turkish and Greek, the conflict is an open wound and the island's partial EU membership has not fully satisfied any of the communities. This chapter then does not claim to expand horizons of knowledge on unrecognized states in general or Northern Cyprus specifically. It listens to the work of scholars who specialize in this field and hopes to translate the meanings of *recognition*, an important key word in discussions on Cyprus, to help better understand denied belongings in Turkey. Such an approach can hopefully show the problems of relying on nonstate actors as primary messengers of democracy and rights in an inter*national* world, one in which a state holds the dominant claims to legitimacy and authority to act. The chapter *does not* propose that lived experience of Turkish Cypriots and Turks is *the same*. It merely suggests that analogies in their institutional relationship with the EU provide another window for reading

---

[3] A number of interlocutors suggested that Turkey should "drop" Cyprus and wondered why I, as someone who obviously supported their concerns about not being treated fairly by the EU, would think of Cyprus as something more than a problem.

belongings in Europe. Reliance on aid makes us forget that that there used to be a thing called rights and obligations.

The Making of a Divided Member State

When and how exactly Cyprus became divided remains contested—what we know for certain is that it did not happen with accession to the European Union. The island had been a part of the Ottoman and later British empires, with decolonial rearrangements resulting in the establishment of the Republic of Cyprus in 1960. According to its constitution, power was to be shared between the Turks and the Greeks.[4] But even before the establishment of the common republic, the leaderships of the two dominant communities presented different proposals for their future—something that certainly mattered in the way the common constitution came apart only three years after its inauguration.[5] In the early spring of 1964, UN sent a peacekeeping force to the island, a mission that remains there at the time of writing, patrolling the so-called Green Line, a space separating its now mostly Greek Cypriot south from the mostly Turkish Cypriot north. As of 1964, the institutions of the republic have been staffed by the Greek Cypriots, and the Turkish Cypriots lived in enclaves for several years.[6] This ethnic separation was solidified in 1974, with intervention by Turkey, a move it justified on the grounds of the then Greek junta's plan to unify the island with Greece (*enosis*) and on the stipulations of the Treaty of Guarantee, part of the 1960 constitution arrangements that established the UK, Greece, and Turkey as guarantors of the republic's territorial integrity.[7] Turkey maintains until today a strong military presence in the island.

In May 2004, the island became the only member state of the Union with a stationed UN force and ongoing talks on reunification. Its capital Nicosia frequently features in news headlines as Europe's "last divided capital." Cyprus' constitutional order was born at international conferences, and there

---

[4]   The residents of Cyprus used to be called Christians and Muslims, later Greeks and Turks. While these markers are valid in some contexts, in this chapter, for the sake of clarity and simplicity I opt for the currently used names for the two constituent communities—Greek Cypriots and Turkish Cypriots.

[5]   Rebecca Bryant, *Imagining the Modern: The Cultures of Nationalism in Cyprus* (London: I.B. Tauris, 2004).

[6]   Rebecca Bryant and Mete Hatay, "Guns and Guitars: Simulating Sovereignty in a State of Siege," *American Ethnologist* 38, no. 4 (2011): 631–49.

[7]   Mensur Akgün, Ayla Gürel, Mete Hatay and Sylvia Tiryaki, "Quo Vadis Cyprus," TESEV Working Paper (Istanbul: TESEV, 2005).

seems to be an expectation that this is where it will be reassembled. Successive Secretary Generals of the UN presented peace plans for reunification without much effect. Until 2003, the Green Line remained closed, and it was very difficult if impossible to move between the south and the north. In the north, Turkish Cypriots have gradually built up their own public institutions, and declared a state, in 1983, the Turkish Republic of Northern Cyprus (TRNC), formally recognized only by Turkey and condemned by United Nations Security Council.[8] Recognition is a more complex issue than reciprocation of diplomatic credentials and opening of representative offices. Turkey and TRNC have diplomatic relations, Turkey is a major donor for TRNC's public sector; at the same time, there are concerns regarding its interventions to Cypriot politics.[9]

Cyprus started accession negotiations as a divided island and entered the Union as such.[10] The Republic of Cyprus applied for associated status with the EU in 1962, when it was still governed jointly by representatives of Greeks and Turks. Yet the next steps, including the application for full membership in the 1990s, were adopted at the time when the country was governed only by the Greek Cypriots. This process was observed with mixed feelings by the Turkish Cypriots, as they were not part of it. While the so-called bi-communal talks were held almost since the beginning of the UN presence on the island, until the EU process moved forward, the voice of the residents of the north was heard only marginally.[11] The debate about the UN arrangement and the EU membership merged when the talks started in the early 2000s about the Annan Plan, the most comprehensive UN-sponsored proposal to that date. In a case of two *yes* votes, a united island would have become an EU member state. When the result of thousands of hours of meetings was put to referendum, the Turkish Cypriots accepted, while the Greek Cypriots rejected it by landslide. Glafkos Clerides, the former Greek Cypriot president, who unlike the president in office at the time

[8] United Nations Security Council, Resolution 367 of 12 March 1975, United Nations Security Council. Resolution 541 of 18 November 1983.
[9] Rebecca Bryant and Christalla Yakinthou, *Cypriot Perceptions of Turkey* (Istanbul: TESEV, 2012). For newer research on the topic, see PRIO Cyprus Centre reports.
[10] For a detailed account of EU policy in the run up to 2004 referenda, see Nathalie Tocci, *EU Accession Dynamics and Conflict Resolution: Catalysing Peace or Consolidating Partition in Cyprus?* (Aldershot: Ashgate, 2004).
[11] For analysis of the Annan Plan and the EU/UN process, see Andrekos Varnava and Hubert Faustmann (eds), *Reunifying Cyprus: The Annan Plan and Beyond* (London: I.B. Tauris, 2009). For up to date perspective on developments in intercommunal relations as well as wider international framework, reports by the Cyprus center of the Peace Research Institute Oslo are probably the best source/starting point. The PRIO Cyprus Center publishes reports covering developments on both sides of the Green Line, authored by Greek and Turkish Cypriot scholars as well as "international" scholars of the conflict.

of referendum, campaigned for a yes vote, said: "The danger we face by voting 'no' in the referendum is the entombment of our country."[12] Several scholars of the conflict have noted that since then, the Greek Cypriot's earlier negotiating position has been losing traction internationally.

After the referendum results were announced, a number of EU representatives voiced their disappointment and spoke of missed opportunities. The EU Commissioner for Enlargement at that time, Gunther Verheugen, said he felt "cheated" by the Greek Cypriot leadership,[13] and the Czech MFA called it a "squandered chance."[14] But while the critique and disappointment were often addressed mainly to Greek Cypriots, it is important to be aware of the fact that the European Union has made choices, which diverged from its standard logic of accession process in which a candidate is invited to join only once it has fulfilled conditions. On the contrary, as Nathalie Tocci described in detail, the process was guided by the expectation that the unconditional promise of acceptance would lead to resolution of the Cyprus issue, not vice versa.[15]

While, arguably, the post-2004 situation did not satisfy any of the constituent communities, it certainly brought a more unconventional regime for the Turkish Cypriots. The UN Secretary General Kofi Annan in his report of June 2004 stated that the "Turkish Cypriot vote has undone any rationale for pressuring and isolating them."[16] As one legal scholar noted, the Turkish Cypriots were in fact subject to economic sanctions by the EU.[17] Yet undoing the isolation proved to be the most difficult thing to do. Shortly after the referenda, the European Commission announced a package of measures for the Turkish Cypriots—aimed to facilitate trade and to disburse aid.[18]

---

[12] Quoted in Niyazi Kizilyurek, *Glafkos Clerides: The Path of a Country* (Nicosia and London: Rimal and Melisende, 2008), 9.

[13] Wright for *The Guardian*, April 22, 2004, http://www.guardian.co.uk/world/2004/apr/22/eu.cyprus.

[14] Statement of the Czech MFA on the Results of Referendums in Cyprus, April 28, 2004, http://www.mzv.cz/jnp/en/issues_and_press/statements/x2004/statement_of_the_czech_mfa_on_the_2.html.

[15] Tocci, *EU Accession Dynamics and Conflict Resolution*.

[16] United Nations Secretary General. Report of the Secretary General on His Mission of Good Offices in Cyprus, June 2, 2004.

[17] Stefan Talmon, "The Cyprus Question Before the European Court of Justice," *European Journal of International Law* 12, no. 4 (2001); See also Tocci, *EU Accession Dynamics and Conflict Resolution*.

[18] Only some of the proposals have materialized. The European Commission website, in a section dedicated to Turkish Cypriot community, announces that "the northern areas are outside the EU's customs and fiscal territory—but this does not affect the personal rights of Turkish Cypriots as EU citizens." Further, the website notes that a "direct trade regulation" which was supposed to facilitate Turkish Cypriot trade beyond Cyprus "remains with the Council for consideration."
https://ec.europa.eu/cyprus/about-us/turkish-cypriots_en (Last updated February 17, 2020).

Experts, Stakeholders, Permissions

A brochure published by the Commission a few years into the launch of the aid projects shows photographs and short texts similar to many other brochures from the world of development: young people in a classroom, men and women behind a conference table, people operating machinery, children smiling, men cutting a tape at the opening ceremony of a renovated monument. The brochure opens with a foreword by the Commissioner serving at the time of its publication. A page just next to the foreword features credits including the copyright and a year of publication. The small text also says: "The contents of this publication do not necessarily reflect the position or opinion of the European Commission."[19] Yet the impact of the aid and other policies on these unrecognized authorities is considerable.[20]

The Commission operates within the rules set out by the member states, to whom it also regularly reports on progress of the program. These reports note difficulties of giving aid in this very specific context and repeatedly encourage a political solution (reunification).[21] They also show hierarchies in the philosophy of the program, such as "there is a need to convince the Turkish Cypriot community of the importance of the reform."[22] The aid regulation is very clear on who can be supported: local bodies, businesses, and nonprofits.[23] While the EU diplomats also consult public and elected authorities, on paper, it is the Turkish Cypriot "community" who is consulted—as "experts" and "stakeholders." The variations of dwelling on "de facto" appear in practices of the member states as well—for example, the German office in the north does not use the official foreign ministry domain @nikosia.diplo.de but a gmail address.

The ambiguity of spaces in which the Turkish Cypriots can *matter* can well be demonstrated on their possibility to participate in international life. In the UN-sponsored conferences on reunification, negotiations are led between the

[19] European Commission, "Closer to the European Union: EU Assistance to the Turkish Cypriot Community" (2012).
[20] George Kyris's research shows that the current mode of EU engagement strengthens the executive as opposed to parliament. George Kyris, "A Model of 'Contested' Europeanization: The European Union and the Turkish-Cypriot administration," *Comparative European Politics* 12, no. 2 (2014): 160–83.
[21] I have reviewed the first five Commission reports on implementation of the aid regulation published in the period 2007–11.
[22] European Commission, 4th report on implementation of the Aid regulation, p.10.
[23] Article 1 of the Aid Regulation lists the following beneficiaries: "local bodies, cooperatives and representatives of civil society, in particular organisations of the social partners, business support organisations, bodies carrying out functions in the general interest in the areas, local or traditional communities, associations, foundations, non-profit organisations, non-governmental organisations, and natural and legal persons."

"leaders" of respective communities, elected in their respective constituencies. Though their local governance structures and processes are deemed illegal, the Turkish Cypriot president (elected in polls organized and managed by the TRNC authorities) is internationally accepted as a *community leader* and participates in the UN-sponsored negotiations with his Greek Cypriot counterpart. Despite being "illegal," the elections in the north always invite international attention and speculation about whether the winner is going to be a "hardliner" or a "pro-solution." Moreover, the EU recognizes Turkish Cypriots[24] not merely as citizens with individual rights but also as a polity—in the end, its assistance is intended for a Turkish Cypriot "community." Yet, the EU cannot officially engage with the elected representatives of the Turkish Cypriots and when it has to refer to any of the TRNC institutions in its documents, it does so with the obligatory prefix "so-called" (as in "so-called court") or uses quotation marks (as in "elections")— to underline that these structures are unrecognized. While other polities have to be democratic *before* they join the EU, it seems that Turkish Cypriot representative institutions can be recognized only *after* the European integration of Northern Cyprus is accomplished. Democracy then can begin only *after* it was shown as existing and functioning.

Even the local authorities, which are not formally illegal, have sometimes problem to access international events. When the Turkish Cypriot municipality of Gönyeli applied to attend a regional summit convened by an EU agency, the Committee of Regions (CoR), the Turkish Cypriot representative in Brussels received a letter, in which the Secretary General of the CoR, after some introductory words of thanks, stated:

> Recalling our previous meeting, I would like to reaffirm the commitment of the Committee of the Regions to welcome representatives of Turkish Cypriots local and regional authorities to participate in various events organized by the Committee of the Regions, such as for conferences or Open Days. Notwithstanding, I regret to inform you that for this particular event we have been applying a strict invitation policy and at this moment we can only accept applications from the CoR Members and European associations which are partners in the organisations of the event.
>
> Should the Turkish Cypriot municipalities be interested in the content of the 5th European Summit of Regions and Cities in Copenhagen, I would like to inform you, that it will be webstreamed, so it will be possible to follow the

---

[24] Turkish-Cypriot is not the only marker of belonging in the north, but the Turkish Cypriots are considered the constituent community.

discussions via the link which will be published on the website of the CoR (www.cor.europa.eu).

Such a situation can well be described by Rita Abrahamsen's notion of "development without democracy."[25] This basically means that the Turkish Cypriots are to be assisted, via a range of projects, but have little opportunity to be officially relevant. They are consulted as "experts" or "stakeholders"—but not in their capacities as government representatives or parliamentarians with a mandate to represent a polity that elected them. The Turkish Cypriots can watch, can "contribute ideas." However, they cannot participate as a matter of their own liking. They have to accept that they will only be part of an unofficial conversation.

This is highly problematic from the perspective of democratic legitimacy. There is a vast literature on the concept of legitimacy in politics, but regardless of their respective nuances, most conceptualizations start with the "the public sense that the regime is a fair one."[26] While the consent of the governed may in itself not be a sufficient condition of legitimacy since the government should "meet certain minimal standards of justice"[27] and has the "responsibility to protect"[28] its citizens, it is an essential one. But what if the governed do not have the means to express their will or their votes are disregarded, as was the case when Turkish Cypriots voted for reunification, and end up with aid instead of membership? In political theory, they are justified to contest the legitimacy of the EU's current policy. In political practice, they do not have official channels to do so. Whether aid is "technical" or "political" is of key concern to scholars of democracy and state-building.[29] How far are the populations concerned consulted about the reforms? Is the political process losing its importance in favor of "the experts"? Is the role of "Western-style" civil society in implementing policy change overemphasized? One of the key problems of development interventions has been, as David Chandler observed, "the belief that the 'rule of law' can be

[25] Rita Abrahamsen, *Disciplining Democracy: Development Discourse and Good Governance in Africa* (London: ZED Books, 2000).
[26] Amitai Etzioni, "The Domestic Sources of Global Adhocracy," *Social Change Review* 10, no. 2 (2012): 99–124. See also Charles Tilly, *Democracy* (New York: Cambridge University Press, 2007); Jean Grugel, *Democratization: A Critical Introduction* (Basingstoke: Palgrave, 2002); John Markoff, "Where and Why Was Democracy Invented?" *Comparative Studies in Society and History* 41, no. 4 (1999): 660–90.
[27] Allen Buchanan, *Justice, Legitimacy and Self-Determination: Moral Foundations for International Law* (Oxford: Oxford University Press, 2004), 4.
[28] ICISS, *Responsibility to Protect. Report of the International Commission on Intervention and State Sovereignty* (Ottawa: International Development Research Centre, 2011).
[29] Olivier Roy, "Development and Political Legitimacy: The Cases of Iraq and Afghanistan," *Conflict, Security and Development* 4, no. 2 (2010): 167–79.

developed and implemented separately from, and counterpoised to, the political process."[30]

In 2012, Cyprus was preparing to assume a rotating EU presidency.[31] That meant higher visibility in the EU policy-making and taking over some responsibilities for structuring of the Union's agenda. It was shortly after the Arab Spring started and also amid difficult economic situation in Cyprus. The EU enlargement was one of the issues the presidency would oversee. A representative of the Greek Cypriot preparatory committee, when asked which country was going to be the biggest challenge answered "Iceland" without deliberation. This was a strange moment. He was sitting at a desk, a map of Europe on the wall behind him. On that map, Turkey is the country closest to Cyprus and clearly more sizeable. Iceland, at that time, was still negotiating with the EU and there were rumors it might want to withdraw from the accession talks. There were of course many other tasks on EU agenda and a diplomacy of any state had to work hard to do a good job on presidency—both in terms of substance and narrative. There is nothing strange that the Greek Cypriot diplomacy, representing a "new member state," was trying to show it has had wider European issues on its radar. But in this specific context, the confidence with which Turkey was not noted is notable. What is perhaps more notable is the absence of Turkish Cypriots. When another member of the preparatory committee was asked whether the Turkish Cypriots would be involved and how, she turned silent for a while. She then suggested that they would certainly be involved as translators. After a while, she remembered that some NGOs would be invited to presidency activities, went to a next door office and returned with a piece of paper on which she jotted a name and an email address of a representative of a cancer prevention association.[32] The denial of Turkish Cypriot presence seemed startling at that particular moment—although it is not a new finding in research on Cyprus.[33] Such reaction may well be considered in light of common diplomatic practice—the effort to show "better face" of the country to international audiences. It is common for diplomatic representations around Europe to avoid questions they consider domestically

---

[30] David Chandler, "Imposing the 'Rule of Law': Lessons of Bosnia-Herzegovina for Peacebuilding in Iraq," *International Peacekeeping* 11, no. 2 (2004): 312–333, 588.

[31] Under the EU Treaty, each member state gets to chair (i.e., prepare agenda on certain relevant issues) Council of the European Union for six months. RoC's first presidency took place July 1–December 31, 2012. "Europe in the world—closer to its neighbors" was one of the priorities of the presidency (see www.cy2012.eu).

[32] Part of the interviews on the EU presidency of Republic of Cyprus was conducted jointly with Tomas Weiss for Institute for European Policy EUROPEUM.

[33] Bryant in *The Past in Pieces*, a work based on long-term ethnographic research, describes how Turkish Cypriot presence and capacity to act is often unnoticed by the Greek Cypriots, that is, they are often portrayed as occupied subject and the main agency is imagined as resting with Turkey.

sensitive. But if the two Cypriot polities are leading *international* talks, can the status of Turkish Cypriots be considered a domestic issue?

Membership of Cyprus in the EU has offered the Turkish Cypriots more platforms to talk to EU-ropeans, but their participation in international life is subject to many permissions and comes with few entitlements. Scholars of the conflict repeatedly noted that *recognition* seems to be central to negotiations between the two Cypriot polities as well as in relation to their standing in international politics. But what and how is to be recognized, and by whom? As the EU institutions and other *recognized* actors walk carefully around putting names on Turkish Cypriot public bodies, Cypriots have developed many strategies of living in their exceptional conditions. Costas Constantinou and Yannis Papadakis share this observation from the village of Pyla:

> For example, Turkish Cypriots living there have refused to pay electricity, water and garbage duties to the Greek Cypriot authorities that provide these resources and services, arguing that they do not wish to recognize the Republic of Cyprus. . . . Greek Cypriots of Pyla sometimes exploited the situation by receiving their own electricity via a clandestine electrical cable from a neighbor Turkish Cypriot who did not pay for it.[34]

Such adjustment to the situation should not be considered as uniquely "Cypriot." Rule-making after all always comes with loopholes and there are many other stories around the world documenting creative strategies adopted by humans who did not feel represented by or satisfied with dominant policy frameworks. Havel's greengrocer, whom we met in Chapter 4 of this book is one of them. Double prices (for locals and foreigners) in the early post–Cold War Czechoslovakia could be another.[35]

Beyond Recognition: Borders, Access, and Accountability

Neither Turkish Cypriots (residents of Northern Cyprus) nor citizens of Turkey can become part of the EU just by expressing the wish—the EU acceptance is needed. Before that acceptance happens, they can appear only if they are invited

---

[34] Costas Constantinou and Yannis Papadakis, "The Cypriot State(s) *in situ*: Cross-Ethnic Contact and the Discourse of Recognition," in Thomas Diez (ed.),*The European Union and the Cyprus Conflict* (Manchester: Manchester University Press, 2002), 73–97. This quote: p. 90.

[35] Joining "the West" in the 1989 many locals experienced a shock at the immense gap in incomes. Many businesses then considered it alright to ask different prices for products and services, depending on whether one was a "poor local" or a "wealthy foreigner."

to present their case. None of them are irrelevant for the EU, both polities play an important role in its aid and security cooperation networks and strategies. Both polities have been given a promise of closer association and eventual membership. Internally, for both polities, the EU is an important theme and a subject of domestic political contestation. Importantly, the EU matters for them not out of a hobby interest—it is an ontological necessity to discuss their relationship with the Union. This is the case in terms of normative frameworks (debating access to rights), in terms of regulation of economy and trade and, finally, in terms of being mobile. So what does it mean to be recognized, accepted, acknowledged, and noted?[36] So far, it seems that while the EU is co-shaping the life of both communities, they have only limited means of shaping the EU and its policy toward them. Importantly, while both polities produce a plurality of perspectives on the EU (and politics in general), their (outsider) relationship to the EU seems to provide stronger incentives to ethno-national platforms.[37]

Let us now consider the notion of citizenship. Turkish Cypriots are EU citizens—and yet their possibility to collectively shape their own affairs is similar, in many respects, to that of citizens of a republic which is negotiating entry into the Union. In some respects, it can be even less sovereign. After all, in relation to the EU, Turkey is a recognized state and its parliament and government are respected as legitimate interlocutors, while Turkish Cypriots are merely a "beneficiary community." Moreover, the self-governance of the Turkish Cypriots is not limited only by the RoC, and by wider EU actions, but also by policies of Turkey, the only state that formally recognizes TRNC.

In the practice of international politics, sovereignty/recognition rarely operates in absolute terms. States' rights have been contingent on a number of factors and certain forms of self-determination have been seen as threatening.[38] As Stuart Elden notes, it has been however more conventional to discuss conditions under which a state's sovereignty might be limited rather than those under which it might be expanded. In Elden's understanding, borders, once set, are almost in-erasable: "In theory, borders themselves may change, but in practice it is more likely that some states may cease to be sovereign within them."[39] Territorial

---

[36] Here I am taking *OED* terms associated to meanings of "recognition."

[37] It is difficult to reconcile this paradox with the supra-national features of the EU and ambitions of many EU policy-makers and citizens to deepen integration towards more supranationalism (federalization).

[38] This is well evidenced in debates on "responsibility to protect," "just war," and "humanitarian intervention," recently addressed by Jessica Whyte, "The 'Dangerous Concept of the Just War': Decolonization, Wars of National Liberation, and the Additional Protocols to the Geneva Conventions," *Humanity* (Winter 2018): 313–41.

[39] Stuart Elden, "Contingent Sovereignty, Territorial Integrity and the Sanctity of Borders," *SAIS Review* 26, no. 1 (2006): 11–24, 22.

understandings of sovereignty might be, as Constantinou and Papadakis state, "a dangerous suggestion,"[40] as they help heat up ethnonationalist competition. They nevertheless remain a dominant site of contestation. In the UN system, territory matters.

Nina Caspersen, author of a comprehensive analysis of polities with contested statehood, observes that polities such as Northern Cyprus are often considered "anomalies of international system."[41] Yet, a visitor to such place will notice that buses run, shops open, people graduate from schools. Elections are held, so are national commemorations or more private ceremonies, such as funerals, weddings, or birthdays. Life is *normal*, as much as it can be, given the many exceptional circumstances Cyprus happens to be in.[42] How then to reconcile the notions of normality and exceptionality? On the one hand, it indeed is uncommon for polities claiming statehood to exist without recognition by other states. If we think territorially, there are maybe two dozen such entities presently.[43] On the other hand, it is not un-normal that people want to govern their affairs and establish institutions for that matter to newspapers, through theaters, to parliaments. Cyprus—both north and south—might be subject to several overlapping states of exception, or, as Costas Constantinou puts it: "What passes off as Cypriot 'normality' nowadays comprises a plurality of states of exception."[44] Yet, as we will see later "exceptionality" (or, "uniqueness," in context of research on Turkey), should not distract us from seeing "longing for normality." It is very "normal" if people do not want to cope with the downsides of exceptional circumstances.

Some political theorists suggest that democracy does not need sovereignty in the form of recognized statehood.[45] This argument is usually not made to dismiss benefits of statehood, but to underline that, even in the absence of formal recognition of governance structures, some type of democratic politics

[40] Constantinou and Papadakis, "The Cypriot State(s) in situ."
[41] Nina Caspersen, *Unrecognized States* (London: Polity, 2002).
[42] Costas Constantinou, "On the Cypriot States of Exception," *International Political Sociology*, no. 2 (2008): 145–64; Constantinou and Papadakis, "Cypriots exceptions in situ"; Bryant and Hatay, "Guns and Guitars."
[43] Caspersen counts seventeen such cases, including two (Taiwan and Kosovo) she considers borderline. Since her book was published, the list became longer. For example, the post-2013 Russian intervention in Ukraine produced contested Crimea, Donetsk, Luhansk. Parts of post–Arab Spring Libya and Syria could probably be added to the list. In Europe, the Spanish Catalonia is another interesting case.
[44] Constantinou, "On the Cypriot States of Exception," 145–64, 145.
[45] Oisin Tansey, "Does Democracy Need Sovereignty?" *Review of International Studies* 37 (2011): 1515–36. See also Nina Caspersen, "Democracy, Nationalism and (Lack Of) Sovereignty: The Complex Dynamics of Democratization in Unrecognized States," *Nations and Nationalism* 17, no. 2 (2011): 337–56.

is necessary to maintain both internal legitimacy and the drive for external recognition.[46] The limits though come in terms of accountability and access. With *accountability* we can imagine that a polity is going to be asked, on a regular basis, to report on mechanisms in which its members negotiate rights. Not being a part of comparative surveys, as Mete Hatay points out, places a polity on a different plane compared to those, which are regularly surveyed.[47] Measurement, reporting, ranking alone can of course hardly deliver. After all, reporting on Turkey's democratization has brought ambiguous results. Thus, measurements do not matter in their own right—it is how they do when one is not part of them. Less accountability in international networks opens more opportunities for subversion or ignoring certain norms. Under access we can imagine the possibility to interact with other representatives of polities recognized in the world system. That is, the possibility to simply appear and establish relations with others.

With accountability and access are under consideration, let us now think about recognition beyond something that comes with the possibility to raise one's flag and establish formal diplomatic relations. Political theorist John Dryzek has recently asked whether there can be a "right to democracy."[48] For Dryzek, the existence of many competing understandings of democracy should not be an obstacle to asking for a "right to formative agency," or a "right to a speech that matters." This proposition is in many respects similar to Appadurai's notion of capacity to aspire.[49] In the encyclopedia of recognitions, questions of aspiration often do not get an entry. Borders are products of specific decisions of people whose voice mattered in crucial historical moments. Yet borders are not the only framework that matters: if Turkey eventually joins the EU, its state borders will not change, nor will those of the EU members.

Consider a hierarchy of democratic credentials, something that matters perhaps most significantly for the present argument about recognized belongings.[50] The EU arguably has developed an upper ground in regulatory standards for access to rights. Yet, the EU record in *allowing* or facilitating democracy in candidate polities is contested. Audra Simpson's observation is helpful here: "Political recognition is, in its simplest terms, to be seen by another

[46] Caspersen, "Democracy, Nationalism and Lack of Sovereignty."
[47] Mete Hatay, "The Problem of Pigeons: Orientalism, Xenophobia and a Rhetoric of the 'Local' in North Cyprus," *The Cyprus Review* 20, no. 2 (2008): 144–71.
[48] Dryzek, "Can There Be a Human Right to an Essentially Contested Concept?" 357–67.
[49] Discussed in the first chapter of this book. Appadurai, "Grassroots Globalization and the Research Imagination"; Appadurai, "The Right to Research."
[50] So is the structure of rules guiding possible union between Greek and Turkish Cypriots, and between Turkish Cypriots and the rest of the EU.

as one wants to be seen."[51] In this case it would be the recognition of unequal positions from which negotiations about the (joint?) future are led. So it is not the recognition of statehood per se but acknowledgement of the unequal starting points—the fact, that one group of interlocutors simply has less leverage.[52]

The Problem of Deadlines: One Day When Things Are Solved (Turkey)

As noted earlier in this book, for Turkey, democracy is something to be achieved by entry into the EU and something to be proven before that entry can actually happen. If there is no deadline, the talks can (don't have to, of course, but they do) expand into recursive loops of blame games—a search for consensus becomes a search for a culprit.[53] Meanwhile, the best the EU can do is to provide aid. Let me emphasize that this is not a problem of intentionality. As we already know, in complex institutions like the EU, a singular intentionality can hardly exist. The focus on aid in case of Northern Cyprus is simply the lowest common denominator the member states were able to agree on. The story of Turkish Cypriots is in many respects similar to the story of Turkey: they are not yet able to shape conversation on EU's future, they have only recently (and partially) been admitted to its presence. It is questionable how far they can be brought "closer to the EU" if the EU puts democracy among its foundational values, and by its very conduct in Northern Cyprus, it seems to suggest that democracy can "start" only once the solution to Cyprus conflict is found. But it can be found only illicitly, as there can officially be no public authority in the north before the solution is found. And while the other actors in international arena have gradually developed more understanding for aspirations of both Turks (in relation to their EU aspiration) and Turkish Cypriots (in terms of political rights more broadly), there still seems to be an infinite postponement of decisive action toward that end. Action is more than a statement—it is a change of space under which authority falls and in which politics can be exercised. There are many ways how this connects to thinking about Turkey's EU bid: for most Turks, the EU is also only web-streamed.

---

[51] Audra Simpson, *Mohawk Interruptus: Political Life Across the Borders of Settler States* (Durham: Duke University Press, 2014), 23.
[52] For discussion of Turkish Cypriot positionality, see Bryant and Hatay, "Guns and Guitars."
[53] Uğur, *The European Union and Turkey*. These observations are discussed in Chapter 4 of the present book.

The philosopher Kelly Oliver proposes alternative analytics to recognition: response ethics. For Oliver, the problem with recognition is that it often "reinforces power structure of dominance insofar as those in power control who is recognized and who is not." Moreover, continues Oliver, "the concept of recognition suggests a moment rather than a process."[54] What she means by response ethics is a "responsibility to promote the ability to respond."[55] Such understanding might lead us to an infinity of responsibilities and responses, perhaps the very core of democratic process. If we, at the same time, accept that recognized statehood and citizenship associated with such statehood remains a key mediating structure for the ability to be mobile, and hence, the ability to speak (and be heard), then those who do not possess it have to wait until those who *do* possess it grant them the permission to speak. Inter*national* frameworks then provide very few exits from the complicated situation and yet they cannot be dismissed.

This can be well evidenced when we go into the nuances of citizenship of those who are in the territory of the Union. In that case, we might need to take a step back and ask again whether citizenship in a (internationally) recognized state significantly alters (every)one's right to speak and to respond. This—the limits of national/citizenship framework—is evident also in other cases and is not as territorial as it seems. Minorities, such as the Roma in Europe, face more restrictions in access to basic public services than citizens belonging to dominant ethnicities and are also more likely targets of deportation if they move to another European state, something they technically have a right to do.[56] Borders then cannot be dismissed in debates about belongings, but neither can ascription of race or membership in an ethno-nation.

On Good Wishes and Hegemonies

It may seem that what is at the center of claims for recognition is the past. But maybe that is not the case—maybe the past, or, things that passed, are repeatedly invoked to resist the presence. Things passed might serve here as irrefutable evidence. Let us now take a page from the literature on settler colonialism. In

---

[54] Kelly Oliver, "Witnessing, Recognition and Response Ethics," *Philosophy and Rhetoric* 48, no. 4 (2015): 473–93, 477.
[55] Oliver, "Witnessing, Recognition and Response Ethics," 484.
[56] Jacqueline Bhabha, "The Politics of Evidence: Roma Citizenship Deficits in Europe," in Benjamin Lawrance and Jacqueline Stevens(eds), *Citizenship in Question: Evidentiary Birthright and Statelessness* (London and Durham: Duke University Press, 2017), 60.

Mohawk Interruptus, the author, Audra Simpson asks: "How to tell a story that is always being told?"[57] The Mohawk, a North American First Nation, were used, before the United States and Canada settled their borders in a current shape, to a different arrangement of checkpoints—places and ways of proving belonging. The Mohawk Simpson worked with "refuse to forget" the lead-up to the current border order. We can see that refusal as a claim on the present—rejection of borders as they are drawn now, and the limits they place on human mobility. We may also see the Mohawk presence as a reminder of foundations of the current set up of borders, citizenships, and dominant ethno-nations.

In Cyprus, there are many ways how participants of dialogues about the future want their present concerns to be recognized. The current institutional and legal framework in which residents of the north can get only some of their personal rights recognized is in many respects similar to the position of Turkey as a country in the process of European integration. Turks, just like the Turkish Cypriots, cannot become full citizens of the EU before they are accepted and they accept. Yet, as there are no deadlines set and no obligation to do things in a particular timeframe, the process can resemble a long polar night from the time before humans learned that polar nights are finite. Joint timeframes and deadlines are essential for rightful belonging in the community.[58] This does not mean that a membership immediately resolves all problems, but it does come with a new regime. Members of EU-rope have more obligations to address the concerns of their fellow members. In this sense, recognition of right to politics is more than a formality—a permission for a particular society to get voting rights in the UN or EU and to raise its flag. This deeper sense of meaning pertains not so much to rights of states to exercise authority over a given territory—this is what the states are already trying to do.[59] Instead, it is more closely linked to vehicles people, as individuals and parts of respective communities, are able to use when they engage with others. Political theorist Patchell Markell proposed to "de-state" recognition:

> [I]t could also mean reconceiving democracy as a pattern of mutual and interlocking relations of dependence among multiple loci of authority or concentrations of power. And it could mean defining democratic citizenship not as the self-control of the people, but as a matter of taking part in the activity of politics, where taking part can refer not only to participation in

---

[57] Simpson, *Mohawk Interruptus*, 177.
[58] The argument builds on Mehmet Uğur's work *The European Union and Turkey*.
[59] Sassen, *Territory Authority Rights*.

authoritative deliberative and decision-making bodies, but also to a range of unofficial activities, both quotidian and extraordinary, through which authoritative acts are subjected to the unpredictable responses of those, whose lives they touch.[60]

If we engage in conversations on what is, in EU reports and brochures documenting relations with polities outside, often called "people-to-people contacts," then yes, spontaneity and creativity have their irreplaceable role. But let us not get distracted from the inter*national* framework. In *The Utopia of Rules* anthropologist David Graeber discusses problematic encounters between bureaucratic systems and humans. Two of his observations might be helpful here to advance the argument. The first one is what he calls "grammar book effect": grammar books are written to capture how people speak at a particular time, yet although languages keep changing, Graeber observes, "once a book exists, [. . .]people feel that the rules are not just descriptions of how people do the talk, but prescriptions for how they *should* talk."[61] Translated into conversation on relations between the EU members and candidates, this could mean that our rule-books need an update to better reflect the lives of the participants of these relations. The second point pertains to "interpretive labor" in relations of systemic inequality:

> Those on the bottom of the heap have to spend a great deal of imaginative energy trying to understand the social dynamics that surrounds them—including having to imagine the perspectives of those on top—while the latter can wander about largely oblivious to much of what is going on around them.[62]

If we translate Graeber's observation to inter*national* framework, and switch top-bottom markers to inside-outside, we could say that a candidate for accession is expected to do more of imaginative work than those inside the Union. It also seems that some polities remain in the queue of candidates even if their individual citizens already belong. The candidate polities have their own internal hegemonies of belonging, in terms of wealth, ethnicity, gender, and other markers. But on *international* maps, because this is what the EU process is about, it is difficult to contend the idea that if the "outsider" wants to be on the map, they have to invest comparably more resources into understanding the European Union than is the case vice versa. Resources in this case do not

[60] Patchen Markell, *Bound by Recognition* (Princeton: Princeton University Press, 2003), 231.
[61] David Graeber, *The Utopia of Rules* (Brooklyn, London: Melville House, 2015), 197.
[62] Graeber, *The Utopia of Rules*, 81.

refer to aid and infrastructure, but to the difficult work of understanding what the one inside requires from the one outside. Thus, we again arrive to similar conclusions as in previous chapters: in an absence of a framework based on rights and obligations, individual participants of the relationship have to figure out things from scratch. Those who are interested in constructive collaboration are often hardest hit by the labor of understanding.

Part Three

Refugees and Crises

There are few themes as defining for European politics as migration. There are few themes as contested as migration. Many Europeans are proud of the opportunities provided by the border-free continent. Many Europeans are concerned that the movement is perhaps too free. Whether one celebrates mobility or is cautious about it always depends on whose mobility is at stake. Are we talking about "our people," or someone from outside, such as the refugees? Are we talking about tourism without long hours of waiting at the borders or about a possibility to change residence? And do we see the connections between the past and the present inhabitants of the continent? In the cacophony of debates about movement, it is easy to forget quite significant pieces of history, such as the fact that the present international regime of refugee protection was established after the Second World War and the experience of Europeans displaced by that war was crucial in its making.[1]

When the anniversary of the end of the Cold War appears in the calendar, news media around the continent reach for archive footage. We watch crumbling of the Berlin Wall and the cutting of the barbed wire at other places that used to separate the East and the West. We watch joyful faces of people who are curious to cross to the other side. And yet, three decades after the end of that war, images of the dismantled fences blend easily with photographs of wires surrounding detention centers for refugees who have just arrived. We could think about refugees as aspiring Europeans, people who have come in search of opportunity to live inside a war-free zone. Absence of armed conflict between member states is after all a major achievement of European integration. Yet not everyone can come to join this dream, and of those who were able to make it, many will be sent back.

---

[1] Lisa Malkki, "Refugees and Exile: From 'Refugee Studies' to the National Order of Things," *Annual Review of Anthropology* 24 (1995): 495–523.

Many things happened before commemoration of Europe's unification could be watched side by side with images of freshly built fences. In the newsreel documenting international politics, the second decade of the twenty-first century started with uprisings in several states on the southern and eastern frontier of the Mediterranean Sea. These events were often called "Arab Spring" and some commentators suggested, in the heat of the moment that this has been an "Arab 1989." As the symbols were travelling between times and spaces, scholars and other curious people took to revise earlier conceptualizations of democracy, security, and stability. Some asked whether "Arabs are ready for democracy," others observed that if the EU's earlier policy had been focused on "stabilizing" the region, the revolts have proved it wrong. This was a time when *stability (security)* and *democracy* were often seen as mutually exclusive. Doubts were also raised about Turkey's "zero problems with neighbors" policy in that same region. In response to the Arab Spring, Turkey and the EU have adopted a range of contradictory policies, yet they soon came together to address what is often called the Syrian refugee crisis. The conflict in Syria has resulted in a diaspora of millions and most of those who searched for refuge outside the country found it in Turkey. The EU has gradually become a major external donor for this diaspora. It has also become a prime target of criticism for failing its international obligations.

In the European Union, discussions about migration gradually evolved into uneasiness with what the anthropologist Dace Dzenovska called a "problem of too many,"[2] because arguably few object to receiving "some" refugees. The panic begins when no one knows what "some" could mean. The year 2015 has been an important milestone for the Union's migration policies and also for its relations with Turkey. Worries were aired that the EU might break up and it seemed that the dominant concern in the policy rooms of many national capitals and the Brussels institutions were to prevent this. While the surge in asylum-applications was often presented as a new development, discussions about who can come and who should not have been shaped by earlier notions of who is already allowed to be home in the EU. As the political representations of the Union's member states debated various options, they soon realized that making most refugees stay outside of their common borders is in fact the main thing they can agree on.

Meanwhile, debates on migration in Turkey have been no less intense. But one needs to keep in mind the angle and the context. As Syria's neighbor, it has over a few years become a host to almost four million Syrians. What matters

---

[2]   Dace Dzenovska, "Coherent Selves, Viable States: Eastern Europe and the 'Migration/Refugee Crisis,'" *Slavic Review* 76, no. 2 (2017): 297–306.

here is not just the number but also the suddenness.[3] With the first hundreds and thousands, this was not a major issue of contestation. People living in the neighborhoods to which Syrians arrived would sometimes note their discomfort: "Why do all the kids have to be on the street at night? Why do so many live in one flat? Why do they throw stuff on the grass?" Many of these same people were at the same time supportive of the Syrians' right to refuge. In Turkey, similarly to the states of the European Union, the Syrians found temporary refuge in some locations and were expelled from (or not let into) others. Let us note that one of the motivations behind setting the international refugee regime has been to avoid a situation in which some countries would have to bear a larger share of responsibility because they happen to be neighbors of conflict-zones.

Part Three looks at anatomy of rights in the early phase of EU-Turkey migration partnership. This partnership has so far been the most significant divergence from accession framework. In late 2015 and early 2016 representatives of Turkey and the EU convened unprecedented number of high-level diplomatic meetings. These eventually led to the infamous agreement under which Turkey pledged to strengthen protection of its borders and the EU committed to increase financial assistance to Turkey. The diplomatic (re)discovery of each other's importance also led to higher presence of the diplomatic relationship in public conversations. Many have campaigned for the deal, asserting EU-rope's right to request that Turkey would prevent any north-bound refugee movements. A few months after the deal was signed, a coup attempt and ensuing state of emergency reshuffled Turkish politics. This part starts with discussion of wider European debates on rights and crisis in the first years of life of the refugee deal. It shows how and why the deal was reported as a success. It engages with recursive loops, such as when some looked for EU-Turkey deal to become a model for EU-Libya deal, while the latter seemed already to have been a model for the former. International petitions circulated asking people to mobilize against "stranding refugees in Turkey," an interesting hierarchy of rights. In this confusing debate, we have seen yet another reversal of model/copy frame, as some of my interlocutors in Turkey showed admiration for exclusion of refugees promoted by several EU politicians. Part Three continues with fragments of proceedings in one EU member state, the Czech Republic. Here, despite their physical absence, refugees have been a central item on political agenda. Czechs were not the only Europeans who rejected refugees. But as recent graduates of EU accession process, they can tell

---

[3] The United Nations High Commissioner for Refugees (UNHCR) maintains a detailed database of registered displaced persons and countries hosting them. https://www.unhcr.org/syria-emergency.html. For a brief (and visual) account of suddenness, see also International Crisis Group, "Turkey's Syrian Refugees: Defusing Metropolitan Tensions," Report No. 248, January 29, 2018.

us things many others cannot. I invite the reader to consider these chapters in light of complexity that has flourished in the relationship since the accession talks have begun. We have already established that the grand narrative of teacher/student has run out of its explanatory potential. We then bring together fragments from conversations with individual actors and record how their experience is not represented by the wider international diplomatic framework.

7

Europe's Very Life Was at Stake

In April 2016, the European Council president Donald Tusk thanked the then prime minister of Turkey Ahmet Davutoğlu for Turkey's treatment of Syrian refugees, adding, amid applause, that "No-one has the right to lecture Turkey on what they should do."[1] The scene is very symbolic as it captures a crucial paradox in the principles guiding the diplomatic relationship. As a candidate for accession, Turkey *is* to be "lectured." In fact, learning about the EU and adapting to it is a defining part of the process. But the European Council president openly suggested that maybe this is not the case. The lecturing paradigm has been based on the assumption that the EU knows better. Yet in migration issues, it perhaps does not.

The meeting took place in Gaziantep, a city in southeastern Turkey, a month after adoption of *Turkey-EU Statement*. In this document, both parties committed "to end the irregular migration from Turkey to the EU" and facilitate safe routes instead. Turkey pledged to strengthen its border, the EU promised to increase funds for Syrians and their host communities.[2] The word *statement*, as the document is called, merits attention. While the partners clearly *agreed* on its terms, the EU policy makers avoid the word *agreement*, because its negotiation did not follow all the rules and procedures necessary for the EU to sign an *agreement* with a third country.[3] Representatives of EU institutions and member states, who I interviewed, often reminded me that calling *"it" an agreement* is not precise. Speaking about *it* with precision, however, requires acknowledgement that the two parties did not just *state* their intentions. They negotiated the terms and acted on (some of) them. I use the expression *refugee deal* to reflect the dynamics, the mutuality, and the dominant content of this action. The maneuvers

---

[1] *BBC News*, "Donald Tusk: Turkey Best Example of How to Treat Refugees," April 23, 2016, http://www.bbc.com/news/world-europe-36122377.

[2] Council of the EU, "EU-Turkey Statement," March 18, 2016, https://www.consilium.europa.eu/en/press/press-releases/2016/03/18/eu-turkey-statement/#.

[3] For rules and procedures under which the EU can reach agreement, see: http://www.consilium.europa.eu/en/council-eu/international-agreements/.

around proper terminology testify to selective responsibility of the EU in what
its various high-level representatives called extraordinary times. Whether the
refugee deal abides by the EU law has been of concern to numerous individuals
and collectives. In the words of one migrant-rights lawyer whom I met in Brussels
in the fall of 2016: "This was a political decision, coming from member states,
and the Council and Commission legal services were asked to somehow find an
acceptable way." While in some settings the deal was considered a satisfactory (if
not ideal) response, in other spaces it has been a subject of recurring criticism.

The Refugee Deal for the Record: "A Steady Delivery of Tangible Results"

The refugee deal was adopted after several summits of highest representatives
of the involved states. Their proceedings have been carefully watched—not least
because in the years leading up to these summits, the relationship has been
declared dead. This new migration cooperation was an act of necessity in the
face of growing demand for asylum in Europe. It was also supposed to give
relations new boost. And so it did—although not one of friendly cooperation.
A Turkish opposition leader noted that the country should not be expected to
become a "concentration camp."[4] The former editor in chief of the opposition
daily *Cumhuriyet* Can Dündar, who served a prison sentence and currently lives
in exile wrote:

> We watched the news conference announcing the win-win agreement with
> bittersweet smiles. We drew lessons from the fact that the most fundamental
> rights were given no voice. Europe paid to rent a far-off refugee camp. Ankara
> received the payment and obliterated its political infamy. As Europe and Ankara
> embraced one another, two things were crushed in between: principles and us.
> Now, in our prison cells built to "western standards" at Silivri prison, we are like
> kids our father and his guests beat together.[5]

---

[4]   CNN Türk, "Kılıçdaroğlu: Türkiye Avrupa'nın toplama kampı olamaz," October 26, 2015, https://ww
      w.cnnturk.com/turkiye/kilicdaroglu-turkiye-avrupanin-toplama-kampi-olamaz. Suggestion that the
      present situation can be labeled "concentration camp" is, especially for West European interlocutors,
      often considered offensive/insulting. In a recent essay, Masha Gessen discusses similar concerns in
      the American context and proposes several explanations for why that sounds so disturbing. Masha
      Gessen, "The Unimaginable Reality of American Concentration Camps," *The New Yorker*, June 21,
      2019.
[5]   Can Dündar, "What's Freedom Worth? Less Than 3 Billion Euros, Apparently," *The Washington Post*,
      December 21, 2015.

But one did not need to be in opposition to contest this agreement. Various public opinion polls showed that also supporters of the government have been uneasy with Turkey hosting so many Syrians.[6] And while, as we will see later, there were certainly voices in Turkey who had understanding for EU's tougher approach on borders, as this is what they would like to see in their own country, one thing was difficult to process for participants across the political spectrum. Regardless of whether one supported the government policy, EU rejection of the refugees was one more blow to the Union's reputation as a rights defender.

But there are also happy accounts of the deal. Browsing through archives of the European Commission, a body that carefully reported on the proceedings, one discovers a story in which things are not all lost. On the contrary, lives are saved and futures are built.[7] In this story, the main enemies are the smugglers and the parties involved take resolute action to defeat them:

> In order to break the business model of the smugglers and to offer migrants an alternative to putting their lives at risk, the EU and Turkey today decided to end the irregular migration from Turkey to the EU.[8]

Navigating the archive requires patience with document names and acronyms. The EU and Turkey have in fact adopted two agreements: a *Joint Action Plan* (JAP) in the fall of 2015 and the *Turkey-EU Statement* (TES) in the spring of 2016. The first plan comes with twenty-four measures to support Syrians in Turkey and their host communities and to cut what is deemed as illegal migration to EU.[9] The second plan presents "additional action points." Only three of these are related to issues beyond migration of "third-country nationals" and cover visa liberalization for Turkish citizens, accession talks, and customs union. Already

[6] Emre Erdogan and Pinar Uyan Semerci, "Attitudes towards Syrian Refugees 2017," Istanbul Bilgi University, https://goc.bilgi.edu.tr/media/uploads/2018/03/15/turkish-perceptions-of-syrian-refug ees-20180315_Y0gYZoI.pdf; EDAM, "Reaction Mounting against Syrian Refugees in Turkey," Public Opinion Surveys of Turkish Foreign Policy 1/2014, http://www.edam.org.tr/en/File?id=1152.

[7] Most of these reports are addressed to the European Parliament, the Council of the EU and the European Council. They constitute a unique record of this cooperation for future reference. While the reports cover mostly third-country migration-related issues, I review also how progress on accession talks has been reported. Of specific interest is the status assigned to Turkey (partner/candidate). Visa liberalization and upgrade of the customs union, other two items on agenda of the summits, are, due to space limitations, not covered in detail in my analysis. I explore what was reported and what was not, and I am specifically interested in how (and whether) the recent history of the relations and the ongoing conflicts in the EU, and in Turkey have been referenced. I reviewed the structure of the reports and space dedicated to specific issues, as well as the timing and frequency, as these provide evidence of prioritization. I explored how efficiency in implementation of the goals was evaluated: What was deemed a success or failure and why?

[8] Council of the EU EU-Turkey Statement, March18, 2016, https://www.consilium.europa.eu/en/press/press-releases/2016/03/18/eu-turkey-statement/# (Accessed December 20, 2017).

[9] European Commission, "EU-Turkey Joint Action Plan," Brussels, October 15, 2015, http://europa.e u/rapid/press-release_MEMO-15-5860_en.htm (Accessed June 15, 2017).

the first agreement sees Turkey as a "negotiating candidate country," it does not, however, spell specific measures related to accession. It also presents a certain idea of togetherness between the parties. The opening passage reads: "This joint action will render the message of Europe stronger and more visible."[10] Within the first eighteen months of these two plans (or one compound agreement), the European Commission has published eight reports on progress in the migration partnership.[11] How and where these reports appear is no less interesting than their content. The first (JAP) report is not available publicly. I could not find it on migration-related websites of the federal institutions nor in the Commission's transparency register, nor in the Council open-data portal. The Commission declined to provide a copy of the report when I requested it, informing me that it is a nonpublic report sent to the member states.[12] The second JAP report was published as an annex to the Commission's communication on implementation of a related policy instrument—the "European agenda on migration."[13] The only report available for public and existing separately (not as an annex to another communication) is the third report on JAP.[14] In April 2016, the sequence gets a new name, and the fourth report on JAP is at the same time a first report on TES adopted the previous month.

Let us now follow up on this slightly disorienting preview of travels between documents, with a different type of precision. How can numbers, quantities, and visuals help us think about what was prioritized? The reports became longer and more detailed after March 2016.[15] From this moment on, the reports also include a few paragraphs on accession talks, although these are considerably shorter than the text discussing migration management.[16] It is not only the word count and depth of coverage of the two issues that shows how migration cooperation gained prominence over accession. It is also the frequency of reporting. The Commission publishes a separate body of progress reports dedicated specifically to accession. These, however, appear annually, while the reports on refugee deal had a frequency of one to three months. The word count of one year of reporting on migration cooperation approaches the length of one annual report

---

[10] European Commission, "EU-Turkey Joint Action Plan," 1.
[11] By April 2017 the Commission has published three reports on implementation of the 2015 JAP and five on the 2016 TES.
[12] Specifically to the Council of permanent representatives (COREPER). I have obtained the report from an EP member.
[13] Second JAP report, published on February 2, 2016.
[14] Published March 3, 2016.
[15] Adoption of TES.
[16] While the earlier reports include graphs, after March 2016 only one report (the third) TES report features a graph – showing rapid decline in sea crossings once the March agreement entered into force.

on the candidate's progress on all of the EU law. In 2015, the Commission even postponed publication of the annual report on Turkey's progress toward accession, until after Turkey's parliamentary elections.[17] This is another evidence that cooperation on prevention of movement to the EU is a matter more urgent than the work of making Turkey a member state.

We should also note what is not discussed in these reports. The cooperation aims at mitigating consequences of problems that originated elsewhere—neither in Turkey, nor in the EU.[18] "Irregular migration" is caused by conflicts in the neighborhood (Syria chiefly), or "in the region"[19] and by activity of smuggler networks. The internal politics in the EU and Turkey that led to adoption of this deal and shaped its implementation are virtually absent from the reporting. There is no reference to disputes in the EU regarding sharing responsibility toward asylum seekers. The reports though do encourage the member states to proceed faster on "resettlement"—an expression used to describe an act when a member state invites refugees registered in a non-EU state. A report published a year after adoption of the refugee deal states: "Member states are advancing well with preparing further resettlement operations, including missions to Turkey to interview resettlement candidates."[20] But while one of the declared goals has been to replace illegal and "dangerous" routes with safe passage, a year into the refugee deal, a total of 4,618 people from Turkey were resettled in the EU with less than a half of its member states taking part.[21] To put the numbers into yet another context—in the period 2015–19, around 65,000 people have been resettled in total (from all countries) to the EU.[22]

The ambiguity of the common "we" shines through the reports. While they often refer to "our joint efforts,"[23] the Union and Turkey are not one polity but

---

[17] *Reuters*, "Withheld EU Report Raps Turkey on Rights, Media, Justice," October 28, 2015, http://www .reuters.com/article/us-turkey-election-eu-idUSKCN0SM2CT20151028 (Accessed April 13, 2017).

[18] This is consistent with Malmvig's findings on reporting of EU neighborhood cooperation in discussed in her article "Caught between democratization and cooperation."

[19] European Commission, "First Report on the Progress Made in the Implementation of the EU-Turkey Statement," April 20, 2016, https://ec.europa.eu/home-affairs/sites/homeaffairs/files/what-we-do/p olicies/european-agenda-migration/proposal-implementation-package/docs/20160420/report_imp lementation_eu-turkey_agreement_nr_01_en.pdf (Accessed April 13, 2017).

[20] European Commission, "First Report on the Progress Made in the Implementation of the EU-Turkey Statement," 8.

[21] European Commission, "Relocation and Resettlement – State of Play," April 12, 2017, https://ec .europa.eu/home-affairs/sites/homeaffairs/files/what-we-do/policies/european-agenda-migration/2 0170412_update_of_the_factsheet_on_relocation_and_resettlement_en.pdf (Accessed April 13, 2017).

[22] European Commission, "Delivering on Resettlement," December 2019, https://ec.europa.eu/home -affairs/sites/homeaffairs/files/what-we-do/policies/european-agenda-migration/201912_deliverin g-on-resettlement.pdf.

[23] European Commission, "First Report on the Progress Made in the Implementation of the EU-Turkey Statement."

two partners with separate roles, resources, and possibilities. One of them offers to rule by decrees—under the JAP, Turkey has committed to issue "a government decree regarding the integration of refugees into the labor market."[24] Migration researchers, however, tell us that labor market integration belongs to the most sensitive and difficult aspects of migration-related policy making.[25] Because if decent jobs are scarce and ethno-nationalist discourses of belonging are dominant, how to make a case that "the other" is not stealing "our" opportunities? Moreover, let us recall that in the logic of the accession process, the EU has stronger institutions guaranteeing rule of law and democracy than the candidate country. This constitutes the backbone of a vast body of Commission and Parliament reports and Council conclusions on Turkey. In the logic of accession partnership, the European Commission has the right and the obligation to report on Turkey's democracy. True to this logic, in reports in which overall progress on democracy is evaluated, the Commission criticizes rule by decree. Yet, if such rule is permissible in migration governance, then migration and accession partnerships are clearly contradictory.

Numbers and statistics constitute prominent part of documentation of the refugee deal, yet not everything and everyone gets counted. The bulk of the reporting concentrates on number of crossings and resources allocated, either for the prevention of further movement or for aid in Turkey. Such selective reporting provides, to use words of de Goede, Leander, and Sullivan, "seemingly objective accounts detached from the messy contextual narratives."[26] A flyer issued by the Commission at the first anniversary of the refugee deal does not mention accession negotiations or visa liberalization. The flyer presents the refugee deal as a success and a "steady delivery of tangible results."[27] The border crossings have been drastically cut and some of the EU funds made it to recipients. Yet almost all Syrians stayed in Turkey and the EU member states' resettlement efforts are meager even when measured against the (already small) commitment. The EU members offered places only for 6 percent of the originally pledged 74,000. Effectively, the commitment to offer safe routes did not materialize and the member states have left the bulk of care for asylum seekers on the candidate country. If smugglers were to be defeated also by provision of

---

[24] European Commission, "EU-Turkey Joint Action Plan, Brussels," October 15, 2015, http://europa.e u/rapid/press-release_MEMO-15-5860_en.htm (Accessed June 15, 2017).

[25] For an insightful ethnographic account see Christopher M. Lawrence, *Blood and Oranges: Immigrant Labor and European Markets in Rural Greece* (New York and Oxford: Berghahn, 2017).

[26] Marieke De Goede, Anna Leander, and Gavin Sullivan, "Introduction: The Politics of the List," *Environment and Planning D: Society and Space* 34, no. 1 (2016): 3–13, 8.

[27] European Commission, "EU-Turkey Statement One Year On," March 17, 2017, https://ec.europa.eu /home-affairs/sites/homeaffairs/files/what-we-do/policies/european-agenda-migration/backgr ound-information/eu_turkey_statement_17032017_en.pdf (Accessed April 13, 2017).

safe routes, the resettlement figures speak loudly that this did not happen. One graph does not feature in the reporting but could help us further to understand the situation.[28] Let us imagine it. We start with the horizontal and the vertical axis. The horizontal will host two bars—one for the EU, one for Turkey. This is a simple graph, let us stay true to the official colors as they appear on their flags. The EU bar will be blue, the Turkish one will be red. The width of the bars will be the same—they are here for purposes of illustration. The height on the vertical axis will show the number of Syrians who were made to stay in Turkey against the number who were allowed to cross via resettlement. Beside the first bar, the second bar would be barely noticeable. In the language of colors: the red bar would be so high that we would know that the blue exists only because of the accompanying legend (index). Many other things are unmeasured in these reports, such as the capacity of Turkish municipalities and other institutions to be able to do the work it takes to host refugees.[29]

Europe's Very Life Was at Stake

In the fall of 2016, more than a year after the beginning of the negotiations and six months into implementation of the refugee deal, the EU institutions representatives I spoke to mostly referred to migration policy making as "stabilized." In one interview, an official who has been closely following the preparation of the refugee deal opened their remarks on consequences of the deal for Turkey with these words: "And then there is the elephant in the room." The official referred to perception of some EU policy makers that the refugee deal might present a negative incentive for Turkey to harmonize with EU law, specifically with the parts on civil liberties. Another official, who was questioned whether she was not concerned about impact of the deal in Turkey asked me to understand that "Europe's very life was at stake." The measure was justifiable because there was no other alternative. The representative did not go into genealogy of Europe-making. This has been Europe and its needs in the present tense. As our conversation progressed, she asked me whether what she had been hearing from colleagues in the Commission about disappointments in Turkey was really true.

---

[28] Correct for the first year and half of the refugee deal, by May 2017.

[29] Some of the concerns raised by municipalities are addressed for example in a 2017 Migration Policy Workshop report "Urban Refugees from 'detachment' to 'harmonization.'" Istanbul: Marmara Belediyeler Birliği Kültür Yayınlari.

The Commission has evaluated the deal as a "success." This was possible only because it focused on a selective set of indicators and disregarded the wider political context. At the time of reporting "success" Turkey-EU talks have been considerably strained and politicians on both sides frequently suggested that the ties should be cut. Since the July 2016 coup attempt Turkey has been under a state of emergency. Many EU policy makers voiced concern over large-scale shutdown of public and nonstate organizations, dismissals from work or imprisonment of people charged with the support of terrorism in Turkey.[30] Other intergovernmental bodies, including the Organization for Security and Cooperation in Europe (OSCE) and the Council of Europe, published reports that criticized the postcoup approach to the rule of law in Turkey.[31] The new situation also emboldened long-time opponents of Turkey's EU membership. "Cultural incompatibility," a long-term justification for impossibility of membership, was replaced (or coupled) with references to divergent approach to law and rights. We cannot, however, say that only Turkey has been selective with reforms—the EU also put varying emphasis on legal harmonization and political inclusion. While conditionality has been repeatedly lauded as the EU's "strongest foreign policy tool," as we saw in earlier chapters, in Turkey the EU partially gave up on it soon after the opening of the accession talks.[32] And although reform was not "dead," it continued in sectors that did not signal immediate membership, such as facilitation of the 2013 asylum law in Turkey.[33]

The achievements in the first year of implementation of the refugee deal do not suggest any significant development bringing Turkey closer to accession. While one of the purposes of numbers is to establish results with certainty, the refugee deal has been implemented in a state of uncertainty. In addition to preexisting conflicts and inequalities, Turkey has been, for most of the implementation of the refugee deal, in a state of emergency. The government ruled by decree and number of checks and balances were suspended. While the

---

[30] The most common justification of dismissal from work or imprisonment has been affiliation to what used to be called "the Gülen network" and came increasingly to be referred to as "FETÖ," an organization suspected of the 2016 coup attempt. Charges also included suspected affiliation to the PKK, an organization outlawed both in Turkey and the EU.

[31] OSCE, "Turkey, Constitutional Referendum, Final Report," June 22, 2017, http://www.osce.org/odihr/elections/turkey/324816; Venice Commission, "Opinion No 865 / 2016," December 12, 2016, http://www.venice.coe.int/webforms/documents/default.aspx?pdffile=CDL-AD(2016)03 7-e, Venice Commission, "Opinion No 875/2017," March 17, 2017, http://www.venice.coe.int/webf orms/documents/default.aspx?pdffile=cdl-ad(2017)005-e.

[32] Tocci, *EU Accession Dynamics and Conflict Resolution*; Diez, *The European Union and the Cyprus Conflict*.

[33] Alexander Bürgin and Derya Asikoglu, "Turkey's New Asylum Law: A Case of EU Influence," *Journal of Balkan and Near Eastern Studies* 19, no. 2 (2017): 121–35.

EU institutions as well as representatives of member states have been critical of these developments, it is important to highlight that the refugee deal itself has been enveloped in legal uncertainty. In February 2017, a year into the refugee deal, the General Court of the European Union declined to hear a complaint of three asylum seekers who submitted a petition that their rights were violated by the deal. The court declared "That measure was not adopted by one of the institutions of the EU."[34] The wording resembles slogans at the entrance of the Ministry of Truth in George Orwell's *1984* ("War is Peace, Freedom is Slavery, Ignorance is Strength").[35] The decision is striking for several reasons. First, the deal has not been known as agreement between Turkey, Austria, Belgium, and the remaining of the (then) twenty-eight member states. In political discussions and media commentary it was always an agreement between EU and Turkey, as two partners. Second, the Commission, clearly an EU institution, regularly reports on progress of the deal and the money for its implementation comes, in a 2:1 ratio, from the member states and the Commission budget. With governing the deal in such an anxious regime, it becomes difficult to defend the EU from critics, who dismiss its credentials in defending human rights. It becomes difficult to see the migration cooperation with Turkey as something that should "save lives."[36]

Moreover, as we recall from previous chapters, many EU public relations bodies and member state policy makers have been working hard to make the Union more legitimate in the eyes of its own citizens. In such narratives, making the Union more legitimate also means that one needs to convince their constituency that the Union is more than a sum of its members. The court opinion, which concluded that such an important measure has not been developed by the EU as a whole, is then contradictory to these legitimation efforts.[37] Candidate countries

---

[34] General Court of the European Union, Press Release 19/17, February 2017, https://curia.europa.eu/jcms/upload/docs/application/pdf/2017-02/cp170019en.pdf.

[35] George Orwell, *1984* (New York: New American Library, 1949 orig, n.d. ed.), 26.

[36] The court did not refer to accession talks or visa liberalization by one word. In the court's view, the deal was purely focused on migration of third-country nationals.

[37] There is a further problem with the grounds on which the Union assists refugees in Turkey and that is the problem of whose knowledge counts. The Steering Committee of the financial leg, the Facility for Refugees in Turkey, is composed of representatives of EU member states and institutions, Turkey has only advisory role in deciding on how the money will be spent, so do civil societies of involved partners. The people who provide the everyday work of attention, welcome, hospitality or care have little say over how the EU funding should be disbursed (see Chapter 5 for wider discussion of role on civil society in aid projects). The fact that even in such a politically important realm as migration partnership Turkish society cannot effectively shape the course of action and co-decide on EU's aid policy is yet another testimony to foundational problems of the relationship. Turkey's (civil) society is not the only one who has been excluded from shaping the framework of the relationship—suggestions of many EU-based groups have also been unheard. An EU official I interviewed in the fall of 2016 explained the observer role of Turkey by stating "we do not do budget support in Turkey"

are often criticized that they cherry-pick, that they would like the perks of EU membership without doing all the work it takes to become a member. But if being a member requires fulfilling all of the obligations, how does one defend an EU whose many members are refusing to do things that a candidate has to do?

Innovations and Recursive Loops

Innovation is an important keyword in the post-2015 European migration architecture.[38] In the fall of 2016, a small group of academics, activists, and diplomats from around Europe accepted an invitation to join a two-day workshop in Sicily. The guiding question announced by the organizers was: "Does the EU-Turkey deal represent a model to be replicated in other contexts?" One such context suggested was Libya-EU cooperation. These were issues dominant on EU agenda at that time and from the perspective of policy practitioners it made perfect sense to convene such a discussion. It was, however, difficult to resist a sense of déjà vu. Does not the Turkey-EU deal resemble an earlier Libya-EU agreement, oft referred as Gaddafi-Berlusconi deal?[39] Are we doing innovation in recursive loops? Is the rush *toward* a new solution in fact an escape *from* something the EU and its members do not really know how to address?

There is an extensive literature discussing state practices of limiting movement to the EU. What is *known*, as far as academic knowledge is concerned, is that aid, investment and cautious rhetoric on domestic politics of the neighbor state have been previously verified practices of limiting migration into the EU.[40] What is also *known* is that migration regime for noncitizens has been linked to emphasis on need to protect domestic peace or what Jef Huysmans called "cultural security."[41] The problem has been shifted "outside" perhaps precisely because the EU societies have trouble negotiating lives with difference.[42]

---

without giving more details. A number of other interlocutors suggested in informal conversations that for the sake of transparency of the spending this indeed is a better system.

[38] It certainly is a trendy word in other realms of public life in this period.

[39] Muammar Quaddafi and Silvio Berlusconi are former leaders of the two states.

[40] Kristina Kausch and Richard Youngs, "The End of the 'Euro-Mediterranean Vision,'" *International Affairs* 85, no. 5 (2009): 963–75. Malmvig, "Free us from Power"; Malmvig, "Caught between Cooperation and Democratization."

[41] Jef Huysmans, "The European Union and the Securitization of Migration," *Journal of Common Market Studies* 38, no. 5 (2000): 751–77.

[42] Paolo Biondi, "Human Security and External Burden-Sharing: The European Approach to Refugee Protection between Past and Present," *The International Journal of Human Rights* 20, no. 2 (2016): 208–22; Nicolas DeGenova, "Spectacles of Migrant 'Illegality': The Scene of Exclusion, the Obscene of Inclusion," *Ethnic and Racial Studies* 36, no. 7 (2013): 1180–98.

Innovation can be thought of as adaptation, in a similar vein, as Václav Havel's greengrocer, whom we met in Chapter 4 of this book, put the "Workers of the World Unite" banner in his shop window. The greengrocer wanted to be left alone by people and circumstances he did not feel able to change. Innovative approaches to policy making can be a strategy of faking novelty, simply an act of putting on the record that we are doing things differently. A scholar of ethics Christopher Groves makes an important point on challenges of innovation: "it is inherently a future-creating activity: by bringing something new into the world, it can change the world itself."[43] Bearing this in mind, Groves insists that responsibility has to be a key consideration for designers of innovations:

> Viewed as part of a political imaginary of care, the "right impacts" of innovation would not just be impacts that address material needs, but ones that enhance human capacities to flourish in the face of uncertainties and surprises, by contributing to the social relationships that are necessary to support these capacities.[44]

The problem with innovations in the overall framework of EU-Turkey relations is that they are too tiny to be conducive to significant change or the flourishing of social relations in the sense as described by Groves. Attempts to innovate can be very genuine—not *saying* we do things differently but *doing* them differently. But if a notion of essential difference underpins the overall framework of the diplomatic relationship, if we have to say Turkey *and* EU, how many small innovations would it take for a transition toward a "common we"? How many and what type of innovations would need to happen to dissolve the assumption that all differences are bad?

Stranded, Exiled, Surprised

A few days before the March 2016 refugee deal, a group called "European March for Refugee Rights" launched an online petition.[45] The signatories, some 75,000 from around the world asked the EU representatives to put a halt to the deal, to

---

[43] Christopher Groves, "Horizons of Care: From Future Imaginaries to Responsible Research and Innovation," in Kornelia Konrad, Christopher Coenen, Anne Dijkstra, Colin Milburn and Hanro van Lente (eds), *Shaping Emerging Technologies: Governance, Innovation, Discourse* (Berlin: IOS Press/AKA, 2013), 185–202, 193.
[44] Groves, "Horizons of Care," 199.
[45] change.org, *Stop EU-Turkey Deal – Safe Passage Now*, March 2016, https://www.change.org/p/stop-eu-turkey-deal-safe-passage-now.

provide safe passage, and to keep the external borders open. They also asked for solidarity with Greece. There is not a word about solidarity with Turkey in the text of the petition. The signatories ask the EU politicians to "refuse to allow push-backs to Turkey or anywhere else" and to "refuse to consider Turkey . . . a safe third country." The petition website included additional comments of signatories who joined after the original text was published. These mostly refer to need for safe passage and appeal to shared humanity. Some are focused specifically on Turkey. A signatory from Oslo writes: "We have to take care of each other. Turkey is not a place for refugees. The refugees are not treated according to international conventions." A supporter from the UK says: "The refugees are people with human rights and are running from war. We need to help them and not send them to Turkey where they are not safe." Gary from the UK adds: "I fear the actions being undertaken in Turkey are not in keeping with the actions of good people in Europe." In this outpouring of shared humanity and concern for refugees, concern for the Turks is somehow left behind.

One Turkish refugee rights activist, with whom I was discussing the deal a few months after it entered into force, remarked: "I don't understand this 'stop the deal.' It is not about stopping the deal. Let's make Turkey a safer country, that's what I want." What she demanded was a commitment. Perhaps a similar commitment as that expressed by the ministers of four EU states (the Visegrad Group, V4) to people in the western Balkans.[46] In November 2015, several dailies in the region published a letter by the V4 foreign ministers titled *We Offer You Our Helping Hand on the EU Path*.[47] Already the word *letter* carries more personal touch than *statement*, and the western Balkan citizens are warmly told that

> It is clear that without you Europe is incomplete. One can never fully understand European history without knowing the rich history of your region. [. . .] We assure you that the crises the EU is facing at the moment, the migration and refugee crisis being one of the most challenging, will not be a cause for hesitation on our side with regard to our support of further EU enlargement.

The letter reassures, it expresses determination to include the region into the EU. It does not come as a surprise. The Visegrad countries have been supporting integration of the region for years and have often used language that suggested sense of ethnic or cultural kinship, shared history, and hopes of similar future.

---

[46] The Visegrad Group is a regional platform established by the Czech Republic, Hungary, Poland and Slovakia in 1991. All four states have been EU members since 2004.
[47] "We Offer You Our Helping Hand on the EU Path"—Joint letter of V4 Foreign Ministers published in Western Balkan dailies; Prague, November 11, 2015.

Turkey, a country also on EU path and one hosting (at that time) some three million Syrians, has not received such a letter, neither have the southern Mediterranean neighbors. It should also be noted here that the western Balkan societies are not thanked for what they have done for refugees. Instead, they are appreciated for reform progress on EU path and for contributing to EU's security. The emphasis here is on completing Europe, the big picture, building European integration. While Turkey was expected to do a good job with refugees, or at least not to remind them too often that it is experiencing problems, the Balkans were offered a default support. Not just in terms of "aid" and "thank you," but a commitment to making their European belonging come true.

While Turkey has been expected to stay outside, as we already know, some Turks have been able and willing to cross the frontier. Some of these people are academics who were uncomfortable for (or with) the regime in Turkey and looked for positions at European institutions. Those who got them, however, did also get a taste of EU academic market. A recent study by Seçkin Özdemir, who interviewed Turkish academics who found temporary refuge at universities in western Europe, presents stories of precarity, including the short-term employment contracts, visa problems, and sense of exclusion. A specific discomfort they experienced was that their situation was often marketed for the needs of the host.[48] This experience of alienation is in many ways similar to concerns voiced by many "native" EU academics. There is a vibrant debate on problems of academic life in the European Union.[49] Experiencing discomfort at the EU universities is in fact a genuine "welcome" to how things are experienced by many "locals." In an article titled *But you don't look Turkish,* Gülay Türkmen explores responses to newly arriving migrants from Turkey, who disrupt the earlier notion of the poor and uneducated guest workers (*Gastarbeiter*), a figure supposedly dissimilar from the local.[50] She notes many surprises experienced by West European interlocutors when they meet the "new Turks." Such encounters can again help us realize that surprises would not be here without situations and policy frameworks that enable them. It is a mutual shock at the gap between what one expects and what one encounters. Just like some in Germany were

[48] Seçkin Özdemir, "Pity the Exiled: Turkish Academics in Exile, the Problem of Compassion in Politics and the Promise of Dis-exile," *Journal of Refugee Studies* 2019 (advance article).

[49] This is a valuable introduction to that debate: Filip Vostal, *Accelerating Academia: The Changing Structure of Academic Time* (London: Palgrave, 2016).

[50] Gülay Türkmen, "'But You Don't Look Turkish!': The Changing Face of Turkish Immigration to Germany," *ResetDOC*, May 27, 2019, https://www.resetdoc.org/story/dont-look-turkish-changing-face-turkish-immigration-germany/.

surprised to meet whom they considered as atypical Turks, those arriving also had to come to terms with the real EU.

Such mutual shock/surprise of an encounter can then be discussed as a moment of differentiation, but also one that potentially offers understanding of similarity. Surprise is a mutual experience, it can happen only in some type of dialogue. This would hardly be possible without moments of interaction, confrontation. It would then be reasonable to assume that if it takes interaction to experience the surprise, it is also in the power of that situation to renegotiate frames, whether those, through which we lead discussions and analyze the world or those that have been enshrined in institutions. But is it really? Can a personal encounter transform deeply entrenched institutional narratives? Can it change established analytical frameworks? Individual encounters may be transformative but often weak in the face of more entrenched and material lines of differentiation. It is helpful to keep in mind that Europeanness is often "proved" by rejecting other affiliations.[51] One can hardly become a legitimate Europe-maker unless they first pledge allegiance to values on which European integration has been built.

Similarities and Appearances: What Is New?

In the summer of 2015, in a conversation with a small hotel owner in Istanbul, I noted that it felt good to escape the anti-refugee rhetoric dominating news from the more western part of Europe. He listened to me in surprise and urged me to understand that I should not object if our leaders try to protect us. My interlocutor felt betrayed by the open-door policy of his country. Writing in *The Guardian* in September 2015, the then prime minister Ahmet Davutoğlu recounted how much Turkey has invested into refugee protection in the past few years and appealed to international audience with the following words:

> The humanitarian crisis that is unfolding day by day is a test of our humanity as well as our morality. It is high time for Europe to look in the mirror, be honest about what it sees in the reflection, to stop procrastinating and start assuming

---

[51] A point made by Maria Todorova in *Imagining the Balkans* and briefly discussed in the first chapter of the present book. In relation to migration, a recent nuanced elaboration was provided by Stef Jansen, "After the Red Passport: Towards an Anthropology of Everyday Geopolitics of Entrapment in EU's 'Immediate Outside,'" *Journal of the Royal Anthropological Institute* 15 (2009): 815–32.

more than its fair share of the burden. Radical politicians must not be allowed to pull the wool over the eyes of the European people.[52]

But leaders of Turkey did not only criticize Europe. Some of their statements expressed the same spirit of joint interest and the need to act together, as we saw in the Commission documentation of the deal presented on previous pages. A few months later, in the same newspaper, the Turkish president Erdoğan wrote:

> To keep illegal migration under control Europe and Turkey must work together to create legal mechanisms such as the March 2016 agreement, for the resettlement of Syrian refugees. By rewarding refugees who play by the rules and making it clear that illegal immigrants will be sent back to Turkey, we can persuade refugees to avoid risking lives at sea.[53]

Several readers commented under the article, objecting to constraints on press freedom in Turkey. At that time, news outlets have been regularly informing on reports by international agencies including the UN and the OSCE on limitations to media freedom. One reader wrote: "I hope Mr. Erdogan appreciates the irony of contributing to a newspaper that he would attempt to ban if it was in his own country." The frontiers of (dis)agreement with this new migration partnership did not follow the land and sea borders and checkpoints.

The 2016 refugee deal certainly brought many novelties into the diplomatic relationship, but also to the many other relationships experienced in its backdrop. Perhaps the most significant novelty has been that a conservation, or stasis, was declared a success. If Turkey was not an acceptable candidate without refugees, and, if refugees are not welcome in the EU, what are Turkey's accession prospects *with refugees*? Re-invention of newness in EU policy making has come full circle and seems to be a policy of resignation. Turkey-EU refugee deal has by then delivered on one major goal: the sea crossings to the EU have dropped substantially. Importantly, the declared goal of "saving lives" from drowning at sea and becoming victims of smugglers by providing safe routes has not materialized at all. Only a handful of asylum seekers have been resettled through "legal" channels. Turkey is, however, no closer to EU accession; on the contrary, prospects for visa liberalization for its citizens seem dim. Moreover, the Union has clearly become more restrained in efforts to support pluralism

---

[52] Ahmet Davutoğlu, "Turkey Cannot Deal with the Refugee Crisis Alone. EU Nations Need to Help," *The Guardian*, September 9, 2015, https://www.theguardian.com/commentisfree/2015/sep/09/turkey-refugee-crisis-christian-fortress-europe.

[53] Recep Tayyip Erdoğan, "When the World Failed Syria, Turkey Stepped In. Now Others Must Help," *The Guardian*, May 23, 2016, https://www.theguardian.com/commentisfree/2016/may/23/world-failed-syria-turkey-refugee-crisis.

in its neighborhood. Turkey is not an exception, yet it is a first country that had a shot at membership. Innovation then seems to be centered on selecting more convenient "indicators of success" rather than building a community in which shared future-making is possible. Planning and investment became a replacement strategy. The conversation about temporalities (what should we do now, what can be postponed to later) thus easily translates into modes of action, which enable or foreclose direct connection and relationships of rights and responsibilities. The 2016 refugee deal has been a yet another reminder that European integration happens with selective approach to rights and obligations of its participants. As we will see in the next chapter, even those are who have freshly graduated from accession process do not feel obliged by many articles of the EU constitution.

8

Can We Trust Turkey?

When in September 2015 a professor from Turkey delivered a keynote address at a dinner in Prague, he left some audience members surprised. Speaking at a foreign policy symposium of a leading research institute, he discussed geopolitical restructuring in the Middle East and the possible end of the Sykes Picot, an agreement that has almost a century earlier redrawn a map of the region. Importantly, he talked about refugees and *criticized* the EU migration policy. The gathering he addressed consisted of delegates of the conference, Czech and foreign diplomats, other government officials, and policy analysts. His remarks were not addressed just to anyone in the world. He was speaking in an EU member state and delivering a message mainly for the EU citizens. A few months earlier the Czech TV screens showed images of tens of thousands of Middle Eastern men and women arriving to Europe, and headlines about hectic policy meetings trying to stop them. Very few eventually found refuge in the Czech Republic. Things were worse than this—top representatives of state openly dismissed the rights of people fleeing the war to claim refuge and repeatedly excluded Arabs and Muslims from the possibility of belonging in Europe. And while the number of participants of this high-level dinner gathering did not endorse the dominant political discourse on migration, they were still struck when the professor reminded them, that *Europe* realized too late that there *are refugees*, and something has to be done to help them. With the speech over and the conversations resuming in smaller groups, one delegate said he was shocked. Another wondered: "Why was he so negative?" The most pressing question seemed to be: "Why did not he talk more about situation in the country?" They *did* expect the professor from Turkey to be critical, but more of his president, or situation with academic freedoms, not of the European Union.

Prague is a city admired by many visitors and cozy for many of its residents. It is rich on greenery and ranks high on various indexes of "good life." By Istanbul standards, its public spaces might be considered quiet. This might not be for the lack of ambition to be otherwise. The airport regularly prides itself in multiplication of flights, new shopping malls and office buildings announce themselves through busy construction work, and the city council has only recently started thinking more loudly about impacts of mass tourism. On New Year's Eve, the blast of petards can easily be confused for sounds of war. On better days, Prague offers peaceful vistas of people socializing on the river-front or riding water-bikes. Visitors from Istanbul often note how soothing it feels to walk around a city where not much seems to be happening. Prague is home to many beautiful palaces, named after members of aristocratic families they used to belong to. Many now serve as schools or other public institutions. Prague can be very Czech and very international. Every single day one can see a unique artwork or attend a talk of a scientist coming from around in the world. Sometimes, the workshop rooms are half empty—so many possibilities the city offers to talk to others.

Many Czech journalists or policy makers have read the news of Turkey in the past years via the prism of suppression of public protest and incarceration of intellectuals. Such news is inseparable from the repeatedly invoked memory of 1989, a time which opened possibility of public speaking, for (almost) anyone on (almost) anything. Many things on post-1989 developments in former state-socialist countries remain contested. There are many debates about disappointments with the process of democratization. Untouchability of freedom of speech and association is one of few things on which the policy circles, and especially the people engaged in debates about European integration, find agreement.

Debates held in Prague offer many productive moments for thinking about Turkey's possibilities of becoming. The city after all is a capital of a state, which has joined the European Union in the so-called "eastern" or "big bang" enlargement. On average, it is one of the wealthiest postsocialist states.[1] It is also often categorized as a very reluctant European.[2] This chapter brings together fragments of discussions held at the time when the EU-Turkey refugee deal was in the making. These were turbulent times. In international forums but also in statements to domestic constituency, the Czech diplomacy vehemently

[1] Question of decent wage and living standards is a regular item on political agenda and so are the concerns about growing precariousness of working conditions.
[2] There is a rich repository of polls showing fragility of the Czech belonging in EU-rope. To provide one illustration: in a recent EU-wide poll (spring 2019 Eurobarometer), citizens were asked "When you think of the EU, what feeling first comes to mind?" They could choose from four options: hope, fear, confidence, doubts. The Czech society scored as the most "doubtful," https://europarl.europa.eu/at-your-service/files/be-heard/eurobarometer/2019/emotions-and-political-engagement-towards-the-eu/report/en-flash-2019.pdf.

argued against EU-wide solidarity mechanisms. While this policy was opposed by many intellectuals and some politicians, rejection of asylum seekers has gradually become a right and so did expectation that the others have a duty to respect this right.[3] The refugees were not rejected because there would already be too many. In fact, in the crisis year, there have been less than two thousand applications and earlier years were not much different. The Prague debates offer an opportunity to think again about knowing and (in)difference. To take advantage of this opportunity, we will need to introduce a few names and places that usually do not make an appearance in books on Turkey and the European Union. I promise to keep only the essentials in, knowing very well that readers interested in Turkey already had to do a lot of work to learn its names and places.

Migrancy in the Czech Context: Some Are Welcome, Most Are Not

There is no easy way to get asylum in the Czech Republic. Those who attempt to get it, or facilitate others' access, stand against a thick fence woven of ethno-nationalist conception of belonging, relative distance from a potential area of flight, and a seemingly endless repertoire of arguments justifying the low numbers. There is no physical barrier preventing entry, the country shares borders only with other EU members. Within the EU, the border checkpoints are used sporadically—in times of emergencies. It is the cluster of national narratives and institutional framework tasked with guarding the territory that serves the purpose. So does the fact that the country's southern neighbors have built walls. And while the Czech numbers cannot be compared to those in Italy or Turkey, they are *related* to them, as activists for the right of entry often remind us. This is what we will explore in this chapter—the relationship between the numbers, or, more precisely, some stories that could explain why there are so few refugees in the Czech Republic. As we will study these stories, the problem of (assuming) intentionality in complex settings that accompanies us from early pages of this book will hopefully be visible from a new angle.

The 2015 "crisis" headlines might have created the impression that migration is something new for the Czechs,[4] yet their recent history has been shaped by multiple flights, expulsions, and shifting borders. In its present borders, the Czech

---

[3] I discuss this in more detail in "Refugees and fish fingers" (in preparation).
[4] Unless otherwise stated, throughout the text I use "Czech" as a marker of citizenship, not of ethnicity.

state exists since 1993. As in the case of any other state, its ethnic make-up has been shaped by earlier histories and subject to repeated reconstructions. Before they established the 1993 republic (or renewed the Czech independence, as the calendar of public holidays tells us), the Czechs were one of the two constituent communities in a state called Czechoslovakia. In this state, established in 1918, as Austro-Hungarian empire was ending, the Czechs and the Slovaks were not the only ethnicities—yet the others, including the Jews, the Roma, the Ruthenians had, as collectives, less say on public affairs.[5] Hierarchies of belonging shaped also the early republican asylum policies. What the historian Michal Frankl called "prejudiced asylum" has been marked by prioritizing ethnic kinship and wider interests of the elite in power.[6] In the Second World War, Czechoslovakia was briefly split—the western part (present Czech Republic) became a protectorate annexed to the German Reich and the eastern part (present Slovakia) became a formally independent Nazi ally. Citizens deemed uncomfortable (including the Jews and the Roma) were sent to death and labor camps. After the war, most of the Germans, almost one-third of the country's population, were deported.[7] In the state-socialist period, many citizens emigrated to the West. When some of them started, after 1989, exploring options of return, they felt unwelcome. As Madeleine Hron described, part of Czech society felt that they had betrayed the nation when they were fleeing to a better life and leaving their compatriots behind.[8] Past migrations are still politically divisive. Migration is a recurring theme in the re-enactments of the Czech(o)Slovak past and it almost always makes an unsettling appearance. In the early 1990s, when Czechoslovakia switched from state-socialism to market-capitalism, support for refugees was not contested. Some of the founders of the first NGOs that worked in this realm were affiliated to the regime opposition during the era of authoritarian socialism. Helping refugees has been a great way of exercising the newly possible freedom of association. In the memories of Czech refugee defenders, refugees from wars in Yugoslavia in the early 1990s were welcomed and helping them was rarely contested. As veterans of the movement recall, Czechs have felt also

---

[5]   An idea of a unitary "Czechoslovak nation" as opposed to Czech and Slovak communities was often floated. Some of this is discussed in Mary Heimann, *Czechoslovakia: The State That Failed* (New Haven: Yale University Press, 2009); Michal Frankl, "Prejudiced Asylum: Czechoslovak Refugee Policy, 1918–1960," *Journal of Contemporary History* 49, no. 3 (2014): 537–55.

[6]   As Frankl notes in "Prejudiced Asylum" Slavs were the preferred group as, among else, the early republican leadership believed this would be a way of bringing democracy to Russia.

[7]   Discussed briefly in Judt, *Postwar* and of course, subject to extensive debate of historians and sociologists, to which, for reasons of space, we will not go in this chapter.

[8]   Madeleine Hron, "The Czech Emigre Experience of Return after 1989," *Slavonic and East European Review* 85, no. 1 (2007): 48–78.

certain cultural affinity to people coming at that time. But that period soon came to close.

In the middle of the second decade of the twenty-first century, a time when the EU-Turkey refugee deal was discussed, public opinion polls showed that the Czechs have been reluctant to accept any refugees at all.[9] But when they were asked about particular ethnicities, the Ukrainians trumped the Middle Easterners by a wide margin. This perception has been shaped by a sense of cultural and historical proximity. While the Ukraine has not made it among the list of countries that could become EU members in the near future, it has certainly received, especially in the post-2013 (Maidan) period, sympathies of significant part of society, who saw analogies between the recent Russian intervention and the 1968 Soviet occupation of Czechoslovakia. It is often said in milieus of people discussing migration, that Muslims do not come here (and are not invited here) because they are not here yet.[10] Ethnic or cultural belongings and respective representations of historical trajectories that bind "ours" with "theirs" are important part of discussions. But all migrants, regardless why they come, and where from, are foreigners, whose presence needs to be justified and explained.[11] Not all justifications get the same level of legitimacy. When Czechs are asked under what conditions foreigners could get residence in the country, options such as education or business are considered more acceptable justifications than staying "just because they like it here."[12]

The entry in the European Union in 2004 is often valued for easing of travel restrictions.[13] For the Czech migration regime this has meant that the country has now become part of a system, in which asylum applications should be processed in the first EU state they reach.[14] This rule is often exculpatory, as most refugees

---

[9] In polls taken by CVVM (The center for public opinion research at the Czech Academy of Sciences) from September 2015 to October 2016, between 50 and 63 percent rejected that the country should take refugees from countries experiencing war. The Roma and the Arabs are the least liked national group (CVVM 2019).

[10] In the last population census, two-thirds of the ten and half million nation declared Czech or Moravian (5 percent) nationality/ethnicity, a little over 1 percent Slovak, with other affiliations (Ukrainian, Vietnamese, Polish, German, Hungarian) under 1 percent. In that same census, dominant religion was no religion. Those who declare as religious are mostly Christian, although significant part of the religious does not claim affiliation to any particular denomination. Dominant foreigner groups are Slovaks and Ukrainians, both counting, according to official records, a few hundred thousand, although the actual numbers, for Slovaks especially, might be higher. While there are some Muslims, their numbers are a negligible portion of population.

[11] Wilding, "Transnational Ethnographies and Anthropological Imaginings of Migrancy," 331–48.

[12] CVVM, "Názory veřejnosti na usazování cizinců—březen 2018," https://cvvm.soc.cas.cz/media/com_form2content/documents/c2/a4586/f9/ov180411.pdf.

[13] In the post-1989 period, Roma have often been blamed for preventing Czechs' free movement—when some of them asked for asylum in West Europe/North America, the latter responded with visa obligations for the country (reference).

[14] In the EU terminology, this is called the Dublin system.

from the south first arrive to the Mediterranean states. As migration scholars note however, this is an internal EU measure—the Geneva refugee convention does not include any such stipulation.[15] The Ministry of Interior has become the key agency making decisions about the Czech migration policy. A comprehensive study of the first two decades of Czech immigration policy argued that one should not overlook that given the pre-1989 tasks of the institution, "already the fact, that it is possible to cross the borders, is perceived as a very accommodating and liberal step."[16] When the 2015 crisis erupted, other institutions, including the prime minister's office and Ministry of Foreign Affairs, were present in the conversation, though the leverage their teams were willing and able to insert into the debate had been much smaller.[17] I am not sure whether this could be explained mainly by the path dependency—political constellation and position (and powers) of the institutions in the public administration system do play a significant role.

What is rather certain is that asylum continues to be something the country awards based on its own needs, not on the needs of those who seek it. Moreover, already in 2011 Alice Szepanikova's research showed preference toward "refugees whose neediness is pre-approved by international humanitarian agencies [. . .] as opposed to those, who come spontaneously in a manner that is hard for authorities to control."[18] The notions of *choice, the right to choose,* has resonated strongly in the post-2015 debate. The low rates of asylum awarded have been justified by claims that the Middle Eastern refugees do not choose to come to the Czech Republic. This is partly true—in some contexts it is more common for migrants to head toward places where they can rely on more support from diaspora communities. At the same time, it was maintained that the country has the right to choose who comes in. This claim has support in the overall set-up of international system: a state has a prerogative to control movement across borders. But things are a bit more complicated. A Czech

[15] Geoff Gilbert, "Why Europe Does Not Have a Refugee Crisis," *International Journal of Refugee Law* 27, no. 4 (2015): 531–5; James Hathaway, "James C. Hathaway on the 1951 Refugee Convention," The Ethics Centre, 2017, https://ethics.org.au/james-c-hathaway-on-the-refugee-convention/.
[16] Tereza Kušníráková a Pavel Čižinský, "Dvacet let české migrační politiky: liberální, restriktivní, anebo ještě jiná?" *Geografie* 116, no. 4 (2011): 497–517, 513. The authors thus urge to abandon the "liberal vs. restrictive" framework often used in Czech literature on migration, as the meaning of those terms often depends on positionality and path dependency, contexts, in which they emerged and cannot grasp current reality.
[17] When, after 2015, the Czech Ministry of Foreign Affairs appointed a plenipotentiary for migration affairs, her office was so understaffed that she was often personally picking up visitors at the reception and preparing tea/coffee for them.
[18] Alice Szcepanikova, "From the Right of Asylum to Migration Management: The Legal-Political Construction of 'a Refugee' in the Post-Communist Czech Republic," *Europe-Asia Studies* 63, no. 5 (2011): 789–806, 804. See also Alice Szczepanikova, "Between Control and Assistance: The Problem of European Accommodation Centres for Asylum Seekers," *International Migration* 51, no. 4 (2012): 130–43.

Migration Policy Strategy introduced in 2015 and prepared, somewhat ironically, with the support of the EU federal funds, stipulates the Czech determination to support "legal" migration—more specifically, one through which "the Czech Republic can satisfy the needs of domestic labor market."[19] This strategy also pledged to "maintain limited level of harmonization on Union level in this area" and rejected "introduction of compulsory tools of solidarity." Thus, when the European Commission proposed a mechanism to relocate some asylum seekers from camps in Greece and Italy, Czech Republic was one of the states that fought vigorously against the measure. High-level government representatives argued that the European Commission "underestimated the explosive effect, hidden in a matter so sensitive, as placing refugees to individual member states."[20] Further, the argument goes, the country has an established track-record in providing aid: "Czech brand works," as a high-level government official put it.[21] Rejection of (any) policy that would bring more refugees to Czech Republic was supported across political spectrum. Yet, while the country already had a multifaceted system of government and nonstate agencies providing development and humanitarian aid abroad, a national platform of NGOs working with migrants pointed out several times that the Czech Republic has not really been meeting its own commitments.[22]

In that crisis year of 2015, as it seemed that number of asylum seekers in the country might increase, the dominant response of the Czech state has been to enact security precautions, with some government representatives engaging in dehumanizing rhetoric.[23] These debates unfolded at the backdrop of regular "breaking news" of terror attacks around Europe. In protest, scientists, housewives, artists, and others signed petitions, penned commentaries, and organized public debates and demonstrations. The groups often overlapped, emerged spontaneously and some of their members were active on various fronts—donating money, traveling to the Balkans, or helping around Prague

---

[19] Ministry of Interior of the Czech Republic, *Strategie migrační politiky ČR*, 2015, http://www.mvcr.cz/clanek/strategie-migracni-politiky-cr.aspx.

[20] Vláda.cz, Komentář předsedy vlády Bohuslava Sobotky k výtkám Evropské komise. Vláda České republiky, June 6, 2017.

[21] Tomáš Prouza,"Kvóty migrační krizi nevyřeší," *Právo*, May 25, 2015.

[22] Consortium of NGOs Working with Migrants "Migration Manifesto," 2015, http://www.migracnim anifest.cz/en/index.html.

[23] Even the more liberal voices in the government made statements justifying outrageous measures. At one point, when the Czech police "registered" a group of new migrants by writing numbers on their forearms, the then prime minister Sobotka responded to a journalist asking whether, for example, the Jewish community might not have reason to be critical of such measures by stating that "But Czech Republic never organized holocaust. We were its victim" (Interview with the PM Sobotka for daily *Pravo*, September 2015, https://www.novinky.cz/domaci/379769-pomahame-ale-ma-to-sve-meze-okrikovani-odmitam-rika-premier-sobotka.html).

Main train station (*Iniciativa Hlavák* notably) through which people were passing further to Germany. Because yes, Czech Republic has mostly been a transit zone—and this posed many dilemmas for volunteers who wanted to support refugees.[24] One activist, a woman in her fifties, who has been a part of several initiatives, and helped around the train station, summed up concerns of many when she said: "We often wondered whether we should just buy them a ticket to go further, or talk them into asking for asylum here. What is the right thing to do?" Her concern was, that if public discourse is dominated by anti-Arab/Islam[25] sentiment, and NGOs have been accused of "importing migrants," maybe it is not responsible to ask anyone to stay. It seemed, however, impossible to convince those who had the power to grant the right to enter that they should do it. Refugee defenders received hate mail and were ridiculed and asked to "take them home"; on one occasion, a minister joked about his more refugee-friendly colleague in government stating that the latter "must have a big flat."[26]

Talking about the EU-Turkey Deal: Capitulation and Pact with the Devil

Discussions about agreement with Turkey have then provided space for airing views about much wider set of questions related to mobilities, future of Europe, and the Czech place in it. Many proposals were made in the debates but their diversity had their limits. Suggestion that the Czech Republic could accept more refugees have been in minority, and those coming from places in decision-making positions have been almost negligible.[27] Similarly, a notion that Turkey could eventually become a member state of the Union has been almost absent from the realm of "realistic" proposals. It seemed that possibilities of Turkey and refugees to become part of the Czech space, or the European space as imagined in the Czech debates, were guided by similar considerations.

---

[24] Some have been recorded at the V4Revue's #humansonthemove blog, for example, Zuzana Pavelkova, "Will Allah Open the Border if the Politicians Don't?" *V4Revue*, 2016, http://visegrad revue.eu/will-allah-open-the-border-if-the-politicians-dont/.

[25] In everyday discussions, the two are often used interchangeably.

[26] For more, see Lucia Najslova, "The Czech Case: Solidarity Yes, But Twelve is Enough for Now," in Tamas Boros and Hedvig Giusto (eds), *The Flexible Solidarity: How Progressive Parties Handled the Migration Crisis in Central Europe* (Brussels and Budapest: FEPS and Policy Solutions, 2017).

[27] The analysis in this chapter builds on material from 2015/16. It is fair to suggest that in the following years refugees found a bit more defenders from the rows of parliamentarians and some government representatives, yet overall policy has not changed.

There are many avenues through which we could describe the anti-refugee campaigns. Not sharing a border with any nonmember state and not having become a home, in previous decades, to any significant number of people from the Middle East could perhaps be some of the reasons that explain reluctance of political leadership to consider incoming Syrians as "our" task. They can, however, barely justify the outbursts of hate speech and its legitimization from highest echelons of state representation, such as when Miloš Zeman, the country's president shared a podium with the leader of far-right initiative named *We don't want Islam in the Czech Republic*, especially as this happened on anniversary of November 17, a Czech national holiday commemorating suppression of student resistance in 1939 (against Nazism) and 1989 (against state-socialist authoritarianism). At the time when the 2015 panic started, the most numerous non-Czech ethnicities—Slovaks and Ukrainians—were also considered European. One of many paradoxes that accompanied debates around 2015 was that one of leaders of antirefugee mobilizations has been Tomio Okamura, a citizen of Czech-Japanese background. Prior to entering politics, Mr. Okamura had been known as an avid promoter of international tourism (mobility). He had also spoken publicly about his own experience with the pain of xenophobia and racism.

We could follow with many other snapshots, but perhaps it is time to turn to a more comprehensive summary of the voice of the people. The parliament discussed agreement with Turkey on several occasions in the fall of 2015 and spring of 2016. Security of the Czech Republic has been a primary frame through which the deal was interpreted. There was little concern for impact of the deal on Turkey. This was a situation in which migrants (especially the Muslim ones) were not supposed to come to Europe, and if they already were in Europe, they were not supposed to come to the Czech Republic. A deal with a third country seemed like an option. But if this book has so far posited that keeping migrants outside of the EU (or a specific member state) had been a preferred trajectory, let me emphasize, that this is not an outcome of a singular intentionality. When the government presented its position and asked for support of the deal, one parliamentarian called it a "capitulation," another a "pact with the devil, in addition signed unfortunately with our own blood."[28] Another asked: "Do we want Europe to be dependent on Turkey?"[29] The Member of the Chamber of

[28] MP Marek Černoch (Usvit), Chamber of Deputies, Session March 22, 2016 (PSP, p. 10).
[29] MP Helena Langšádlová, Chamber of Deputies, Session March 22, 2016 (PSP, p. 27).

Deputies Zdeněk Soukup said that after watching a television report on EU-TR summit:

> As a European, and, I emphasize European by rational choice (*Evropan z rozumu*), it has been long since I felt so humiliated. The Turkish president is giving us ethics lessons on a TV screen.[30]

But Soukup's sense of humiliation does not spring from understanding that the EU states have done little for people fleeing war. He continues his intervention with a list of Turkey's leaders' statements and human rights violations (including those not committed), finishing with a question for the Czech PM: "Mr. Prime Minister, do you trust such a partner?"

The proceedings in both chambers placed demands on Turkey and the EU institutions. And while it was generally accepted that the Czechs should also help, taking any significant number of refugees was not on the agenda. The help was supposed to happen outside the territory. In fact, when the Chamber of Deputies voted on a related resolution, the article stipulating opposition to EU-wide relocation mechanism received the biggest number of votes (149 of the 150 present). The Chamber of Deputies rejected visa liberalization for Turkish citizens and did not say a word on accession process. The first article stipulates the parliamentarians' opposition to compulsory relocation, the second asks the Czech government to provide humanitarian assistance maintaining security of the EU—such as by provision assistance in camps in Jordan.[31] Another parliamentary chamber, the Senate, asked Turkey to do more work for refugees. It also stipulated that aid has to be controlled and visa liberalization cannot receive a green light without fulfillment of conditions. Again, there is not a word on accession process.[32] Many representatives did not hide their uneasiness at not being able to choose who can come in. The late senator Kubera was cheered up to hear that number of young Spaniards are moving to the Czech Republic:

> [I]f they would, Mr Prime Minister, count into those quotas also the young Spaniards, Swedes and Germans, IT crowd, young people who are moving here, that would be quite nice. Those are the people we would need here.[33]

---

[30] MP Zdeněk Soukup (ANO movement), Chamber of Deputies, Session March 22, 2016 (PSP, p. 26).

[31] Poslanecká sněmovna ČR, "Usnesení PS č. 1144," March 22, 2016, https://www.psp.cz/sqw/text/te xt2.sqw?idd=82733.

[32] Senát Parlamentu ČR, "373. Usnesení Senátu," March 16, 2016, http://senat.cz/xqw/webdav/pss enat/original/79174/66562.

[33] Senate of the Czech Republic, p 17; In May 2019, Mr Kubera (ODS) as the head of the Senate attended a commemoration event for victims of Holocaust in Terezín (Theresienstadt). A speech he gave there included a line: "Totality, intolerance to other races, other opinions, can and does have

In the parliamentary proceedings, the accession process has been brought up rarely and if so, it was mainly by parliamentarians who wanted to make a point that Turkey does not belong to Europe. Some portrayed the visa liberalization as a security threat and a "too expensive bribe," for which "we" are anyway not going to get anything long lasting. Importantly, none of the chambers of the parliament reflected the dynamics the EU approach creates in Turkey. The pledge to help Turkey's democracy seemed to have evaporated completely. There was little reflection that the EU cannot possibly have a leverage to support human rights and democratic standards if it fails the refugee test and if its main priority regarding Turkey is that the latter keeps the refugees in.

The rhetoric that dominated in and after 2015 has been one of self-defense, as if people and things were being imposed on the country. As noted earlier, in the fall of 2015, the country's diplomacy rejected a proposal for an EU-wide relocation system.[34] In one interview for a newspaper, a deputy prime minister and chairman of the Christian Democratic Party compared the relocation scheme to the "Munich agreement"—a national trauma from the times before the outbreak of the Second World War remembered as a betrayal, a decision about Czechoslovakia without its presence and something forced upon it.[35] With a bit of simplification we could see analogies between symbolism of Munich and Sèvres in the respective Czech and Turkish debates.[36]

Trust has been an important term in these proceedings. Coincidentally, in 2015/16 the Czech Republic presided over meetings of the Visegrad Group. The main slogan of its program was "trust" and "togetherness." One of the seven priorities read: "active practicing of the solidarity principle in the EU."[37] Parliamentarians questioned whether Turkey can be trusted and insisted that

---

a very different shape today. For example veiled in words such as ecology, environment, gender equality, political correctness and multiculturalism."

[34] The mechanism became EU law despite the Czech (and three other members') "no" vote. And while the Czech reluctance to share responsibility has been a subject of much critique, the European Commission filed a lawsuit against the Czech position only in January 2018. "Žaloba za kvóty Česko netěší, pořád je ale možná dohoda, tvrdí ministerstvo zahraničí," January 4, 2018, https://www.iro zhlas.cz/zpravy-domov/cesko-migrace-kvoty-zaloba_1801041814_mos.

[35] Lidovky.cz, "O nás bez nás. Kvóty jsou jako Mnichov," May 5, 2016. https://www.lidovky.cz/belobra dek-o-nas-bez-nas-kvoty-jsou-jako-mnichov-rusko-pouziva-migraci-jako-zbran-g1u-/zpravy-dom ov.aspx?c=A160505_110041_ln_domov_ELE. (The vice-PM also adds, that it is unfair to say the Czechs are not showing solidarity).

[36] I am not suggesting that the Sèvres treaty and Munich agreement had similar drivers and consequences. The point of analogy is to make the Czech context a bit more comprehensible for a reader primarily familiar with Turkish/Ottoman realia.

[37] Ministry of Foreign Affairs of the Czech Republic, *Program of the Czech Presidency of the Visegrad Group 2015–2016*.

the money has to be controlled. As noted in previous chapter, the money sent to Turkey for Syrians is mainly controlled by the EU as Turkey has only advisory role in the trust fund.

Refugees were not supposed to come to the Czech Republic, and thus there have been continued doubts whether Turkey would really use the EU money in a proper way. Such question resonated in media coverage of the issue. More than once a journalist would start the conversation with a variation of "Can we trust Turkey?" What they meant was, whether Turkey would use the EU funds to *really* make sure that refugees would stop coming. When I was asked for a comment, I sometimes responded with a counter-question: "Can Turkey trust the EU?" What often followed were a few seconds of silence and then a variation on *What do you mean*? Sometimes I would follow with an answer right after the question and say that the European Union is not perceived as a credible interlocutor due to steps it has taken earlier in the accession process. And often I wondered, how is it possible that conclusions reached by the many scholars of the relationship get permanently questioned, and have to be explained from scratch.

Friends and acquaintances in Turkey to whom I recounted such conversations were genuinely entertained. *Do they really ask you that?* From a perspective of an academic or a practitioner of refugee integration programs in Turkey, such questions, posed in Prague, can surprise, often entertain, but mostly sound absurd. As already noted, many supporters of Turkey's European integration have seen the refugee deal as a betrayal—of both the EU (declared) values and of its commitment to Turkey. Questioning Turkey's trustworthiness by interlocutors who themselves reject refugees cannot be seen as a credible attempt to defend refugee rights. As we have seen in earlier chapters, Turkey's accession process is based on a future-oriented imaginary that it could belong if it meets the criteria. Debates about refugees in the EU show that trust is a problematic issue between the member states—it is not just a thing disputed between the EU and Turkey. If one reads these discussions through a lens of the accession process, one cannot help mourning for a possibly lost future. Moreover, rejecting refugees and rejecting Turkey seem to have similar drivers.

There is another angle to the story. It was often suggested by Czech (and other EU) policy makers and commentators that Turkey is "blackmailing" them. This referred to repeated announcements by the Turkish president that he would send the refugees EU-rope's way. If we think about blackmail in the conventional meaning of the word, then it is a situation in which one party is in possession of some information about the other party and threatens to disclose it publicly unless the former obliges with demands for financial settlement or other favors.[38] But the present situation is different. It is not a secret that the EU states are reluctant to admit more refugees, hence, one cannot blackmail them by revealing this. At the same time, even if we consider "blackmail" a problematic label in this context, EU policy makers read statements of Turkey's leadership as acts of intimidation. Suggestions that if the EU does not satisfy demands, Turkey will send refugees its way are not exactly in line with the standard script of amicable conversation between friends who claim to be building a shared future. Moreover, in a situation in which it is clear that conversations about migration and cultural cohesion are a weak spot for the EU, something it is not able to handle, announcements that Turkey might send refugees Europe's way sound to many observers as an exploitation of an already difficult situation.

Suggestion of possibility to "threaten by refugees" then perhaps requires separate attention. The literature on migration abounds with texts documenting government practices of presenting refugees as an extra toll on the (potential) host societies. After all, already the 1951 Geneva convention binding signatory states to cooperate in managing situations in which large groups suddenly have to flee one territory speaks of "burden-sharing" rather than "responsibility-sharing." But what would eventually be the difference between *being the one who threatens by refugees* and *being the one who is threatened*? This mere act is a unifying moment, one which brings both interlocutors to a shared registry of meanings.[39] It is here that the architecture of similarity emerges in its most obvious form.

Worlds of History: Everything Is Charles

The violence of exclusion often shows itself in acts made with an intention to include. This has been well-grasped by the French Lebanese writer Amin Maalouf:

---

[38] *Oxford Dictionary* of English: "the action, treated as criminal offence, of demanding money from someone in return for not revealing compromising information which one has about them."

[39] Suspicion and distrust has already been discussed in this book. The EU's growing reluctance to give a green light to Turkey's membership disappointed many an EU defender in Turkey. At the time of writing migration agenda has replaced accession and this has perhaps meant a frame reversal and different types of questions: "Can we trust Turkey?" instead of (or in parallel to) "Can we trust the EU?" Policy makers in the EU relied on Turkey and other neighbors to provide for/manage the refugees. Thus, focus on whether Turkey can be trusted bears perhaps some denial of failed commitments of the other side. For wider discussion of Orientalism in Central European context see Miloš Mendel, Bronislav Ostřanský and Tomáš Rataj (eds.), *Islám v srdci Evropy* (Praha: Academia, 2007).

I happened to be in Prague in December 1989, as the demonstrations against Ceausescu were beginning in Bucharest. Immediately there was a spontaneous expression of solidarity with the Romanian people in the Czech capital, which had recently been liberated in the "Velvet Revolution." On a sign near the cathedral someone had written in English: "Ceausescu, you don't belong in Europe!" The anger of the anonymous sign-writer was understandable, but his way of expressing it shocked me. I wanted to ask him on what continent a dictator *would* belong.[40]

As the second decade of the present century was coming to its close, Prague has again seen mass demonstrations, often called the biggest since the 1989. Yet, some observers might be similarly puzzled. Participants of some of the largest public protests in the recent Czech history asked for resignation of Prime Minister Babiš, some chanting, that he should "go back to Slovakia." Babiš was born in the Slovak part of former federation, something revealed in his accent and vocabulary, which often mixes Czech and Slovak words. Had Maalouf attended these demonstrations, he would probably have questions again.

We may continue with some more questions local observers were asking. While the country is a republic, a former minister and presidential candidate is often referred to as a *kníže* (duke/prince). This is not factually incorrect—he is a descendant of an aristocratic family. At the same time, while some address this politician as *kníže* to show respect and admiration, others use the same word in quotation marks to express disdain. In 2016, the Czech Republic celebrated 700th anniversary of the birth of Emperor Charles IV, who was just a decade earlier selected as "the greatest Czech" in a TV contest by viewers.[41] The then minister of culture remarked for a television:

> It is once in 700 years that we commemorate a personality, who is, also by the majority of the nation, considered the biggest personality of our history. Even after seven centuries there is still a lot here from Charles IV legacy.[42]

Commenting on the related celebrations for the emperor, historian Jan Adamec noted that "his name magically opens public budgets."[43] According to Adamec,

---

[40] Amin Maalouf, *Disordered World: A vision for the Post-9/11 World* (London: Bloomsbury, 2012), 41.

[41] This is a TV show modeled after the BBC original "the Greatest Britons," the Czech version aired in 2005. The TV audience can vote on historical personalities. In the Czech version, many votes (the exact number has not been publicized) were sent for one Jára Cimrman, a fictional figure. The team at the Czech TV (Česká televize) however decided to allow only "real" contestants. On a related note—a similar show ("The Greatest Slovak") aired over a decade later in the neighboring Slovakia, the public Slovak TV (RTVS) used Jozef Tiso, the president of the Nazi-affiliated Slovak state that existed during the Second World War, in one of the teasers, asking viewers to consider whether he was "a hero or a traitor." After uproar from intellectual quarters the teaser was withdrawn.

[42] http://tn.nova.cz/clanek/cesko-oslavi-700-narozeniny-karla-iv-bude-to-stat-71-5-milionu.html.

[43] Jan Adamec, "Was Charles IV. the Greatest Czech?" *visegradrevue.eu*, May 23, 2016.

The commemoration of 700th birthday anniversary of a medieval ruler unleashed old ethnocentric discourse and intensified the call for a wise, all-mighty and paternalistic sovereign.

The art historian Milena Bartlová observed that several parliamentarians proposed to commemorate not the king's birthday, but the wedding night of his parents as "merging of the Przemysl and Luxembourg dynasties."[44] Reflecting on wider debates on the theme held at this time, Bartlová wrote:

> To be sure—Charles IV of Luxemburgh certainly was, in the 14th century, a very important medieval king in the lands of the Czech crown. He was also a central figure in European politics at that time—as a Roman king and a caesar. But whichever operation of politics of memory, including a clear-cut case such as legislating on days to be officially remembered, are not concerned with how he "really" was. They only and solely relate to our present and power relations in it.[45]

The Czech cultural production is rich on fairy tales about good and wise kings and beautiful (and often also wise) princesses. It should not strike us that there are efforts to commemorate some. In Prague, Charles is everywhere—a bridge, a university, a square, a club/spa is named after him. It is just that the very same people who commemorate the kings with sweet nostalgia as a kind of fairy-tale heroes, often use the short-cut "sultan" to express their views on current Turkish politics. And while it is also citizens of Turkey who use that same word (sultan) to express their dissatisfaction with state of public affairs, we should not underestimate the element of "othering" in these debates, which, as we have already established, goes a long way. We should also note that not everyone in Czech society celebrates kings. The problematic point arises in the moment, when the very same speaker uses the word "sultan" as a shorthand for the *bad past* (and bad presence), while "kings" are symbols of something benevolent or benign. After all, the times of Charles IV as recorded by historians, would not be called a paradise of democracy by today's standards.[46] The differentiation, the us and them, the EU and Turkey, is a very complex process that involves several temporalities. "We" are not different only today—"our" pasts are also different. The stories of good kings and bad sultans are not just a random act of imagination. They fit naturally within the long-term reproduced institutionalized narratives.

---

[44] This, as the historian Jan Adamec reminded me, was also to symbolize the merging of the "Czech" (ours) with the "strange" (or, powerful and a European) dynasty, in result, an ideal combination.

[45] Milena Bartlová, "Slavit narození Karla IV. je nebezpečná hloupost," *a2larm.cz*, February 17, 2016. (Quote edited for clarity.)

[46] Adamec, "Was Charles IV the Greatest Czech?"; Milena Bartlová "Otec vlasti a stavitel mostu" Salon *Právo*, May 14, 2016.

Intermezzo / Interruption

We are sitting in a friend's kitchen in Ankara. A long conversation suddenly comes to a halt. We are looking at each other in disbelief. In the past few hours we rapidly went through music, common acquaintances, future of the world; one cup of tea replaced another. Now there are a few moments of silence. These come after the friend, Zehra, asked: "Why are you defending Muslims?" I wondered what she meant. Zehra, as long as I'd known her, has been critical of the Western Islamophobia. She has also been critical of Turkish Islamophobia. One of the first public protests she has ever joined was in support of the right of headscarf-wearing women to enter public institutions such as colleges, something they have been banned from doing until the beginning of the second decade of twenty-first century. So when she asked "Why are you defending Muslims," I first thought I did not hear her right and once she repeated the question, I simply did not understand it. Shortly before the question, I was describing to her the atmosphere in Czech public space, one in which anti-Muslim mobilization bore more than one similarity to the 1930s. Zehra's surprise was of a different order: she wondered whether I have noticed that there was now a strong demand from several public places in Turkey to adjust lifestyles to be more in line with the dominant religion, or political version thereof. Zehra expected me to know that some of those in Turkey who used to actively defend rights of the more conservative part of their society, now felt that their own lifestyles were under threat. I did know that. Or, perhaps it is more precise to say that I did hear and read about this concern and the question "Why are you defending Muslims" was one more reminder how deep it ran. In short, it has been difficult for the Czechs to understand or know about nuances of debates in Turkey. It has also been difficult for the Turks to understand discussions in Prague. Zehra did not know that many of the West European defenders of "our women" from the "Middle East invasion" were nowhere in sight when the rights of these women have been violated by the locals. Zehra did not know that the Charles University co-hosted a conference on the "MeToo" movement featuring speakers who openly dismissed and ridiculed any claims of people who have experienced gendered violence. Our misunderstanding happened between contexts in which we were speaking. It was a product of those contexts, the histories we saw and lived, the symbols we had been expected to defend. How could one conversation, even if it was long, sort out the pile of national narratives we lived in?

Knowing and In/difference

Let us now make a bit more sense of what the Czech debate about EU-Turkey relations tells us about wider framework of those relations. In the Czech debate about refugees and the EU-Turkey 2016 deal we have seen both acts of differentiation and acts of indifference. The former would be decisions on who does and does not belong informed by categories such as race or religion. The latter would be the act of not taking into account what happens elsewhere, such as the refusal to consider or even to see that if the Czechs do not accept the refugees, someone else has to. This indifference could well be categorized as something that "just happens." We have after all reviewed a few moments in which people realize during the conversation with one another that what they held as unimaginable can be often perfectly explained and justified. Although it is not always the case, surprises may result in understandings.

Indifference could, however, be considered as an active act. Let us start with three premises. First, there is no shortage of academic knowledge that migration is a difficult topic in every state in Europe. Researchers have amassed thick dossiers of notes and observations on various nuances on why migration is difficult to negotiate within the societies they studied—ranging from ethnic insecurities to economic uncertainty.[47] Second, this knowledge is not classified, one does not need a security clearance to access it. The findings are diffused in a variety of publications and public panels. Scientists are often invited to comment for wider audience, they also convene events for wider audience. Academics of course are not the only ones observing migration-related issues. The theme is of interest to a wide range of writers—travelers, NGO workers, parliamentarians, and citizens taking the opportunity to express their views on blogs or social media. And even if the nuances of the latest scientific work do not immediately reach wider audiences, the theme is out there. The stories of refugees as well as of the people who migrate for other reasons are publicly available, together with commentaries and more systematic research on their lives, and the joys, anger, frustration, and opportunities related to mobility. Third, while individuals may have selective access to knowledge about migration, the state bureaucracy should know it all. I do not suggest that the state has to be a repository that integrates all available knowledge. That has so far been the case probably only in science fiction, such as the Czech series *Návštěvníci* (The Visitors) that features an entity

---

[47] Referenced in previous chapter.

called *centrální mozek lidstva* (central brain of mankind).[48] In the current EU, including the Czech Republic, citizens can (but don't have to) read stories and scientific books. The state has a large enough apparatus to do this and clearly a constitutional commitment to make judgments based on careful consideration of evidence. The state also has the supreme authority to regulate movement of humans. It can pass and enforce laws and decide on who is (not) allowed to enter. Citizens can have opinions but only the state can decide which migration is permissible.

From these three premises, the grounds for seeing ignorance as an active disregard should be clear. But it all comes down back to knowledge. The apparatus that has the supreme right to decide upon movement also has the highest access to information, the highest capacity to analyze, centralize, to know. And if we do not dispute this thesis, then decisions on (denial of) entry have to be considered as active acts of indifference. Whereas any of the citizens spontaneously encountering each other have the right to ignore the particulars of the other's condition, the state, by the virtue of claims it makes on legitimacy and authority, cannot claim such right. So if individuals, including state servants, say "I do not really know what is going on," this could well be within the sphere of a rightful ignorance. A public servant can be as lost and confused as any citizen. But if we see that confusion and eventual rejection as a framework of state policy, then this is a different matter.

It is, however, also clear that a state is unlikely to lose its international legitimacy solely on the grounds of rejecting refugees. Representatives of states, the main units in system of regular meetings and adoption of actions, are legitimized by the assumption that they are speaking for the polities that appointed them. EU or UN meetings and voting sessions are not supposed to be random conventions of people who had a good idea or wanted to speak on an issue. They are guided by strict rules of national representation. In these meetings, claims are often made on shaping the universal, the worldly. By this recognized being in the world, a state also gets the ticket to shape the world, in ways that cross state borders. In the present system, states can potentially lose basic privileges related to recognition if they fail to sustain rights of their citizens or if they otherwise present a danger to other states.[49] It, however, seems from debate on migration that offering refuge to noncitizens is not an act that could shake state rights. In fact, refusal is accepted, disregarding refugees is something one can get away

---

[48] We will meet "the Visitors" again in Coda.
[49] This theme is discussed in Chapter 6 of the present book.

with. This again well documented. Scholars have written widely about growing focus on borders in search for an ability to control at least something.

And yet, if we put aside questions of intentionality and short-term benefits offered by political cycle such as points gained on anti-immigration rhetoric, it may well be the case that the state as a collective *does not know everything*. The collective singular is here to indicate that while the many individuals working at or providing services for public institutions can have various types of specific knowledge, as we saw in the fragments from Czech debates, the state as a body composed of these numerous institutions and practices *does not know* how to manage mobility in a nonviolent way. The 2015 panic in Europe after all showed that even borders, the state prerogative, could not be managed. So the only way to look at this with understanding is to accept that a state perhaps does not have one voice. Moreover, climate science and related sociopolitical analysis have already outlined futility of certain sovereignty discourses. The geographer Reece Jones aptly summed up these considerations: "climate change will be the border control of the future."[50] This necessarily brings us back to where this book started—to the fissures between particularistic and universal belongings. An avenue that offers itself as a path out of the seemingly irresolvable dilemmas of modernity and modernization is to give more attention to thinking about mobilities and belongings beyond the measurements of travels of people between places. If we understand, together with Anthropocene scholar David Chandler, "life itself as a mobility,"[51] then perhaps we are a step closer to seeing refugees, Turkey in the EU, or belongings in general more as a fact that needs to be recognized than as a problem to be solved. The misunderstandings as we saw them in stories presented in this chapter are not necessarily a product of active intention. While the EU and member state institutions do have an active policy of prevention of entry of refugees, this does not come with active policy of leaving them in one particular country. Barely anyone notices, that the EU-ropean "no entry" means that the people will still be somewhere. The individual participants of the relationship could hardly possess all the knowledge on the big picture. They can hardly understand everything and everyone. But what does the confusion tell us about states that represent them?

[50] Reece Jones, "Climate Change Will be the Border Control of the Future," *Quartz*, November 9, 2017, https://qz.com/1124055/climate-change-will-be-the-border-control-of-the-future/.
[51] David Chandler, "Forum 2: The Migrant Climate: Resilience, Adaptation and the Ontopolitics of Mobility in the Anthropocene," *Mobilities* 14, no. 3 (2019): 381–7.

Coda

A photograph captures four men in suits. Some are smiling, some are laughing, the vocabulary really depends on the viewer. One can also wonder whether what they are doing is a handshake or a fist-bump. The protagonists are high-level representatives of the Union and Turkey who have just held a summit and agreed to "accelerate relations."[1] How can this photograph help us make sense of what has been said on earlier pages of the present book? Some time ago the writer Susan Sontag observed that "Photographs may be more memorable than moving images, because they are a neat slice of time, not a flow."[2] But flows are what we live—although rarely on a constant speed and often with a pause when we get stuck on a particular image. For many readers, who regularly scroll the news from the world of diplomacy, this photograph might seem unremarkable. Summit results are usually presented by men, who wear suits and show a range of emotions—including anger, happiness, or neutrality. It is the pledge to "accelerate relations" that is perhaps more noteworthy. To a long-time student of Turkey-EU relations perhaps even this does not come as news. Have not such commitments been made many times? And yet this acceleration might become more difficult to imagine once we recall the multiplicity of relations between Turks and other Europeans. As the historian Charles King observed:

> People live the present as a grand improvisation—misunderstanding their predicaments, laughing when they ought to mourn, staying when they should leave and packing up their belongings when it would be better to stay at home.[3]

Institutions of course move in a different tempo than individuals, and the leaders in the photograph did not pledge to accelerate their personal trajectories but those of countries they represent. If we speak about the speed, we should also consider destination. Where exactly should the faster relationship take us? Let

---

[1]   Hande Fırat, "Turkey, EU Agree to Accelerate Relations: Erdoğan," *Hurriyet Daily News*, March 28, 2018.

[2]   Susan Sontag, *On Photography* (London: Penguin, 1977), 17.

[3]   Charles King, *Midnight at the Pera Palace: The Birth of Modern Istanbul* (New York: W.W. Norton & Co, 2014), 374.

us get help from basic physics, and the words it uses to describe movement.[4] Physicists distinguish between speed and velocity. Speed is a ratio of distance traveled over time; velocity takes into account whether one has actually moved away from the starting point. Acceleration then, is a measurement of velocity, not speed. To accelerate, one needs to change location. This could be up or down, left or right, forward or backward. If one just jumps up and returns to the same place, by the force of gravity, this will not mean changing location. In debates about movement of human collectives, it is fair to expect that the end point will be different than the starting point. While physicists can work with negative acceleration, in conversations about human belonging, moving on implies moving forward, toward something, or away from a difficult situation. But then, since human trajectories are messy, moving on could also mean returning to past, "to go back to the way things once were," as Rebecca Bryant vividly described in her ethnography of Cyprus.[5]

Where does *acceleration* stand in wider debates about social meanings of time, and our belonging in various time zones? Doing things fast and at faster pace has not been always considered as a good thing, on the contrary. The core of the critique seems to be that technological development and organization of economic production and exchange has made it increasingly difficult for an individual to make decisions or to be in control and the field of knowledge has not been an exception.[6] Speed can be oppressive. As the anthropologist Thomas H. Eriksen put it: "Everything that can be done quickly, threatens to do away with everything that must be done slowly."[7] What connects these critiques of speed of changes is an argument in defense of a possibility to choose. Such possibility, however, does not lie only in our individual psychologies, nor can it be "empowered" only by targeted trainings and teachings. It relies on wider socioeconomic processes, including access to material resources and the possibility (rather than necessity) of being mobile.[8] From this perspective, the world already is fast, and calls to accelerate deserve further attention.

---

[4] The website *The Physics Classroom* developed by Tom Henderson, a high school teacher in Illinois, provides useful tutorials for students and teachers of physics including kinetics, https://www.phy sicsclassroom.com/class/1DKin/Lesson-1/Acceleration.

[5] Bryant, *Past in Pieces*, 41.

[6] Graeber, *The Utopia of Rules*; Gary Cross, "A Right to Be Lazy? Busyness in Retrospective," *Social Research* 72, no. 2 (2005): 263–86. Appadurai, "The Right to Research"; Filip Vostal, *Accelerating Academia: The Changing Structure of Academic Time* (London: Palgrave, 2016).

[7] Thomas Hylland Eriksen, *The Tyranny of the Moment: Fast and Slow Time in the Information Age* (London: Pluto Press, 2001), 161.

[8] Some of this has also been addressed by Appadurai, "Grassroot Globalization and Research Imagination."

Before We Drift Toward Time Travel

This book walked through fragments of some of the many conversations happening in and about Turkey-EU relations. The detours into seemingly marginal spaces were not meant to suggest that the international (in which nation means the state) framework does not matter. On the contrary—the detours showed us just how important the decisions adopted by representatives of states are. They can enable fruitful exchanges between citizens or discourage them. We have also seen how every single decision builds upon or cannot really escape the thick network of earlier narratives, including Orientalist and Occidentalist, and very firm materialities of belonging. Manuscripts that let the states speak with one voice are still common in the library of international studies yet there is no dearth of accounts digging into "domestic dynamics" of the states and its impact on outcomes of their international cooperation. Scholars study political parties, civil society, public opinion, businesses, or social movements. The present ethnography of misunderstandings and denied belonging ventured into reporting on interactions of people who have tried to cross into the transnational space. Theirs has often been a rewarding journey— but not an easy one, as they have regularly been reminded of strength of the inter*national* framework. That framework might be enabling in many respects, as it offers protection and rights. But it can leave some protagonists abandoned when they strive to have conversations with counterparts from "the other side." In such transnational conversations, people are often expected to defend notions they did not subscribe to and reject beliefs they actually hold dear.

Understanding, as we saw on the previous pages, is perhaps the most difficult thing to do for many participants of Turkey-EU relations. It is not that they actively refuse—it just sometimes be comes too hard. In complex relations, there are way too many things to be understood. But if there are too many things and too little time, it is handy to have a compass. Such as assuming that if things do not work well, it is because one or more of the protagonists, or even the whole countries, came to the table with bad intentions. People of course *do* have various motivations. They sometimes come in peace and sometimes in anger. It is difficult, for a student of the international relations, to think of countries not as people but as complex systems composed of many people and objects. Even the best-informed students of politics cannot avoid shortcuts such as *Turkey wants this, the EU (or Germany, Slovakia, etc.) is not willing to provide that.* Perhaps it is not even possible to have conversations without such shortcuts. One cannot talk if every word should come with a footnote or an explanation in brackets. One cannot have a conversation without assuming that at least some meanings are shared. And this is where my point enters: the shared meaning I often witnessed in conversations on the relationship includes suggestions that *the EU does not want Turkey* and *Turkey does not want to reform*. It is on purpose that I do not say *Turks think the EU does not want them* and *EU-ropeans think Turkey does not want to reform*. Because such meanings and suggestions are shared across the national divide. Many Turks are skeptical of their governments' commitment to accession process, many EU-ropeans are disappointed with how their representative institutions have handled the accession process. And yet, it can be hard to avoid ascribing intentions. When participants of the relationship try to make sense of it, they can hardly avoid making claims on who is right and who is wrong. They can also hardly avoid being put into specific national boxes by other interlocutors. Sometimes, they end up defending those boxes (national markers) not because they would believe everything that has been ascribed to these markers, but because that is the way of defending their own specific liminal place in the world. They might not agree with all the structures and markers defining them in the eyes of the others. Saying "the EU is unfair to Turkey" does not mean that the speaker agrees with everything Turkey ever did. It means that the speaker feels the EU has not understood the context in which things in Turkey happen. Saying "Turkey is not European" does not have to be an act of hostility and exclusion. It can simply be a reflection on how the speaker understands Europeanness from what they have been socialized into throughout the many years of living in and with an entity built on the notion that it is "not like the East." In what follows, we will simply drift. I cannot be sure, but perhaps drifting is a good exercise in imagination—it might help us see what happens, if we discard hierarchies of analytical planes.

Synchronization: Can We Be on the Same Page?

We check the clock or a calendar when we run errands, when we want to meet others or agree with them on future visits or cooperation. As the sociologists John Berger and Thomas Luckmann observe, we also do it to "re-enter the reality of everyday life" after events that made us "disoriented" such as accidents.[9] Measurement units such as days or hours seem neutral and universal. It is probably not common to think of each and every time we

---

[9] Berger and Luckmann, *The Social Construction of Reality*, 40–2.

do this about *how* the clock and calendar were invented, or, to consider, that they *were* invented. Historians have noted linkages between the rise of mass capitalist production and standardization of time; international relations scholar Andrew Hom has in a recent article showed how the processes of standardization were connected to colonialities and establishment of sovereignty as a norm.[10]

Clocks continue to be political—not just because of how they were invented but also in their sensitivity to ongoing conflicts. In early spring of 2018, several newspapers ran a story of a six-minute slowdown in clocks across Europe. A dispute between Kosovo and Serbia had a bearing on the voltage in one European power grid.[11] A representative of ENTSO-E, a transmissions system operator, told *The Guardian*:

> [T]his average frequency deviation, that has never happened in any similar way in the Continental European power system, must cease. . . . This is beyond the technical world. Now there needs to be an agreement between Serbia and Kosovo about this lack of energy in the Kosovo system. You need to solve it politically and then technically.

The delay did not affect all countries. This European grid does not really respect EU frontiers and consists of five regional groups, which take the liberty to ignore even national borders. The biggest of the five is a continental group, which spans majority of EU states, parts of the Balkans and Turkey has an observer status. The second (not in order of importance) is the Nordic countries, which includes east Denmark, Finland, Norway, and Sweden. The third is the Baltic (and includes Estonia, Latvia, and Lithuania). The fourth is for part of the UK. Finally, Ireland and Northern Ireland have their own group.[12] As we express our surprise at the breach of conventional borders (Why is Turkey in the continental group? Why are the UK and Denmark split into different groups?), let us also note the

---

[10] Andrew Hom, "Hegemonic Metronome: The Ascendancy of Western Standard Time," *Review of International Studies* 36 (2010): 1145–70. Hom's article brings together an extensive amount of literatures on time. For an insightful recent fieldwork-based study that complicates the "Western hegemony" accounts of time see Matti Erasaari, "Time and the Other Time: Trajectories of Fiji Time," *History and Anthropology* (2018), DOI: 10.1080/02757206.2018.1445624.

[11] BBC, "Kosovo-Serbia Row Makes Europe Clocks Go Slow," March 7, 2018, https://www.bbc.com/news/world-europe-43321113; The Guardian, "European Clocks Lose Six Minutes After Dispute Saps Power from Electricity Grid," March 8, 2018, https://www.theguardian.com/world/2018/mar/08/european-clocks-lose-six-minutes-dispute-power-electricity-grid (Accessed March 22, 2019); I find it interesting that both BBC and *The Guardian* introduced the story with suggestion that there is now excuse for being late to work. Late modernity, always catching up. See also ENTSO web and consultations on risk preparedness https://www.entsoe.eu/news/2019/06/14/risk-preparedness-regulation/.

[12] The European Network of Transmission System Operators for Electricity (ENTSO-E) https://www.entsoe.eu/about/system-operations/.

suddenness with which the delay occurred. We rarely question the reliability of metrics or devices keeping us up to date. And yet, it happened, time just slowed down, no prior notice given. Or perhaps time continued undisturbed—it was just our knowing of it that went out of sync briefly.

We could find a number of other cases showing troubles of synchronization. In summer of 2018, a while after the Kosovo-Serbia incident, the European Commission opened a public consultation on question of summertime.[13] The purpose of such consultation was to solicit views of citizens on issues on agenda of policy makers. After receiving over four million responses (mostly from German citizens)[14] the Commission proposed that the summertime, sometimes called daylight savings time, be abolished. By April 2019 member states were expected to adopt the provisions, yet, at the time of writing, the process seems to be postponed. The European Parliament discussed the issue in spring of 2019, and it was then up to the member states to present their positions. At the time of the last edit of this coda, 2021 was scheduled as the year when seasonal changes could be discontinued. It is important to keep in mind that regardless of whether and when the change will happen, the EU will still be in three different time zones: GMT for the UK, Ireland and Portugal, GMT-1 for most of the continent, and GMT-2 for the states on its eastern end (from the Baltics in the north down to the Balkans).

The debate that accompanied this particular policy proposal showed how powerful the symbolism of clocks is and how much it invites reflection on wider societal issues. The EU as a collective can abolish seasonal time only if its members agree which time will be the default one, winter or summer? The member states have to carefully consider their options. Trade interests have been high on agenda in their proceedings. In Slovakia, some suggested to adjust to the decision taken by Austria, an important trading partner. A popular cartoon portal Cynical Monster (*Cynická obluda*)[15] posted an image of a peasant saying to himself: "Now we'll have bloody fights whether to introduce the same time as the Austrians will. . . . As if that one hour mattered with our twenty years of delay." The image and the tone are a common language the portal uses to comment on questions of country's modernity and catching up with the West. Austria has been for many Slovaks the first Western country they could visit after the fall of the Iron curtain.

[13] European Commission documents portal on the issue https://ec.europa.eu/transport/themes/summertime_en.

[14] Around 70 percent of the responses came from citizens of Germany, according to the Commission report "Public consultation on EU summertime arrangements, a report on the results" SWD(2018) 406 final.

[15] cynickaobluda.sme.sk.

The developments of 1989 did not change the land distance between Vienna and Bratislava but removed some physical barriers, including the barbed wire. Thirty years later one can commute easily, even faster, but some frontiers remain. The awareness of this lag is subject of vibrant debates in literatures on time and place called "post-socialism."[16] Becoming an EU member *is* a major change for both the (former) candidate and the older members. The act of granting/accepting membership, however, does not resolve all outstanding disputes. Membership, in other words, is not an ultimate arbiter of who and what belongs where.

Distance and Good Velocity: How Do We Know When We Are Closer?

Bearing in mind the problems of acceleration and complications of synchronization, let us now return to the wishes expressed by participants of the Turkey-EU summit who smiled at us from the image that opened this coda. A call for acceleration has often been made in conversations about Turkey and the EU. The accession process is frequently lamented as stalled, not really moving anywhere. For some participants of the relationship, such call expresses a sense of being left out or behind. It is a demand for proximity. At the same time, in conversations about Turkey and the EU, calls are often made to stop the accession process. The latter is often justified by protagonists' perception that a full accession is not possible and, thus, the participants should liberate themselves from the pressure and stop pretending. But what would it mean if things either stopped or started happening faster? In the more diplomatic routines, going faster often means that Turkey should "do the reforms" and Western Europe should "stop closing its door." In the fifteen years of accession talks, the participants of the relationship have, however, become increasingly aware that the "West" seems to have started walking backward. The perceptions of proximity, inclusion and exclusion, are informed also by this awareness.

If we take proximity as a possible endpoint of moving faster, there is not much good news. At the time of writing, accession talks are formally on and they continue in timelines shaped by domestic politics in the candidate and the member states and their expectations from EU cooperation. Toward candidate countries, the Union acts as *one* decision-maker, yet that decision is a product of

---

[16] Bailyn, Jelača and Lugarić, *The Future of (Post)Socialism*; Larisa Kurtović and Nelli Sargsyan, "After Utopia: Leftist Imaginaries and Activist Politics in the Postsocialist World," *History and Anthropology* 30, no. 1 (2019): 1–19.

relations and processes too messy to be calculated, predicted, or separated from each other. The election and campaign dynamics in member states, distribution of votes in federal institutions, as well as the many forms of bilateral relations these states and institutions have with Turkey move in pathways that link up to reinforce, or sometimes silence, each other. The public discourses in member states have different rhythms, clauses of EU law are enforced in varying intensity. Turkey, or any other candidate state, can rarely get priority attention and when they do become part of discussion, their aspirations are often read through layers of decision-making on other issues.

As we saw in the chapters of the Part Three, the 2016 refugee deal was a policy aimed at bringing the EU and Turkey closer. Eventually, the official reports ended up counting the bodies of those who did and did not cross and were used as evidence to report success. The drop in numbers of sea crossings has been presented as the most convincing evidence of success of this cooperation. The safe routes for refugees that were supposed to replace "irregular" ones barely materialized. Moreover, the movement across the EU-Turkey border, for refugees and citizens alike, continues to be regulated by permissions issued by the respective governments policing these borders and, arguably, there are hierarchies of privilege in crossing the border.

Temporalities in the multitude of overlapping Turkey-EU relationships can well be expressed through juxtaposing of *now* and *later*. What are the partners doing and what are they postponing? In diplomatic exchanges we see phases, fragments, iterations of mutual lecturing, and common concerns. Yet some of the joint policies do not seem to address commonalities. In the many conversations held at the theatrical stage of the EU-Turkey framework, we often see a combination of paternalism and recognition of the other's specific positionality. The latter perhaps opens more space for synchronization.[17] Acting jointly requires a common awareness of what has to be done now, and what can be postponed. Without such common awareness, connectivity does not disappear, but different expectations are placed on participants of the relationship.

Planning, in the debates about acceleration, has an irreplaceable role. Planning and development are a common part of nation-state toolkit. They are also core tools of the EU' being in the world, as an institution, ever since its founding declaration, all the way up to the present neighborhood, accession, and migration partnerships. Let us recall the hopeful language in the videos accompanying the

---

[17] For a conceptual discussion of patronizing versus recognizing discourses through the lens of "care," see Robinson, *Ethics of Care.*

Union's 2016 global strategy. The vision of a future as a destination where things fall into each other, make sense, and where everyone wins. This destination will be reached if we follow the outlined principles and causalities. The problem with this future is that things distant from now are projected in sets of relations we cannot really know will be there later. It is a form of seeing the future like we are used to seeing the past, through present optics and categories. But if planning is to prepare us for both the expected and the unexpected, and if nothing can be planned because the world is too complex, than what eventually would be the purpose of institutions?[18] Planning is not a bad thing. It is just that sometimes not much happens between the moment plans are announced and the (possibly very distant) moment in which that future is supposed to happen. If we take a page from scholarship of disasters (an appropriate diversion, as the relationship studied in this book is often discussed as one mired in crises), Roberto Barrios's observations are very telling: "defining what it means to recover successfully or rebuild better is sometimes more a matter of discursive power, hegemonic imagination, and the politics of knowledge that it is about disaster affected people."[19] Moreover, Barrios continues, "if disasters are products of a social system, then resilience building that emphasizes perseverance may, in effect, perpetuate development practices that shape disasters."[20] In the time between now and future, people are expected to adjust, but not at the same speed and not providing the same work.[21]

This, however, does not seem to be only a discourse of policy planners; it is also we as commentators, students, critics of policies who establish hierarchies of problems often based on insufficient understanding of what is at stake in issues/people/regions we choose to exclude or unintentionally do not take into account. As we have seen in several scenes described on previous pages, the growing abundance of information channels, acceleration in potential for connections, and reading each other's lives has not brought interlocutors of the many Turkey-EU relations on the same page. On the contrary, the communicative space abounds with hierarchies. A recent editorial attention-getter to a text urging Central European policy makers to take a tougher stance on their authoritarian allies reads:

> The most profound crisis facing the European Union today is the crisis of democracy in Central and Eastern Europe. Other EU crises such as the refugee

---

[18] Chandler, "Digital Governance in the Anthropocene."
[19] Roberto Barrios, "Resilience: A Commentary from the Vantage Point of Anthropology," *Annals of Anthropological Practice* 40, no. 1 (2016): 28–38, this quote p. 33.
[20] Barrios, "Resilience, a Commentary," 35.
[21] Including the work of interpretation (Graeber, *Utopia of Rules*).

crisis or the Eurozone crisis have—at least for the time being—abated, and Brexit has turned out to be more of a costly annoyance for the EU than the existential crisis many had feared.[22]

What is interesting is not just the emphasis on Central Europe, as the crisis that needs to be prioritized, but also the explicit statement that the other crises are not important anymore. It takes a few clicks to read, listen, and learn about everyday politics and life in neighboring or a more far-off state, but the technical connectivity has not delivered an unambiguous sense of common *we*. Saying, to a resident or a worker in an asylum camp in Greece, that "the refugee crisis has . . . abated" would sound like a suggestion from someone who must have read a very different newspaper, to put it diplomatically.

We are then left with a complex terrain in which the all-encompassing policy narratives and plans coexist with suggestions of people commenting on these plans to come up with different hierarchies of problems, often prioritizing one's immediate environ. As demonstrated by Ginette Verstraete, some of the existing connectivity networks enable artistic interventions that show precisely the limits of thinking about connectivity mainly in transactional terms.[23]

The Visitors and Their Differences

In *Návštěvníci* (The Visitors), a Czechoslovak TV series from the 1980s, an expedition from earth in the year 2484 travels to the earth of 1984.[24] Those coming from the future believe that if they manage to save one particular notebook belonging to a school kid who later, as they know from archives, became a respected scientist, they could prevent the impending catastrophe in 2484. Before taking the journey into the past, the visitors undergo preparation. They learn from museums about the peculiarities of life in the period, 500 years before their time, that are supposed to provide clues for their future survival. Yet even the best efforts to plan and adjust leave them with a few unexpected situations. The future humans are surprised that mankind uses money, because

---

[22] Visegradinfo.eu, "Friends Do Not Let Friends Kill Democracy," 2019, http://visegradinfo.eu/index.p hp/icon-articles/592-friends-don-t-let-friends-kill-democracy (Accessed July 10, 2019).

[23] Some of these are described by Ginette Verstraete, "Timescapes: An Artistic Challenge to the European Union Paradigm," *European Journal of Cultural Studies* 12, no. 2 (2009): 157–72. (There is a surprising lack of WoS records on cultural cooperation projects.)

[24] The show was coproduced with France, Switzerland, and West Germany. While the plot does happen in 1984, it does not contain any explicit references to George Orwell's book *1984*. Orwell's work was not widely available, this was a series for a wider audience.

in 2484 cash is considered obsolete. In one episode, when the visitors realize they need more of this old-fashioned means of exchange, they submit a request to *Centrální mozek lidstva* (the Central Brain of Mankind), an omniscient entity with many tasks in their time zone, which delivers banknotes not corresponding to the time they visited by mistake. Visitors travel to humanity's past to accomplish a particular mission, to save that notebook from fire, but the flash and thrill of the series is maintained by the many encounters between the world they know and the world they have entered. The series is rich on moments of discovery, crossing from the known and comfortable, perceived as "normal" to the unknown and potentially mind-opening.

Theirs is a journey between times, centuries, and yet, difference and encountering the unfamiliar is not scary, violent, or conflict-ridden. The encounters as presented by screenwriters are mostly in good faith; if misunderstandings occur, they can be easily explained. An observation that probably matters is that the twenty-fifth-century humans do all they can to cover up the markers that distinguish them from the twenty-first-century humans. They do their best to be incognito, to pass to others as from the space and era they are visiting. To a twenty-first-century viewer it may perhaps seem striking how openly the series questions certain ways of planning and designing the future. The show was, after all, made and broadcast in 1983 Czechoslovakia, at the time when the Iron Curtain was still up and the path to communism was considered to be the desired and the better state of being of mankind. *The Visitors* was not a banned series—it was broadcast by the state TV and has been (and still is) very popular.[25]

This may lead us toward considering "difference" as something enabling and world-expanding. At the time of writing, one can observe architectures of similarity on both sides of *and* in the sets of relationships we commonly refer to as Turkey *and* the EU. The similarity lies in the problem of coping with *difference*. Instead of using the latter as a something that could expand the world, it is often dismissed or discouraged outright. The debates held at the time of writing seem to be sending us toward endless reconfigurations of our pasts. To take one more page from *The Visitors*: before travelling to the earth of 1984, they discuss whether this is ethical and permissible, noting that in the twenty-fourth century such trips are banned because they had previously been abused.

---

[25] This has not been the only popular series nested in the theme of travel between worlds. Another would be *Arabela*—in which the main protagonists travel between *svět lidí* (the world of humans) and *svět pohádek* (the world of fairy tales), the latter inhabited by a diverse set of beings including Cinderella, Little Red Riding Hood, and the Sleeping Beauty.

Bibliography

Books and journal articles

Abrahamsen, Rita. *Disciplining Democracy: Development Discourse and Good Governance in Africa*. London: ZED Books, 2002.

Abu Lughod, Lila. "Do Muslim Women Really Need Saving? Anthropological Reflections on Cultural Relativism and its Others." *American Anthropologist* 104, no. 3 (2002): 783–90.

Ahıska, Meltem. "Occidentalism: The Historical Fantasy of the Modern." *The South Atlantic Quarterly* 102, nos. 2-3 (2003): 351–79.

Ahıska, Meltem. *Occidentalism in Turkey: Questions of Modernity and National Identity in Turkish Radio Broadcasts*. London: I.B. Tauris, 2010.

Ahıska, Meltem. *The Person You Have Called Cannot Be Reached at the Moment: Representations of Lifestyles in Turkey 1980–2005*. Istanbul: Ottoman Bank Archives and Research Centre, 2006.

Ahmad, Feroz. *The Making of Modern Turkey*. London and New York: Routledge, 1996.

Akgün, Mensur, Ayla Gürel, Mete Hatay and Sylvia Tiryaki. "Quo Vadis Cyprus." TESEV Working Paper. Istanbul: TESEV, 2005.

Amygdalou, Kalliopi. "Building the Nation at the Crossroads of 'East' and 'West': Ernest Hébrard and Henri Prost in the Near East." *Opticon1826* 16, no. 15 (2014): 1–19.

Anderson, Benedict. *Imagined Communities* (New edn). London and New York: Verso, 2006.

Appadurai, Arjun. "Grassroots Globalization and the Research Imagination." *Public Culture* 12, no. 1 (2000): 1–19.

Appadurai, Arjun. "The Right to Research." *Globalisation, Societies and Education* 4, no. 2 (2006): 167–77.

Arsel, Murat, Bengi Akbulut and Fikret Adaman. "Environmentalism of the Malcontent: Anti-Coal Power Plant Struggle in Turkey." *Journal of Peasant Studies* 42, no. 2 (2015): 371–95.

Baban, Feyzi and Fuat Keyman. "Turkey and Postnational Europe: Challenges for the Cosmopolitan Political Community." *European Journal of Social Theory* 11, no. 1 (2008): 107–24.

Babül, Elif. *Bureaucratic Intimacies*. Stanford: Stanford University Press, 2017.

Bache, Ian. "Theories of European Integration." In Ian Bache, Stephen George and Simon Bulmer (eds.), *Politics in the European Union*. Oxford: Oxford University Press, 2011.

Bailyn, John F., Dijana Jelača and Danijela Lugarić (eds.). *The Future of (Post)Socialism: Eastern European Perspectives.* Albany: SUNY Press, 2018.

Barrios, Roberto. "Resilience: A Commentary from the Vantage Point of Anthropology." *Annals of Anthropological Practice*40, no. 1 (2016): 28–38.

Beaulieu, Jill and Mary Roberts (eds.). *Orientalism's Interlocutors: Painting, Architecture, Photography.* Durham and London: Duke University Press, 2002.

Behar, Ruth. "Ethnography and the Book that Was Lost." *Ethnography*4, no. 1 (2003): 15–39.

Behr, Hartmut. "The European Union in the Legacies of Imperial Rule? EU Accession Politics Viewed from a Historical Comparative Perspective." *European Journal of International Relations*13, no. 2 (2007): 239–62.

Berger, John, , Sven Blomberg, Chris Fox, Michael Dibb and Richard Hollis. *Ways of Seeing.* London: British Broadcasting Corporation and Penguin Books, 2008.

Berger, Peter and Thomas Luckmann. *The Social Construction of Reality: A Treatise in the Sociology of Knowledge.* Penguin, 1991 [1966].

Bhabha, Jacqueline. "The Politics of Evidence: Roma Citizenship Deficits in Europe." In Benjamin Lawrance and Jacqueline Stevens (eds.), *Citizenship in Question: Evidentiary Birthright and Statelessness.* London and Durham: Duke University Press, 2017, 43–59.

Billig, Michael. *Banal Nationalism.* London: Sage, 1995.

Billig, Michael. *Laughter and Ridicule: Towards a Social Critique of Humour.* London: Sage and Theory, Culture and Society, 2005.

Biondi, Paolo. "Human Security and External Burden-sharing: The European Approach to Refugee Protection between Past and Present." *The International Journal of Human Rights*20, no. 2: 208–22.

Bisaha, Nancy. *Creating East and West: Renaissance Humanists and the Ottoman Turks.* Philadelphia: University of Pennsylvania Press, 2004.

Boşnak, Büke. "Europeanisation and De-Europeanisation Dynamics in Turkey: The Case of Environmental Organisations." *South European Society and Politics*21, no. 1 (2016): 75–90.

Brubaker, Roger. "Myths and Misconceptions in the Study of Nationalism." In J. A. Hall (ed.), *The State of the Nation: Ernest Gellner and the Theory of Nationalism.* Cambridge: Cambridge University Press, 1998, 272–306.

Brubaker, Roger. "Categories of Analysis and Categories of Practice: A Note on the Study of Muslims in European Countries of Immigration." *Ethnic and Racial Studies*36, no. 1 (2013): 1–8.

Bryant, Rebecca. *Imagining the Modern: The Cultures of Nationalism in Cyprus.* London: I.B. Tauris, 2004.

Bryant, Rebecca. *The Past in Pieces: Belonging in the New Cyprus.* Philadelphia: University of Pennsylvania Press, 2010.

Bryant, Rebecca. "On Critical Times: Return, Repetition, and the Uncanny Present." *History and Anthropology* 27, no. 1 (2017): 19–31.

Bryant, Rebecca and Mete Hatay. "Guns and Guitars: Simulating Sovereignty in a State of Siege." *American Ethnologist* 38, no. 4 (2011): 631–49.

Buchanan, Allen. *Justice, Legitimacy and Self-Determination: Moral Foundations for International Law*. Oxford: Oxford University Press, 2004.

Bürgin, Alexander and Derya Asikoglu. "Turkey's New Asylum Law: A Case of EU Influence." *Journal of Balkan and Near Eastern Studies* 19, no. 2 (2017): 121–35.

Buruma, Ian and Avishai Margalit. *Occidentalism: The West in the Eyes of Its Enemies*. London: Penguin, 2005.

Çagaptay, Söner. *Islam, Secularism and Nationalism in Modern Turkey: Who is a Turk?* New York: Routledge, 2006.

Calhoun, Craig. "Belonging in the Cosmopolitan Imaginary." *Ethnicities*3, no. 4 (2003): 531–53.

Calhoun, Craig. "The Class Consciousness of Frequent Travelers: Toward a Critique of Actually Existing Cosmopolitanism." *The South Atlantic Quarterly* 101, no. 4 (2002): 869–97.

Calhoun, Craig. "Imagining Solidarity: Cosmopolitanism, Constitutional Patriotism and the Public Sphere." *Public Culture* 14, no. 1 (2002): 141–71.

Carey, Matthew. *Mistrust: An Ethnographic Theory*. Chicago: HAU Books, 2017.

Carrier, James G. "Occidentalism: The World Turned Upside Down." *American Ethnologist* 19, no. 2 (1992): 195–212.

Caspersen, Nina. "Democracy, Nationalism and (Lack Of) Sovereignty: The Complex Dynamics of Democratization in Unrecognized States." *Nations and Nationalism* 17, no. 2 (2011): 337–56.

Caspersen, Nina. *Unrecognized States*. London: Polity, 2012.

Çelik, Zeynep and Edhem Eldem (eds.). *Camera Ottomana: Photography and Modernity in the Ottoman Empire1840–1914*. Istanbul: Koç University Press, 2015.

Chandler, David. *Constructing the Global Civil Society: Power and Morality in International Relations*. London: Palgrave Macmillan, 2004.

Chandler, David. "Democracy Unbound? Non-linear Politics and the Politicization of Everyday Life." *European Journal of Social Theory* 17, no. 1 (2014): 42–59.

Chandler, David. "Digital Governance in the Anthropocene: The Rise of the Correlational Machine." In David Chandler and C. Fuchs (eds.), *Digital Objects, Digital Subjects: Interdisciplinary Perspectives on Capitalism, Labour and Politics in the Age of Big Data*. London: University of Westminster, 2019, 23–42.

Chandler, David. *Empire in Denial: The Politics of State-building*. London: Pluto, 2006.

Chandler, David. "Forum 2: The Migrant Climate: Resilience, Adaptation and the Ontopolitics of Mobility in the Anthropocene." *Mobilities* 14, no. 3 (2019): 381–87.

Chandler, David. "Imposing the 'Rule of Law': Lessons of Bosnia-Herzegovina for Peacebuilding in Iraq." *International Peacekeeping* 11, no. 2 (2004): 312–33.

Chandler, David. "New Rights for Old? Cosmopolitan Citizenship and the Critique of State Sovereignty." *Political Studies* 51 (2003): 332–49.

Chandler, David. "Rhetoric Without Responsibility: The Attraction of 'Ethical' Foreign Policy." *British Journal of Politics and International Relations* 5, no. 3 (2003): 295–316.

Chandler, David. "The Security-development Nexus and the Rise of 'Anti-foreign Policy." *Journal of International Relations and Development* 10 (2007): 362–86.

Chatterjee, Partha. "Anderson's Utopia." *Diacritics* 29, no. 4 (1999): 128–34.

Clark, Bruce. *Twice a Stranger: How Mass Expulsions Forged Modern Greece and Turkey.* London: Granta Books, 2006.

Commaroff, Jean and John L. Commaroff. "Millennial Capitalism: First Thoughts on a Second Coming." *Public Culture* 12, no. 2 (2000): 291–343.

Constantinou, Costas and Yanis Papadakis. "The Cypriot State(s) *in situ*: Cross-ethnic Contact and the Discourse of Recognition." In Thomas Diez (ed.), *The European Union and the Cyprus Conflict.* Manchester: Manchester University Press, 2002, 73–97.

Constantinou, Costas. "On the Cypriot States of Exception." *International Political Sociology* 2 (2008): 145–64.

Cross, Gary. "A Right to Be Lazy? Busyness in Retrospective." *Social Research* 72, no. 2 (2005): 263–86.

Damro, Chad. "Market Power Europe." *Journal of European Public Policy* 19, no. 5 (2012): 682–99.

DeGenova, Nicolas. "Spectacles of Migrant 'Illegality': The Scene of Exclusion, the Obscene of Inclusion." *Ethnic and Racial Studies* 36, no. 7 (2013): 1180–98.

De Goede, Marieke, Anna Leander and Gavin Sullivan. "Introduction: The Politics of the List." *Environment and Planning D: Society and Space* 34, no. 1 (2016): 3–13.

Delanty, Gerard. *Inventing Europe: Idea, Identity and Reality.* Basingstoke: Macmillan Press Ltd, 1995.

De Waal, Thomas. *Great Catastrophe: Armenians and Turks in the Shadow of Genocide.* Oxford: Oxford University Press, 2015.

Diez, Thomas (ed.). *The European Union and the Cyprus Conflict.* Manchester: Manchester University Press, 2002.

Dink, Hrant. *Two Close Peoples, Two Distant Neighbors.* Istanbul: Hrant Dink Foundation, 2014.

Dönmez-Colin, Gönül. *Turkish Cinema: Identity, Distance and Belonging.* London: Reaktion Books, 2008.

Döşemeci, Mehmet. *Debating Turkey's Modernity: Civilization, Nationalism and the EEC.* Cambridge: Cambridge University Press, 2013.

Doxiadis, Constantinos A. "Ecumenopolis: Tomorrow's City" (From Britannica Book of the Year 1968, Encyclopaedia Britannica, available at www.doxiadis.org

Dryzek, John. "Can There Be a Human Right to an Essentially Contested Concept? The Case of Democracy." *The Journal of Politics* 78, no. 2 (2016): 357–67.

Düzgit, Senem A. *Seeing Kant in the EU's Relations with Turkey.* Istanbul: TESEV, 2006.

Dzenovska, Dace. "Coherent Selves, Viable States: Eastern Europe and the 'Migration/ Refugee Crisis." *Slavic Review* 76, no. 2 (2017): 297–306.

Eder, Klaus. "The EU in Search of its People: The Birth of Society Out of the Crisis of Europe." *European Journal of Social Theory* 17, no. 3 (2014): 219–37.

Ekmekçioğlu, Lerna. *Recovering Armenia: The Limits of Belonging in Post-genocide Turkey*. Stanford: Stanford University Press, 2016.

Elden, Stuart. "Contingent Sovereignty, Territorial Integrity and the Sanctity of Borders." *SAIS Review* 26, no. 1 (2006): 11–24, p. 22.

Erasaari, Matti. "Time and the Other Time: Trajectories of Fiji Time." *History and Anthropology* 29, no. 4 (2018): 407–24.

Eric, Hobsbawm and Terence Ranger (eds.), *The Invention of Tradition*. Cambridge: Cambridge University Press, 1983.

Eriksen, Thomas Hylland. *The Tyranny of the Moment: Fast and Slow Time in the Information Age*. London: Pluto Press, 2001.

Eriksen, Thomas Hylland. *What is Anthropology?* 2nd ed. London: Pluto Press, 2017.

Etzioni, Amitai. "The Domestic Sources of Global Adhocracy." *Social Change Review* 10, no. 2 (2012): 99–124.

Evin, Ahmet. *Origins and Development of Turkish Novel*. Minneapolis: Bibliotheca Islamica, 1983.

Evin, Ahmet and Nora Fisher Onar. "Convergence and Resistance: The European Dilemma of Turkish Intellectuals." In Justine Lacroix and Kalypso Nicolaïdis (eds.), *European Stories: Intellectual Debates on Europe in National Contexts*. Oxford: Oxford University Press, 2010.

Fanon, Franz. *The Wretched of the Earth*. London: Penguin Classics, 2001 [1961 French orig.].

Faroqhi, Suraiya. *Approaching Ottoman History: An Introduction to Sources*. Cambridge: Cambridge University Press, 1999.

Finkel, Caroline. *Osman's Dream*. London: John Murray, 2006.

Firat, Bilge. "Political Documents and Bureaucratic Entrepreneurs: Lobbying the European Parliament During Turkey's EU Integration." *Political and Legal Anthropology Review* 39, no. 2 (2016): 190–205.

Fisher Onar, Nora. "Echoes of a Universalism Lost: Rival Representations of the Ottomans in Today's Turkey." *Middle Eastern Studies* 45, no. 2 (2009): 229–41.

Fisher Onar, Nora and Hande Paker. "Towards Cosmopolitan Citizenship? Women's Rights in Divided Turkey." *Theory and Society* 41 (2012): 375–94.

Fisher, William. "Doing Good? The Politics and Antipolitics of NGO Practices." *Annual Review of Anthropology* 26 (1997): 439–64.

Frankl, Michal. "Prejudiced Asylum: Czechoslovak Refugee Policy, 1918–1960." *Journal of Contemporary History* 49, no. 3 (2014): 537–55.

Fukuyama, Francis. "The End of History?" *The National Interest* no. 16 (Summer 1989): 3–18

Göçek, Fatma M.*The Transformation of Modern Turkey*. London: I.B. Tauris, 2011.

Goffman, Daniel. *The Ottoman Empire and Early Modern Europe*. Cambridge: Cambridge University Press, 2002.

Goffman, Erwing. *Frame Analysis: An Essay on the Organization of Experience*. Boston: Northeastern University Press, 1974.

Göle, Nilüfer. *The Forbidden Modern: Civilization and Veiling.* Ann Arbor: University of Michigan Press, 1996.

Goody, Jack. *The East in the West.* Cambridge: Cambridge University Press, 1996.

Goody, Jack. *The Theft of History.* Cambridge: Cambridge University Press, 2006.

Goody, Jack. *The Eurasian Miracle.* Cambridge: Polity Press, 2010.

Graeber, David. *The Utopia of Rules.* Brooklyn, London: Melville House, 2015.

Groves, Christopher. "Horizons of Care: From Future Imaginaries to Responsible Research and Innovation." In Kornelia Konrad, Christopher Coenen, Anne Dijkstra, Colin Milburn and Hanrovan Lente (eds.), *Shaping Emerging Technologies: Governance, Innovation, Discourse.* Berlin: IOS Press/AKA, 2013, 185–202; p. 193.

Grugel, Jean. *Democratization: A Critical Introduction.* Basingstoke: Palgrave, 2002.

Gürbilek, Nurdan. "Dandies and Originals: Authenticity, Belatedness, and the Turkish Novel." *The South Atlantic Quarterly* 102, no. 2/3 (2003): 599–628.

Gürbilek, Nurdan. *The New Cultural Climate in Turkey: Living in a Shop Window.* London: Zed Books, 2011.

Hall, Stuart (ed.). *Representation: Cultural Representation and Signifying Practices.* London, Thousand Oaks and New Delhi: Sage Publications and Open University, 1997.

Haraway, Donna. "Situated Knowledges: The Science Question in Feminism and the Privilege of Partial Perspective." *Feminist Studies* 14, no. 3 (Autumn 1988): 575–99.

Harrington, Cameron. "The Ends of the World: International Relations and the Anthropocene." *Millennium: Journal of International Studies* 44, no. 3 (2016): 478–98.

Hatay, Mete. "The Problem of Pigeons: Orientalism, Xenophobia and a Rhetoric of the 'Local' in North Cyprus." *The Cyprus Review* 20, no. 2 (2008): 144–71.

Havel, Václav. *The Power of the Powerless,* 1978. Available at http://www.vaclavhavel.cz/ showtrans.php?cat=eseje&val=2_aj_eseje.html&typ=HTML.

Herzfeld, Michael. "The Hypocrisy of European Moralism." *Anthropology Today* 32, no. 2 (2016): 10–13.

Hillebrand, Ernst and Anna M. Kellner (eds.). *Shaping a Different Europe.* Bonn: Dietzt, 2014.

Hobsbawm, Eric. *The Age of Empire 1875–1914.* New York: Vintage, 1989.

Hobson, John. *The Eastern Origins of Western Civilization.* Cambridge: Cambridge University Press, 2004.

Hobson, John. "The Postcolonial Paradox of Eastern Agency." *Perceptions* 29, no. 1 (2014): 121–34.

Hom, Andrew. "Hegemonic Metronome: The Ascendancy of Western Standard Time." *Review of International Studies* 36 (2010): 1145–70.

Horky, Ondrej and Simon Lightfoot. "From Aid Recipients to Aid Donors? Development policies of Central and Eastern European States." *Perspectives on European Politics and Society* 13, no. 1 (2012): 1–16.

Hron, Madeleine. "The Czech Emigre Experience of Return after 1989." *Slavonic and East European Review* 85, no. 1 (2007): 48–78.

Huysmans, Jef. "The European Union and the Securitization of Migration." *Journal of Common Market Studies* 38, no. 5 (2000): 751–77.

Iğsız, Aslı. "Polyphony and Geographic Kinship in Anatolia." In Esra Özyürek (ed.), *The Politics of Public Memory in Turkey*. New York: Syracuse University Press, 2007, 162–190.

James, Erica Caple. *Democratic Insecurities*. Berkeley, Los Angeles and London: University of California Press, 2010.

Jansen, Stef. "After the Red Passport: Towards an Anthropology of Everyday Geopolitics of Entrapment in EU's 'Immediate Outside.'" *Journal of the Royal Anthropological Institute* 15 (2009): 815–32.

Jeffery, Renée. "Tradition as Invention: The 'Traditions Tradition' and the History of Ideas in International Relations." *Millennium: Journal of International Relations* 34, no. 1 (2005): 57–84.

Johanisova, Nadia and Stephan Wolf. "Economic Democracy: A Path for the Future?" *Futures*44 (2012): 562–70.

Judt, Tony. *Postwar*. London: William Heinemann, 2005.

Judt, Tony (with Timothy Snyder). *Thinking the Twentieth Century*. London: William Heinemann, 2012.

Jung, Yuson. "The Inability Not to Follow: Western Hegemonies and the Notion of 'Complaisance' in the Enlarged Europe." *Anthropological Quarterly* 83, no. 2 (2010): 317–53.

Karahasanoğlu, Selim and Deniz Cenk Demir (eds.). *History from Below: A Tribute in Memory of Donald Quataert*. Istanbul: Istanbul Bilgi University Press, 2016.

Karlsson, Bengt G. "Writing Development." *Anthropology Today* 29, no. 2 (2013): 4–7.

Kausch, Kristina and Richard Youngs. "The End of Euro-Mediterranean Vision." *International Affairs* 85, no. 5 (2009): 963–75.

Keyder, Çağlar. "Capital City Resurgent: Istanbul since the 1980s." *New Perspectives on Turkey* 43 (2010): 177–86.

King, Charles. *Midnight at the Pera Palace: The Birth of Modern Istanbul*. New York and London: Norton, 2014.

Kizilyurek, Niyazi. *Glafkos Clerides: The Path of a Country*. Nicosia and London: Rimal and Melisende, 2008.

Klinke, Ian. "European Integration Studies and the European Union's Eastern Gaze." *Millennium: Journal of International Studies* 43, no. 2 (2015): 567–83.

Konuk, Kader. *East-West Mimesis: Auerbach in Turkey*. Stanford: Stanford University Press, 2014.

Kurtović, Larisa and Nelli Sargsyan. 2019. "After Utopia: Leftist Imaginaries and Activist Politics in the Postsocialist World." *History and Anthropology* 30, no. 1: 1–19.

Kušníráková, Tereza and Čižinský, Pavel. "Dvacet let české migrační politiky: liberální, restriktivní, anebo ještě jiná?" *Geografie* 116, no. 4 (2011): 497–517.

Kutter, Amelie. "A Catalytic Moment: The Greek Crisis in the German Financial Press." *Discourse and Society* 25, no. 4 (2014): 446–66.

Kuus, Merje. *Geopolitics and Expertise*. Chichester: John Wiley and Sons, 2014.

Kuzmanovic, Daniela. *Refractions of Civil Society in Turkey*. New York: Palgrave Macmillan, 2012.

Kyris, George. "A Model of 'Contested' Europeanization: The European Union and the Turkish-Cypriot Administration." *Comparative European Politics* 12, no. 2 (2014): 160–83.

Lawrence, Christopher. *Blood and Oranges: Immigrant Labor and European Markets in Rural Greece*. New York and Oxford: Berghahn Books, 2007.

Levin, Paul. *Turkey and the European Union: Christian and Secular Images of Islam*. New York: Palgrave Macmillan, 2011.

Levin, Paul and Sinan Ciddi. "Interdisciplinarity and Comparison in Turkish Studies." *Turkish Studies*15, no. 4 (2014): 557–70.

Lindstrom, Lamont. "Cargoism and Occidentalism." In J. G. Carrier (ed.), *Occidentalism: Images of the West*. Oxford: Clarendon Press, 1995, 33–60.

Long, A. A. "The Concept of the Cosmopolitan in Greek and Roman Thought." *Daedalus* 137, no. 1 (2008): 50–58.

Maalouf, Amin. *Disordered World: A vision for the Post-9/11 World*. London: Bloomsbury, 2012.

Malkki, Lisa. "Refugees and Exile: From 'Refugee Studies' to the National Order of Things."*Annual Review of Anthropology* 24 (1995): 495–523.

Malmvig, Helle. "Caught Between Cooperation and Democratization: The Barcelona Process and the EU's Double-Discursive Approach." *Journal of International Relations and Development* 9, no. 4 (2006): 343–70.

Malmvig, Helle. "Free Us from Power: Governmentality, Counter-conduct, and Simulation in European Democracy and Reform Promotion in the Arab World." *International Political Sociology* 8, no. 3 (2014): 293–310.

Manners, Ian. "Normative Power Europe: A Contradiction in Terms?" *Journal of Common Market Studies* 40, no. 2 (2002): 235–58.

Markell, Patchen. *Bound by Recognition*. Princeton: Princeton University Press, 2003.

Markoff, John. "Where and Why Was Democracy Invented?" *Comparative Studies in Society and History* 41, no. 4 (1999): 660–90.

McMahon, Darrin. "Fear and Trembling, Strangers and Strange Lands." *Daedalus*137, no. 1 (2008): 5–17.

Michael, Merlingen. "Everything is Dangerous: A Critique of 'Normative Power Europe." *Security Dialogue* 38, no. 4 (2007): 435–53.

Mitchell, Timothy. *Carbon Democracy: Political Power in the Age of Oil*. London: Verso, 2013.

Moscovici, Serge. "Questions for the Twenty-First Century." *Theory, Culture & Society* 7, no. 1 (1990): 1–19.

Moscovici, Serge. "Social Representations and Pragmatic Communication." *Social Science Information* 33, no. 2 (1994): 163–77.

Moyn, Samuel. *Last Utopia: Human Rights in History*. Boston: Harvard University Press, 2012.

Mutlu, Can. "How (Not) to Disappear Completely: Pedagogical Potential of Research Methods in International Relations."*Millennium: Journal of International Studies* 43, no. 3 (2015): 931–41.

Nader, Laura. *The Life of the Law*. Berkeley: University of California Press, 2002.

Naimark, Norman M. "How Historians Repeat Themselves." *Hoover Digest* no. 3 (2009). https://www.hoover.org/research/how-historians-repeat-themselves.

Najslova, Lucia. "The Czech Case: Solidarity Yes, But Twelve is Enough for Now." In Tamas Boros and Hedvig Giusto (eds.), *The Flexible Solidarity: How Progressive Parties Handled the Migration Crisis in Central Europe*. Brussels and Budapest: FEPS and Policy Solutions, 2017.

Najslova, Lucia. *Foreign Democracy Assistance in the Czech and Slovak Transitions: What Lessons for the Arab World?* Madrid: FRIDE, 2013.

Najslova, Lucia. "Slovakia in the East: Pragmatic Follower, Occasional Leader." *Perspectives: Review of International Affairs* 19, no. 2 (2011): 101–22.

Nereid, Camilla Trud. "Domesticating Modernity: The Turkish Magazine *Yedigün*, 1933–39." *Journal of Contemporary History* 47, no. 3 (2012): 483–504.

Neumann, Iver. *Uses of the Other: The 'East' in European Identity Formation*. Minneapolis: University of Minnesota Press, 1999.

Nicolaïdis, Kalypso. "Southern Barbarians? A Postcolonial Critique of Univeralism." In Kalypso Nicolaïdis, Berny Sèbe and Gabrielle Maas (eds.), *Echoes of Empire*. London: I.B. Tauris, 2015.

Nicolaïdis, Kalypso and Robert Howse. "'This is My Utopia …': Narrative as Power." *Journal of Common Market Studies* 40, no. 4 (2002): 767–92.

Nicolaïdis, Kalypso, Berny Sèbe and Gabrielle Maas (eds.). *Echoes of Empire: Memory, Identity and Colonial Legacies*. London: I.B. Tauris, 2015.

Oliver, Kelly. "Witnessing, Recognition and Response Ethics." *Philosophy and Rhetoric* 48, no. 4 (2015): 473–93.

O'Hagan, Jacinta. *Conceptualizing the West in International Relations: From Spengler to Said*. Houndmills, Basingstoke, Hampshire and New York: Palgrave,2002.

Öner, Selcen. "Internal Factors in the EU's Transformative Power over Turkey: The Role of Turkish Civil Society." *Southeast European and Black Sea Studies* 14, no. 1 (2014): 23–42.

Orwell, George. 1984. New York: New American Library [1949 orig., this edition n.d].

Özdemir, Seçkin. "Pity the Exiled: Turkish Academics in Exile, the Problem of Compassion in Politics and the Promise of Dis-exile." *Journal of Refugee Studies* (2019, advance article). https://doi.org/10.1093/jrs/fey076.

Özyürek, Esra (ed.). *The Politics of Public Memory in Turkey*. New York: Syracuse University Press.

Phelan, William. "What is Sui Generis about the European Union? Costly International Cooperation in a Self-Contained Regime." *International Studies Review* 14, no. 3 (2012): 367–85.

Philips, David L. *Diplomatic History: The Turkey-Armenia Protocols*. New York: Columbia University, 2012.

Pieterse, Jan Nederveen. "Globalisation Goes in Circles: Hybridities East and West." In
    D.Schirmer, G.Saalman and C.Kessler (eds.), *Hybridising East and West*. Munster:
    LIT Verlag, 2006.

Pirický, Gabriel. "The Ottoman Age on Southern Central Europe as Represented in
    Secondary School History Textbooks in the Czech Republic, Hungary, Poland and
    Slovakia." *Journal of Educational Media, Memory & Society* 5, no. 1 (2013): 108–29.

Powers, Theodore and Theodoros Rakopoulos. "The Anthropology of Austerity: An
    Introduction." *Focaal: Journal of Global and Historical Anthropology* 29, no. 83
    (2019): 1–12.

Probyn, Elspeth. *Outside Belongings*. London: Routledge, 1996.

Rancatore Jason A."It Is Strange: A Reply to Vrasti."*Millennium: Journal of International
    Studies* 39, no. 1 (2010): 65–77.

Rigney, Ann. "Reconciliation and Remembering: (How) Does it Work?" *Memory
    Studies* 5, no. 3 (2012): 251–8.

Robinson, Fiona. *The Ethics of Care: A Feminist Approach to Human Security.*
    Philadelphia: Temple University Press, 2011.

Rosaldo, Renato. "Imperialist Nostalgia." *Representations* 26 (1989): 107–22.

Roy, Olivier. "Development and Political Legitimacy: The Cases of Iraq and
    Afghanistan." *Conflict, Security and Development* 4, no. 2 (2010): 167–79.

Reuben,Rose-Redwood. "With Numbers in Place: Security, Territory, and the
    Production of Calculable Space." *Annals of Association of American Geographers* 102,
    no. 2 (2012): 295–319.

Rumelili, Bahar. "Liminality and Perpetuation of Conflicts: Turkish-Greek Relations in
    the Context of Community-Building by the EU." *European Journal of International
    Relations* 9, no. 2 (2003): 213–48.

Rumelili, Bahar. "Constructing Identity and Relating to Difference: Understanding the
    EU's Mode of Differentiation." *Review of International Studies* 30 (2004): 27–47.

Rumelili, Bahar and Viyacheslav Morozov. "The External Constitution of European
    Identity: Russia and Turkey as Europe-makers." *Cooperation and Conflict* 47, no. 1
    (2012): 28–48.

Rutz, H. J. *The Politics of Time*. American Ethnological Society Monograph Series, 1992.

Said, Edward. *Orientalism*. 25th anniversary edn. New York: Vintage Books, 1994.[1979
    orig.]

Said, Edward. "Reflections on Exile." In Edward Said (ed.), *Reflections on Exile and
    Other Essays*. Boston, MA: Harvard University Press, 1984, 137–49.

Sassen, Saskia. *Territory, Authority, Rights: From Medieval to Global Assemblages.*
    Princeton and Oxford: Princeton University Press, 2008.

Scarry, Elaine1998. "On Beauty and Being Just." *The Tanner Lectures on Human Values*,
    delivered at Yale University, March 25 and 26.

Schwartz, Joan and Terry Cook. "Archives, Records and Power: The Making of Modern
    Memory." *Archival Science* 2 (2002): 1–19.

Shore, Cris, Susan Wright and Davide Pero (eds.). *Policy Worlds: Anthropology and the Analysis of Contemporary Power*. New York and Oxford: Berghahn Books, 2011.

Shore, Cris. *Building Europe: The Cultural Politics of European Integration*. London and New York: Routledge, 2006.

Simpson, Audra. *Mohawk Interruptus: Political Life Across the Borders of Settler States*. Durham: Duke University Press, 2014.

Sjursen, Helen. "Why Expand? The Question of Legitimacy and Justification in the EU's Enlargement Policy." *Journal of Common Market Studies* 40, no. 3 (2001): 491–513.

Somer, Murat. "Theory-consuming or Theory-Producing? Studying Turkey as a Theory-developing Critical Case." *Turkish Studies* 15, no. 4 (2014): 571–88.

Sontag, Susan. *Regarding the Pain of Others*. New York: Picador, 2003.

Spencer, Jonathan. "Occidentalism in the East: The Uses of the West in Politics and Anthropology of South Asia." In J. G. Carrier (ed.), *Occidentalism: Images of the West*. Oxford: Clarendon Press, 1995, 234–57.

Stoler, Ann Laura. "Colonial Aphasia: Race and Disabled Histories in France." *Public Culture* 23, no. 1 (2011): 121–56.

Stoler, Ann Laura. "Rethinking Colonial Categories: European Communities and the Boundaries of Rule." *Comparative Studies in Society and History* 31, no. 1 (1989): 134–61.

Strathern, Marilyn. *Before and After Gender*. Chicago: HAU Books, 2016.

Suny, Ronald G., Fatma M. Göçek and Norman M. Naimark. *A Question of Genocide: Armenians and Turks at the End of Ottoman Empire*. Oxford: Oxford University Press, 2011.

Szczepanikova, Alice. "Between Control and Assistance: The Problem of European Accommodation Centres for Asylum Seekers." *International Migration* 51, no. 4 (2012): 130–43.

Szcepanikova, Alice. "From the Right of Asylum to Migration Management: The Legal-Political Construction of 'a Refugee' in the Post-Communist Czech Republic." *Europe-Asia Studies* 63, no. 5 (2011): 789–806.

Tajfel, Henri and J. C. Turner. "The Social Identity Theory of Inter-group Behavior." In S. Worchel and L. W. Austin (eds.), *Psychology of Intergroup Relations*. Chicago: Nelson-Hall, 1986.

Talmon, Stefan. "The Cyprus Question Before the European Court of Justice." *European Journal of International Law* 12, no. 4 (2001): 727–50.

Tansey, Oisin. "Does Democracy Need Sovereignty?" *Review of International Studies* 37 (2011): 1515–36.

Tilly, Charles. *Democracy*. Cambridge: Cambridge University Press, 2007.

Tocci, Nathalie. *EU Accession Dynamics and Conflict Resolution: Catalysing Peace or Consolidating Partition in Cyprus?* Aldershot: Ashgate, 2004.

Todorova, Maria. *Imagining the Balkans*. Updated edn. Oxford: Oxford University Press, 2009.

Tsing, Anna Lowenhaupt. *The Mushroom at the End of the World: On the Possibility of Life in Capitalist Ruins*. Princeton and Oxford: Princeton University Press, 2015.

Tuğal, Cihan. *The Fall of the Turkish Model: How the Arab Uprisings Brought Down Islamic Liberalism*. London: Verso, 2016.

Uğur, Mehmet. *The European Union and Turkey: Anchor-Credibility Dilemma*. Aldershot: Ashgate, 1999.

Ulusoy, Kivanç. "Turkey's Reform Effort Reconsidered, 1987–2004." *EUI Working Paper RSCAS* 28 (2005).

Vachudova, Milada A. *Europe Undivided: Democracy, Leverage and Integration after Communism*. Oxford: Oxford University Press, 2005.

Van Middelaar, Luuk. "The Return of Politics—The European Union after the Crises in the Eurozone and Ukraine." *Journal of Common Market Studies* 54, no. 3 (2016): 495–507.

Varisco, Daniel Martin. *Reading Orientalism: The Said and the Unsaid*. Seattle: University of Washington Press, 2007.

Varnava, Andrekos and Hubert Faustmann (eds.). *Reunifying Cyprus: The Annan Plan and Beyond*. London: I.B. Tauris, 2009.

Verovšek, Peter J. "Expanding Europe through Memory: The Shifting Content of the Ever-Salient Past." *Millennium: Journal of International Studies* 43, no. 2 (2015): 531–50.

Verstraete, Ginette. "Timescapes: An Artistic Challenge to the European Union Paradigm." *European Journal of Cultural Studies* 12, no. 2 (2009): 157–72.

Vostal, Filip. *Accelerating Academia: The Changing Structure of Academic Time*. London: Palgrave, 2016.

Vrasti, Vanda. "Dr. Strangelove, or How I Learned to Stop Worrying about Methodology and Love Writing." *Millennium – Journal of International Studies* 39, no. 1 (2010): 79–88.

Wallace, Helen, Mark A. Pollack and Alasdair Young. Eds. *Policy-Making in the European Union*. 6th Edition. Oxford: Oxford University Press, 2010.

Whyte, Jessica. "The 'Dangerous Concept of the Just War': Decolonization, Wars of National Liberation, and the Additional Protocols to the Geneva Conventions." *Humanity* (Winter 2018): 313–41.

Wilding, Raelene. "Transnational Ethnographies and Anthropological Imaginings of Migrancy." *Journal of Ethnic and Migration Studies* 33, no. 2 (2007): 331–48.

Yesil, Bilge. *Media in New Turkey: The Origins of an Authoritarian Neoliberal State*. Champaign, IL: University of Illinois Press, 2016.

Yılmaz, Gözde. "EU Conditionality is Not the Only Game in Town! Domestic Drivers of Turkey's Europeanization." *Turkish Studies* 15, no. 2 (2014): 303–21.

Yılmaz, Hale. "Learning to Read (Again): The Social Experiences of Turkey's 1928 Alphabet Reform." *International Journal of Middle East Studies* 43, no. 4 (2011): 677–97.

Yıldırım, Onur. *Diplomacy and Displacement: Reconsidering the Turco-Greek Exchange of Populations, 1922–1934*. New York and London: Routledge, 2006.

Yurchak, Alexei. "Introduction." In *Everything Was Forever Until it Was No More*. Princeton: Princeton University Press, 2005.

Yuval Davis, Nira. "Belonging and the Politics of Belonging." *Patterns of Prejudice* 40, no. 3 (2006): 197–214.

Zurcher, Erik Ian. *The Young Turk Legacy and Nation Building: From the Ottoman Empire to Atatürk's Turkey*. London: I.B. Tauris, 2010.

Research reports

Alessandri, Emiliano, Ian Lesser and Kadri Tastan. "EU-Turkey Relations: Steering in Stormy Seas." The German Marshall Fund of the United States Turkey, Europe and Global Issues Report No. 31 (2018). Available at: http://www.gmfus.org/sites/def ault/files/publications/pdf/EU-Turkey%20Relations-%20Steering%20in%20Stormy %20Seas_July%2031.pdf.

Aydin, Senem, Gergana Noutcheva, Michael Emerson, and Julia De Clerck-Sachsse. "Just What is this 'Absorption Capacity' of the European Union?" *CEPS Policy Brief No. 113* (2006). https://www.ceps.eu/publications/just-what-absorption-capacity-eu ropean-union.

Aydintaşbaş, Asli. "The Discreet Charm of Hypocrisy: An EU-Turkey Power Audit." European Council on Foreign Relations, March 2018. https://www.ecfr.eu/page/-/ EU_TURKEY_POWER_AUDIT.pdf.

Békés, Márton (ed.). *The Future of Europe. Hungary: Brave and Free*. Budapest: Public Endowment for Research on Central and Eastern European History and Society, 2018.

Bertoncini, Yves. "Differentiated Integration and the EU: A Variable Geometry Legitimacy." Instituto Affari Internazionali, March 2017. https://www.iai.it/sites/ default/files/eu60_7.pdf.

Bryant, Rebecca and Christalla Yakinthou. *Cypriot Perceptions of Turkey*. Istanbul: TESEV, 2012.

Centrum pro výzkum veřejného mínění. "Důvěra vybraným politikům v mezinárodním kontextu – prosinec 2015." https://cvvm.soc.cas.cz/media/com_form2content/doc uments/c2/a2000/f9/pm160127.pdf.

EDAM. "Reaction Mounting against Syrian Refugees in Turkey." *Public Opinion Surveys of Turkish Foreign Policy* 1/2014. http://www.edam.org.tr/en/File?id=1152.

Erdogan, Emre and Pinar Uyan Semerci. "Attitudes towards Syrian Refugees 2017." Istanbul Bilgi University. https://goc.bilgi.edu.tr/media/uploads/2018/03/15/turki sh-perceptions-of-syrian-refugees-20180315_Y0gYZoI.pdf.

Hatay, Mete. *Beyond Numbers: An Inquiry into the Political Integration of the Turkish 'Settlers' in Northern Cyprus*. PRIO Report 4/2005. Nicosia: PRIO Cyprus Centre.

International Commission on Intervention and State Sovereignty. *Responsibility to Protect. Report of the International Commission on Intervention and State Sovereignty*. Ottawa: International Development Research Centre, 2011.

International Crisis Group. "Turkey's Syrian Refugees: Defusing Metropolitan Tensions." Report No. 248, January 29, 2018.

Ludlow, Peter. *Dealing with Turkey: The European Council of 16–17 December 2004.* Brussels: Eurocomment, 2005.

Migration Policy Workshop. "Urban Refugees from 'Detachment' to "Harmonization." Istanbul: Marmara Belediyeler Birliği Kültür Yayınlari, 2017.

Tocci, Nathalie. *The Baffling Short-sightedness in the EU-Turkey-Cyprus Triangle.* Documenti IAI 1021 (2010). Available at: http://www.iai.it/sites/default/files/iai1021.pdf.

Tulmets, Elsa (ed.). "Identity and Solidarity in Foreign Policy: Investigating East Central European Relations with Eastern Neighborhood." A special issues of *Perspectives: Review of International Affairs* 19, no. 2 (2011): 5–191.

Türkmen, Gülay. "'But You Don't Look Turkish!': The Changing Face of Turkish Immigration to Germany." *ResetDOC*, May 27, 2019. https://www.resetdoc.org/story /dont-look-turkish-changing-face-turkish-immigration-germany/.

Documents and PR materials (select list of those directly cited in the text)

AKP. *Political Vision of AK Parti (Justice and Development Party) 2023: Politics, Society and the World.* 2012. http://www.akparti.org.tr/english/akparti/2023-political-vis ion#bolum_.

change.org. *Stop EU-Turkey Deal—Safe Passage Now.* March 2016. https://www.change. org/p/stop-eu-turkey-deal-safe-passage-now.

Council of the European Union, Presidency Conclusions, Brussels European Council 16/17 December 2004.

Council of the European Union. "EU-Turkey Statement." March 18, 2016, Available at: «https://www.consilium.europa.eu/en/press/press-releases/2016/03/18/eu-turkey-st atement/#», Accessed December 20, 2017.

EEAS. *Shared Vision, Common Action: A Stronger Europe. A Global Strategy for the European Union's Foreign and Security Policy.* 2016. http://europa.eu/globalstrategy/ en/global-strategy-foreign-and-security-policy-european-union.

EEAS. "EU Foreign Policy Matters to You." http://europa.eu/globalstrategy/en/globa l-strategy-foreign-and-security-policy-european-union.

European Commission. "Civil Society Dialogue between EU and the Candidate Countries." Brussels June 29, 2005, COM (2005) 290 final.

European Commission. "Screening Report Turkey. Chapter 25: Science and Research." February 3, 2006.

European Commission. "Closer to the European Union: EU Assistance to the Turkish Cypriot Community" (2012).

European Commission. EU Enlargement Strategy, COM 2015 (611final).

European Commission. (11.3.2015) Seventh FP7 Monitoring Report. Directorate General for Research and Innovation 2015—Evaluation.

European Commission. (2015) EU-Turkey Joint Action Plan, Brussels, October 15, 2015. Available at: «http://europa.eu/rapid/press-release_MEMO-15-5860_en.htm." Accessed June 15, 2017.

European Commission. "Communication on Establishing a New Partnership Framework with Third Countries under the European Agenda on Migration." COM (2016) 385 final, Strasbourg, June 7, 2016, https://ec.europa.eu/home-affairs/sites/homeaffairs/files/what-we-do/policies/european-agenda-migration/proposal-implementation-package/docs/20160607/communication_external_aspects_eam_towards_new:migration_ompact_en.pdf.

European Commission (2016) First Report on the Progress Made in the Implementation of the EU-Turkey Statement, 20. April. Available at « https://ec.europa.eu/home-affairs/sites/homeaffairs/files/what-we-do/policies/european-agenda-migration/proposal-implementation-package/docs/20160420/report_implementation_eu-turkey_agreement_nr_01_en.pdf ». Accessed April 13, 2017.

European Commission (2017) EU-Turkey Statement One Year On, 17 March. Available at «https://ec.europa.eu/home-affairs/sites/homeaffairs/files/what-we-do/policies/european-agenda-migration/background-information/eu_turkey_statement_17032017_en.pdf. Accessed April 13, 2017.

European Commission (2017) Relocation and Resettlement – State of Play, 12 April. Available at «https://ec.europa.eu/home-affairs/sites/homeaffairs/files/what-we-do/policies/european-agenda-migration/20170412_update_of_the_factsheet_on_relocation_and_resettlement_en.pdf», Accessed April 13, 2017.

European Commission. "Public Consultation on EU Summertime Arrangements, a Report on the Results." SWD (2018) 406 final, Brussels, September 12, 2018.

European Commission. Program for Turkish Cypriot community. https://eur-lex.europa.eu/legal-content/EN/TXT/?uri=CELEX:32006R0389

The European Network of Transmission System Operators for Electricity (ENTSO-E). https://www.entsoe.eu/about/system-operations/.

General Court of the European Union, Press Release 19/17, February 2017, https://curia.europa.eu/jcms/upload/docs/application/pdf/2017-02/cp170019en.pdf

La Fontaine, Oscar*EU in 12 Lessons*, 2014, https://publications.europa.eu/en/publication-detail/-/publication/2d85274b-0093-4e38-896a-12518d629057.

Ministry for EU Affairs of the Republic of Turkey, Press Statement by H.E. Egemen Bağış on Turkey's Progress Report, December 31, 2012.

Ministry of Foreign Affairs of the Czech Republic. Statement of the Czech MFA on the Results of Referendums in Cyprus, April 28, 2004, http://www.mzv.cz/jnp/en/issues_and_press/statements/x2004/statement_of_the_czech_mfa_on_the_2.html

Ministry of Foreign Affairs of the Czech Republic. *Programme of the Czech Presidency of the Visegrad Group 2015–2016.*

OSCE. "Turkey, Constitutional Referendum, Final Report." June 22, 2017. «http://www.osce.org/odihr/elections/turkey/324816 ».

Parliament of the Czech Republic Poslanecká sněmovna ČR (22.3.2016) Usnesení PS č. 1144, March 22, 2016, https://www.psp.cz/sqw/text/text2.sqw?idd=82733.

Parliament of the Czech Republic Senát Parlamentu ČR 373. Usnesení Senátu, March 16, 2016, http://senat.cz/xqw/webdav/pssenat/original/79174/66562.

Republic of Cyprus. Cyprus EU presidency 'Europe in the world – closer to its neighbors' was one of the priorities of the presidency (see www.cy2012.eu).

Schuman Declaration May 9, 1950, http://ec.europa.eu/publications/booklets/eu_documentation/04/txt07_en.htm#declaration

United Nations Security Council (1975). Resolution 367 of 12 March 1975.

United Nations Security Council (1983). Resolution 541 of 18 November 1983.

United Nations Secretary General (2004). Report of the Secretary General on His Mission of Good Offices in Cyprus, June 2, 2004.

Venice Commission. "Opinion No 865 / 2016." December 12, 2016. Available at «http://www.venice.coe.int/webforms/documents/default.aspx?pdffile=CDL-AD(2016)037-e.

Venice Commission. "Opinion No 875/2017." March 17, 2017. Available at «http://www.venice.coe.int/webforms/documents/default.aspx?pdffile=cdl-ad(2017)005-e ».

Visegrad Group. "We Offer You Our Helping Hand on the EU Path." Joint letter of V4 Foreign Ministers published in Western Balkan dailies; Prague, November 11, 2015.

Magazine and newspaper articles

Adamec, Jan. "Was Charles IV the Greatest Czech?" *visegradrevue.eu*, May 23, 2016.

Andrea, Petö. "Attack on freedom of education in Hungary: The case of gender studies." *Engenderings*, September 24, 2018, https://blogs.lse.ac.uk/gender/2018/09/24/attack-on-freedom-of-education-in-hungary-the-case-of-gender-studies/

Ash, Timothy Garton. "Europe's True Stories." *The Prospect Magazine*, Issue 131, http://www.prospect-magazine.co.uk/article_details.php?id=8214

BBC News (2016) "Donald Tusk: "Turkey Best Example of How to Treat Refugees." April 23, 2016 Available at «http://www.bbc.com/news/world-europe-36122377 » Accessed September 16, 2016.

BBC News. "Kosovo-Serbia Row Makes Europe Clocks Go Slow." March 7, 2018 https://www.bbc.com/news/world-europe-43321113.

BIA News. "EP Passes Resolution Condemning Turkey, Ankara Declares It Null and Void." February 9, 2018, https://bianet.org/english/politics/194175-ep-passes-resolution-condemning-turkey-ankara-declares-it-null-and-void.

CNN Türk. "Kılıçdaroğlu: Türkiye Avrupa'nın toplama kampı olamaz." October 26, 2015. https://www.cnnturk.com/turkiye/kilicdaroglu-turkiye-avrupanin-toplama-kampi-olamaz.

Davutoğlu, Ahmet. "Turkey cannot deal with the refugee crisis alone. EU nations need to help." *The Guardian*, September 9, 2015, https://www.theguardian.com/commentisfree/2015/sep/09/turkey-refugee-crisis-christian-fortress-europe

Dundar, Can. "What's Freedom Worth? Less Than 3 Billion Euros, Apparently." *The Washington Post*, December 21, 2015.

Erdoğan, Recep Tayyip. "When the World Failed Syria, Turkey Stepped in. Now Others Must Help." *The Guardian*, May 23, 2016, https://www.theguardian.com/comment isfree/2016/may/23/world-failed-syria-turkey-refugee-crisis

Fırat, Hande. "Turkey, EU agree to accelerate relations: Erdoğan." *HurriyetDaily News*, March 28, 2018.

For gender studies "reform" see Andrea Pető, "Attack on freedom of education in Hungary: the case of gender studies." *Engenderings*, September 24, 2018, https:// blogs.lse.ac.uk/gender/2018/09/24/attack-on-freedom-of-education-in-hungary-t he-case-of-gender-studies/

Gessen, Masha. "The Unimaginable reality of American concentration camps." *The New Yorker*, June 21, 2019.

Günersel, Tarik. "Earth Day and Earth Civilization Project." *Sampsonia Way*, April 17, 2014, http://www.sampsoniaway.org/fearless-ink/tarik-gunersel/2014/04/17/ear th-day-and-earth-civilization-project/

Herszenhorn, David. "Thousands Demand Resignation of Ukraine Leader." *The New York Times*, December 1, 2013, http://nyti.ms/ICFuS4

Higgins, Charlotte. "There is no such thing as past or future: physicist Carlo Rovelli on changing how we think about time." *The Guardian*, April 14, 2018.

Hubinger, Vaclav. "Rakouská hra s tureckým míčkem na evropský účet" [Austrians play with a Turkish ball, Europeans will pay the bill], 2016, http://blog.aktualne.cz/blogy/ vaclav-hubinger.php?itemid=27787

HurriyetDailyNews, Turkish Parliament OKs general budget for 2015, December 23, 2014, http://www.hurriyetdailynews.com/turkish-parliament-oks-general-budget -for-2015.aspx?pageID=238&nID=75997&NewsCatID=344

Idiz, Semih. "Article 301 and its European Cousins." *Turkish Daily News*, October 19, 2006.

In't Veld, Sophie. "Threat to European Way of Life is not migrants. It's populists." *Politico*, September 13, 2019, https://www.politico.eu/article/populist-threat-to-euro pean-way-of-life-sophie-int-veld-ursula-von-der-leyen/

irozhlas.cz. "Žaloba za kvóty Česko netěší, pořád je ale možná dohoda, tvrdí ministerstvo zahraničí." January 4, 2018, https://www.irozhlas.cz/zpravy-domov/ces ko-migrace-kvoty-zaloba_1801041814_mos

Jones, Reece „Climate Change Will be the Border Control of the Future." *Quartz*, November 9, 2017, https://qz.com/1124055/climate-change-will-be-the-border-con trol-of-the-future/

Leyshon, Cressida. "This week in fiction: Zadie Smith." *The New Yorker*, February 3, 2013.

lidovky.cz. "Bělobrádek: O nás bez nás. Povinné kvóty na uprchlíky jsou jako Mnichov." May, 2016. https://www.lidovky.cz/belobradek-o-nas-bez-nas-kvoty-jsou-jako-m

nichov-rusko-pouziva-migraci-jako-zbran-g1u-/zpravy-domov.aspx?c=A160505_11
0041_ln_domov_ELE.

Miloš, Mendel, Bronislav Ostřanský and Tomáš Rataj (eds.), Islám v srdci Evropy
(Praha: Academia, 2007).

Özkök, Ertuğrul. "Çok güldüm ama." *Hürriyet*, March 9, 2008. https://www.hurriyet
.com.tr/cok-guldum-ama-8410329

Pogatsa, Zoltan. "Open Letter to anti-Greek Eastern European Bloc." July 8, 2015, https
://www.sigmalive.com/en/news/greece/131867/open-letter-to-antigreek-eastern
-european-bloc

Prouza, Tomáš. "Kvóty migrační krizi nevyřeší." *Právo*, 25 May 2015.

Reuters. "Withheld EU Report Raps Turkey on Rights, Media, Justice." October 28,
2015, Available at «http://www.reuters.com/article/us-turkey-election-eu-idUSKC
N0SM2CT20151028 », Accessed April 13, 2017.

Sobotka, Bohuslav. Komentář předsedy vlády Bohuslava Sobotky k výtkám Evropské
komise. Vláda České republiky, June 6, 2017

Şafak, Elif. "Finaly Turkey Looks East." *The New York Times*, February 23, 2011.

Sönmez, Mustafa. "The political gain of the construction boom." *Hurriyet Daily News*,
January 19, 2015, http://mustafasonmez.net/?p=4768.

Sönmez, Mustafa. "Too many payroll workers, but too few unions in Turkey." *Hurriyet
Daily News*, February 9, 2015, p. 10.

The Guardian. "European Clocks Lose Six Minutes After Dispute Saps Power from
Electricity Grid." March 8, 2018, https://www.theguardian.com/world/2018/mar/08
/european-clocks-lose-six-minutes-dispute-power-electricity-grid (Accessed March
22, 2019

Tidley, Alice. "What's the European Way of Life? EU chief's new Commission portfolio
draws criticisms." *Euronews*, September 12, 2019, https://www.euronews.com/2019/
09/10/what-s-the-european-way-of-life-eu-chief-s-new-commission-portfolio-d
raws-criticism

Visegradinfo.eu. "Friends Do Not Let Friends Kill Democracy." 2019 http://visegrad
info.eu/index.php/icon-articles/592-friends-don-t-let-friends-kill-democracy
(Accessed July 10, 2019)

Wright, George. "Greek Cypriot Leaders Reject Annan Plan." *The Guardian*, April 22,
2004, http://www.guardian.co.uk/world/2004/apr/22/eu.cyprus

Index

www.ingramcontent.com/pod-product-compliance
Lightning Source LLC
Chambersburg PA
CBHW050439280326
41932CB00013BA/2175